Taste *of* Home

more
GRANDMA'S FAVORITES

TASTE OF HOME BOOKS • RDA ENTHUSIAST BRANDS, LLC • MILWAUKEE, WI

Visit us at **tasteofhome.com** for other
Taste of Home books and products.

International Standard Book Number:
978-1-62145-792-3

Component Number:
117600104H

Executive Editor: Mark Hagen
Senior Art Director: Raeann Thompson
Editor: Amy Glander
Art Director: Courtney Lovetere
Senior Designer: Jazmin Delgado
Deputy Editor, Copy Desk:
Dulcie Shoener
Senior Copy Editor: Ann Walter

Cover Photography:
Photographer: Mark Derse
Set Stylist: Melissa Franco
Food Stylist: Shannon Norris

Pictured on front cover:
Herb-Glazed Turkey, p. 121

Pattern: Spiderplay/Getty Images

Pictured on back cover:
Lemon Spiced Tea, p. 36;
Lemony Chicken Noodle Soup, p. 189;
Roasted Strawberry Sheet Cake, p. 239

Printed in China
1 3 5 7 9 10 8 6 4 2

CONTENTS

LAMB STEW,
PAGE 198

Grandma always had the best food waiting to welcome you into her home. Whether she knew a dish by heart or had a box of smudged recipe cards jotted with notes for getting it *just right*, her tried-and-true standbys are the ones to cherish for a lifetime.

These are the recipes that conjure up heavenly aromas, stir up sweet memories of holidays and Sunday dinners, and bring loved ones happily dashing to the table. Whether you're feeding a crowd or just your own hungry crew, capture the essence of authentic down-home cooking with the hundreds of classic recipes inside *More Grandma's Favorites*.

Savor the goodness...

• **Grandma's Favorite Breakfasts.** No one could bring a little morning magic to the table quite like Grandma. Dig into stacks of fluffy pancakes, savory egg bakes and other sunny staples that will start the day off right.

• **Grandma's Favorite Main Courses.** Relish her signature dinner dishes—from potpies, meat loaf and hearty roasts to savory soups, stews and other cozy comfort foods she was proud to include in her repertoire.

• **Grandma's Favorite Breads, Rolls & More!** With muffins, quick breads, breakfast rolls, braided loaves and other freshly baked wonders, this chapter has all the tasty breads Grandma created for every meal.

• **Grandma's Favorite Desserts.** Grandma knew there was nothing as heavenly as a warm, bubbly mixture of butter, sugar and flour. Savor her best cakes and pies, as well as cookies, bars and other sweet treats.

Relive treasured moments, and the comforting flavors behind them, with the 291 recipes inside *Taste of Home More Grandma's Favorites*. This nostalgic collection offers homespun favorites that will bring back fond memories of Grandma's kitchen with every fork-worthy bite.

SUNDAY DINNER MENUS

Whether you're new to meal planning or a longtime pro, consider this handy guide that relies on recipes from this book to create complete meals.

Perfect Four-Cheese Lasagna, p. 107 • Savory Biscuit-Breadsticks, p. 87 • Butter Pecan Cheesecake, p. 293

Slow-Cooker Milk-Can Supper, p.129 • Emily's Honey Lime Coleslaw, p. 173 • Gran's Apple Cake, p. 241

Salmon with Brown Sugar Glaze, p. 108 • Green Bean-Cherry Tomato Salad, p. 151 • Lemon Berry Dump Cake, p. 297

Squash & Lentil Lamb Stew, p. 110 • Cheddar/ Squash Cloverleaf Rolls, p. 92 • Vermont Maple Cookies, p. 225

Skillet-Grilled Catfish, p. 123 • Best Hush Puppies, p. 161 • Black-Eyed Peas with Collard Greens, p. 170 • Mom's Peach Pie, p. 257

New Zealand Rosemary Lamb Shanks, p. 113 • Garlic Roasted Brussels Sprouts, p. 159 • Coconut Creme Chocolates, p. 289

Puff Pastry Chicken Potpie, p. 116 • Cornmeal Parker House Rolls, p. 95 • Homemade Butterscotch Pudding, p. 278

Slow-Cooked Ham with Pineapple Sauce, p. 115 • Grandma's Favorite Hot Cross Buns, p. 74 • Orange-Glazed Carrots, Onions & Radishes, p. 146

Grandma Edna's Cajun Pork, p. 118 • Super Simple Scalloped Potatoes, p. 156 • Chocolate Cake with Chocolate Frosting, p. 265

Pronto Vegetarian Peppers, p. 124 • Winter Beet Salad, p. 141 • Roasted Strawberry Sheet Cake, p. 239

Herb-Glazed Turkey, p. 121 • Buttermilk Smashed Potatoes, p. 164 • Grandma's Poultry Dressing, p. 160 • The Best Sweet Potato Pie, p. 250

Country Cassoulet, p. 100 • Golden Crescents, p. 79 • Grandma's Spinach Salad, p. 157 • Rhubarb Custard Bars, p. 223

SHEET-PAN BACON & EGGS
BREAKFAST, PAGE 16

BREAKFAST

Rise and shine! Everyone wakes up happy when breakfast is at Grandma's house. Whether it's a special occasion or just an opportunity to break out of the daily milk-and-cereal routine, it's destined to be a meal to remember. With an assortment of comforting dishes, you won't be able to resist these nostalgic classics.

BAKED BLUEBERRY GINGER PANCAKE

My kids love pancakes, so I came up with this baked version that saves a lot of time in the morning. They gobble these ginger-kissed breakfast squares right up!
—*Erin Wright, Wallace, KS*

TAKES: 30 MIN. • MAKES: 9 SERVINGS

2 large eggs, room
  temperature
1½ cups 2% milk
¼ cup butter, melted
2 cups all-purpose flour
2 Tbsp. sugar
3 tsp. baking powder
1½ tsp. ground ginger
½ tsp. salt
2 cups fresh or frozen
  unsweetened
  blueberries
  Maple syrup

1. Preheat oven to 350°. Combine eggs, milk and butter. Whisk the next 5 ingredients; add to egg mixture. Spoon batter into a 9-in. square baking pan coated with cooking spray. Sprinkle blueberries over top.

2. Bake until a toothpick inserted in center comes out clean, 20-25 minutes. Cut into squares; serve with warm maple syrup.

1 PIECE: 213 cal., 7g fat (4g sat. fat), 58mg chol., 368mg sod., 31g carb. (8g sugars, 2g fiber), 6g pro. **DIABETIC EXCHANGES:** 2 starch, 1½ fat.

OVERNIGHT OATMEAL

Start this breakfast the night before so you can get some extra sleep the next morning. My husband adds coconut to his, and I stir in dried fruit.
—*June Thomas, Chesterton, IN*

PREP: 10 MIN. + CHILLING • MAKES: 1 SERVING

⅓ cup old-fashioned oats
3 Tbsp. fat-free milk
3 Tbsp. reduced-fat plain
  yogurt
1 Tbsp. honey
½ cup assorted fresh fruit
2 Tbsp. chopped walnuts,
  toasted

1. In a small container or Mason jar, combine oats, milk, yogurt and honey. Top with fruit and nuts. Seal; refrigerate overnight.

NOTE: To toast nuts, bake in a shallow pan in a 350° oven for 5-10 minutes or cook in a skillet over low heat until nuts are lightly browned, stirring occasionally.

1 SERVING: 345 cal., 13g fat (2g sat. fat), 4mg chol., 53mg sod., 53g carb. (31g sugars, 5g fiber), 10g pro.

BAKED BLUEBERRY
GINGER PANCAKE

ROASTED VEGETABLE STRATA

With the abundance of zucchini my family has in the fall,
this is the perfect dish to use some of what we have. Cheesy
and rich, the warm breakfast dish is sure to please!
—*Colleen Doucette, Truro, NS*

PREP: 55 MIN. + CHILLING • **BAKE:** 40 MIN. • **MAKES:** 8 SERVINGS

- 3 large zucchini, halved lengthwise and cut into ¾-in. slices
- 1 each medium red, yellow and orange peppers, cut into 1-in. pieces
- 2 Tbsp. olive oil
- 1 tsp. dried oregano
- ½ tsp. salt
- ½ tsp. pepper
- ½ tsp. dried basil
- 1 medium tomato, chopped
- 1 loaf (1 lb.) unsliced crusty Italian bread
- ½ cup shredded sharp cheddar cheese
- ½ cup shredded Asiago cheese
- 6 large eggs
- 2 cups fat-free milk

1. Preheat oven to 400°. Toss zucchini and peppers with oil and seasonings; transfer to a 15x10x1-in. pan. Roast until tender, 25-30 minutes, stirring once. Stir in tomato; cool slightly.

2. Trim ends from bread; cut bread into 1-in. slices. In a greased 13x9-in. baking dish, layer half of each of the following: bread, roasted vegetables and cheeses. Repeat layers. Whisk together eggs and milk; pour evenly over top. Refrigerate, covered, 6 hours or overnight.

3. Preheat oven to 375°. Remove the casserole from refrigerator while oven heats. Bake, uncovered, 40-50 minutes or until golden brown. Let stand 5-10 minutes before cutting.

FREEZE OPTION: Cover and freeze the unbaked casserole. To use, partially thaw in refrigerator overnight. Remove from refrigerator 30 minutes before baking. Preheat oven to 375°. Bake casserole as directed, increasing time as necessary to heat through and for a thermometer inserted in center to read 165°.

1 PIECE: 349 cal., 14g fat (5g sat. fat), 154mg chol., 642mg sod., 40g carb. (9g sugars, 4g fiber), 17g pro. **DIABETIC EXCHANGES:** 2 starch, 1 vegetable, 1 medium-fat meat, 1 fat.

SWEET POTATO DUTCH BABY WITH PRALINE SYRUP

This recipe reminds me of my favorite Dutch baby breakfast from
when I was a child. It's a perfect comfort dish morning or evening.
—*Angela Spengler, Niceville, FL*

PREP: 10 MIN. • COOK: 30 MIN. • MAKES: 6 SERVINGS

4 **Tbsp. butter, divided**
3 **large eggs, room**
  temperature
½ **cup 2% milk**
¼ **cup mashed canned**
  sweet potatoes in syrup
½ **cup all-purpose flour**
¼ **tsp. salt**
½ **cup maple syrup**
¼ **cup chopped pecans**

1. Preheat oven to 400°. Place 2 Tbsp. butter in a 10-in. cast-iron or other ovenproof skillet. Place in oven until the butter is melted, 4-5 minutes; carefully swirl butter to coat pan evenly.

2. Meanwhile, in a large bowl, whisk the eggs, milk and sweet potatoes until blended. Whisk in flour and salt. Pour into hot skillet. Bake until puffed and sides are golden brown and crisp, 20-25 minutes.

3. In a small saucepan, combine the syrup, pecans and remaining 2 Tbsp. butter. Cook and stir over medium heat until butter is melted. Remove the pancake from oven; serve immediately with syrup.

1 SERVING: 261 cal., 14g fat (6g sat. fat), 115mg chol., 210mg sod., 30g carb. (19g sugars, 1g fiber), 5g pro.

SLOW-COOKER HAM & EGGS

This dish is appreciated any time of the year, but I love serving it on holiday mornings.
Once started, it requires little attention—and it's a fun meal for the family.
—*Andrea Schaak, Jordan, MN*

PREP: 15 MIN. • COOK: 3 HOURS • MAKES: 6 SERVINGS

6 **large eggs**
1 **cup biscuit/baking mix**
⅔ **cup 2% milk**
⅓ **cup sour cream**
2 **Tbsp. minced fresh**
  parsley
2 **garlic cloves, minced**
½ **tsp. salt**
½ **tsp. pepper**
1 **cup cubed fully**
  cooked ham
1 **cup shredded**
  Swiss cheese
1 **small onion, finely**
  chopped
⅓ **cup shredded**
  Parmesan cheese

1. In a large bowl, whisk the first 8 ingredients until blended; stir in remaining ingredients. Pour mixture into a greased 3- or 4-qt. slow cooker.

2. Cook, covered, on low 3-4 hours or until the eggs are set. Cut into wedges.

1 SERVING: 315 cal., 18g fat (9g sat. fat), 256mg chol., 942mg sod., 17g carb. (4g sugars, 1g fiber), 21g pro.

"Very delicious! I didn't have ham so I fried up some turkey bacon and the onion. I also added mushrooms. I served it with asparagus. It was done in 3 hours. I will be making it again."
—BIG EYES, TASTEOFHOME.COM

SLOW-COOKED
BIG BREAKFAST

SLOW-COOKED BIG BREAKFAST

We make this during holidays or on mornings when we know we're going to have a busy day. You can set this to cook overnight on low for an early breakfast, or for three hours on high for a leisurely brunch.
—Delisha Paris, Elizabeth City, NC

PREP: 30 MIN. • COOK: 3 HOURS + STANDING • MAKES: 12 SERVINGS

1 lb. bulk pork sausage
2 lbs. potatoes (about 4 medium), peeled and cut into ½-in. cubes
1 large onion, finely chopped
1 medium sweet red pepper, chopped
2 cups fresh spinach
1 cup chopped fresh mushrooms
1 lb. deli ham, cubed
1 cup shredded cheddar cheese
12 large eggs
½ cup 2% milk
1 tsp. garlic powder
1 tsp. pepper
½ tsp. salt

1. In a large skillet, cook and crumble sausage over medium heat for 5-7 minutes or until no longer pink; drain.

2. Meanwhile, place the potatoes and ¼ cup water in a large microwave-safe dish. Microwave, covered, on high until potatoes are tender, about 6 minutes; stir halfway. Drain potatoes and add to the sausage.

3. Stir in onion, sweet red pepper, spinach, mushrooms, ham and cheese. Transfer to a greased 6-qt. slow cooker.

4. Whisk together remaining ingredients until blended; pour over sausage mixture. Cook, covered, on low 3-4 hours or until eggs are set. Let stand, uncovered, 10 minutes.

1 CUP: 303 cal., 18g fat (6g sat. fat), 236mg chol., 873mg sod., 14g carb. (3g sugars, 1g fiber), 21g pro.

BLUEBERRY CORNMEAL PANCAKES

These blueberry cornmeal pancakes are one of my family's favorite breakfasts. No time to make it from scratch? No problem! My grandmother's standby of store-bought corn muffin mix makes quick work of the job.
—Carolyn Eskew, Dayton, OH

TAKES: 30 MIN. • MAKES: 10 PANCAKES

1 pkg. (8½ oz.) cornbread/ muffin mix
1 cup fresh or frozen blueberries
⅓ cup canned white or shoepeg corn
Maple syrup

In a large bowl, prepare muffin mix according to the package directions. Gently stir in blueberries and corn. Lightly grease a griddle; warm over medium heat. Pour batter by ¼ cupfuls onto griddle; flatten slightly. Cook until bottoms are golden brown. Turn; cook until second sides are golden brown. Serve with syrup.

2 PANCAKES: 251 cal., 7g fat (2g sat. fat), 39mg chol., 454mg sod., 41g carb. (14g sugars, 4g fiber), 6g pro.

HEARTY SLOW-COOKER BREAKFAST HASH

This sweet and savory hash certainly won't leave you hungry—the sausage, veggies and eggs will fill you up. The hint of maple syrup makes it extra cozy.
—*Colleen Delawder, Herndon, VA*

PREP: 25 MIN. • COOK: 5 HOURS • MAKES: 4 SERVINGS

8 **to 10 frozen fully cooked breakfast sausage links**
4 **cups diced red potatoes (about 1½ lbs.)**
4 **medium carrots, diced**
2 **green onions, thinly sliced (white and pale green parts only)**
2 **Tbsp. extra virgin olive oil**
1 **Tbsp. red wine vinegar**
1 **Tbsp. plus 2 tsp. snipped fresh dill, divided**
1 **tsp. kosher salt**
½ **tsp. coarsely ground pepper, divided**
¼ **tsp. crushed red pepper flakes**
2 **Tbsp. crumbled feta cheese**
1 **Tbsp. butter**
4 **large eggs**
2 **Tbsp. maple syrup**

1. In a large skillet over medium heat, cook sausages, turning occasionally, until heated through, 8-9 minutes. Combine next 5 ingredients in a 3-qt. slow cooker. Add 1 Tbsp. dill, kosher salt, ¼ tsp. pepper and red pepper flakes. Arrange sausages on top of vegetable mixture. Cook, covered, on low until vegetables are tender, 5-6 hours. Transfer vegetables to a serving platter; sprinkle with feta cheese. Top with sausages.

2. Meanwhile, in a large skillet, heat butter over medium heat. Add eggs; cook to desired doneness. Arrange the eggs over vegetables. Sprinkle with remaining dill and pepper; drizzle with maple syrup.

1 SERVING: 446 cal., 25g fat (8g sat. fat), 212mg chol., 911mg sod., 42g carb. (12g sugars, 5g fiber), 14g pro.

"One of our favorite 'breakfast for dinner' recipes! So easy to make and the veggies with feta is simply irresistible."
—KYMBERLYFLEWELLING, TASTEOFHOME.COM

PEPPERONI HOPPLE-POPPLE

My grandma and I created this kid-friendly version of a German breakfast dish. Serve it with toast or English muffins.
—*Jaycee Gfeller, Russell, KS*

TAKES: 30 MIN. • MAKES: 6 SERVINGS

2½ **cups frozen shredded hash brown potatoes**
⅓ **cup chopped onion**
3 **Tbsp. butter**
5 **large eggs**
½ **cup 2% milk**
1 **tsp. Italian seasoning**
½ **tsp. salt**
½ **tsp. pepper**
25 **slices pepperoni**
1 **cup shredded Mexican cheese blend**

1. In a large skillet, cook potatoes and onion in butter until tender and lightly browned. Meanwhile, in a large bowl, beat eggs, milk, Italian seasoning, salt and pepper.

2. Pour over potato mixture. Sprinkle with pepperoni. Cover and cook on medium-low heat until eggs are set, 10-12 minutes. Remove from the heat. Sprinkle with cheese; cover and let stand for 2 minutes. Cut into wedges.

1 PIECE: 267 cal., 20g fat (11g sat. fat), 219mg chol., 608mg sod., 9g carb. (2g sugars, 1g fiber), 12g pro.

FLUFFY BANANA PANCAKES

I love to make pancakes for my family on Saturday mornings. Since we often have ripe bananas, I decided to add them to a batch of pancake batter. The results were delicious!
—*Lori Stevens, Riverton, UT*

TAKES: 30 MIN. • MAKES: 7 SERVINGS

1 cup all-purpose flour
1 cup whole wheat flour
3 Tbsp. brown sugar
1 tsp. baking powder
1 tsp. baking soda
1 tsp. ground cinnamon
½ tsp. salt

2 large eggs, room temperature
2 cups buttermilk
2 Tbsp. canola oil
1 tsp. vanilla extract
1 ripe medium banana, finely chopped
⅓ cup finely chopped walnuts

1. In a large bowl, combine the first 7 ingredients. In another bowl, whisk eggs, buttermilk, oil and vanilla until blended. Add to the dry ingredients, stirring just until moistened. Fold in banana and walnuts.

2. Pour batter by ¼ cupfuls onto a hot griddle coated with cooking spray. Cook until bubbles begin to form on top and bottoms are golden brown. Turn; cook until second side is golden brown.

FREEZE OPTION: Freeze cooled pancakes between layers of waxed paper in a freezer container. To use, place the pancakes on an ungreased baking sheet, cover with foil and reheat in a preheated 375° oven 5-10 minutes. Or place 2 pancakes on a microwave-safe plate and microwave on high for 40-50 seconds or until heated through.

2 PANCAKES: 283 cal., 10g fat (2g sat. fat), 63mg chol., 503mg sod., 40g carb. (12g sugars, 4g fiber), 9g pro. DIABETIC EXCHANGES: 2½ starch, 1½ fat.

APPLE PIE STEEL-CUT OATMEAL

I love this slow-cooker oatmeal. The steel-cut oats have so much flavor
and texture. My family loves to sprinkle toasted pecans on top.
—*Angela Lively, Conroe, TX*

PREP: 10 MIN. • **COOK:** 6 HOURS • **MAKES:** 8 SERVINGS

6 cups water
1½ cups steel-cut oats
**1½ cups unsweetened
    applesauce**
¼ cup maple syrup
1½ tsp. ground cinnamon
½ tsp. ground nutmeg
⅛ tsp. salt
**1 large apple, chopped
    Optional: Sliced apples,
    toasted pecans and
    additional maple syrup**

In a 4-qt. slow cooker, combine the first 7 ingredients. Cover and
cook on low for 6-8 hours or until liquid is absorbed. Stir in the
chopped apple. If desired, top servings with apple slices, pecans
and syrup.

1¼ CUPS: 171 cal., 2g fat (0 sat. fat), 0 chol., 39mg sod., 36g carb.
(13g sugars, 4g fiber), 4g pro.

SHEET-PAN BACON & EGGS BREAKFAST

PICTURED ON PAGE 6

I re-created this recipe from inspiration I saw on social media, and it was a huge hit!
Use any cheeses and spices you like—you can even try seasoned potatoes.
—*Bonnie Hawkins, Elkhorn, WI*

PREP: 20 MIN. • **BAKE:** 40 MIN. • **MAKES:** 8 SERVINGS

10 bacon strips
**1 pkg. (30 oz.) frozen
    shredded hash brown
    potatoes, thawed**
1 tsp. garlic powder
1 tsp. dried basil
1 tsp. dried oregano
½ tsp. salt
**½ tsp. crushed red pepper
    flakes**
**1½ cups shredded
    pepper jack cheese**
**1 cup shredded
    cheddar cheese**
¼ tsp. pepper
8 large eggs
**¼ cup chopped green
    onions**

1. Preheat oven to 400°. Place bacon strips in a single layer in a
15x10x1-in. baking sheet. Bake until partially cooked but not crisp,
about 10 minutes. Remove to paper towels to drain. When cool
enough to handle, chop bacon; set aside.

2. In a large bowl, combine the potatoes and seasonings; spread
evenly into bacon drippings in pan. Bake until potatoes are golden
brown, 25-30 minutes.

3. Sprinkle with cheeses. With the back of a spoon, make 8 wells
in potato mixture. Break an egg in each well; sprinkle with pepper
and reserved bacon. Bake until egg whites are completely set and
yolks begin to thicken but are not hard, 12-14 minutes. Sprinkle
with green onions.

1 SERVING: 446 cal., 30g fat (13g sat. fat), 246mg chol., 695mg sod.,
22g carb. (2g sugars, 1g fiber), 22g pro.

APPLE PIE
STEEL-CUT
OATMEAL

GRANDMA'S SECRET

Boost protein by adding a dollop of vanilla Greek yogurt on top of these oats (it will help you feel full longer).

SAUSAGE & EGGS OVER CHEDDAR-PARMESAN GRITS

These creamy grits topped with Italian sausage, peppers, onions and a fried egg on top are total comfort food. Perfect for brunch or dinner, they are easy to put together and will satisfy a hungry crew.

—*Debbie Glasscock, Conway, AR*

PREP: 20 MIN. • **COOK:** 20 MIN. • **MAKES:** 6 SERVINGS

- 1 lb. bulk Italian sausage
- 1 large sweet onion, chopped
- 1 medium sweet yellow pepper, chopped
- 1 medium sweet red pepper, chopped
- 6 cups water
- 1½ cups quick-cooking grits
- 1 cup shredded sharp cheddar cheese
- ½ cup shredded Parmesan cheese
- 2 Tbsp. half-and-half cream
- ½ tsp. salt
- ¼ tsp. pepper
- 2 tsp. olive oil
- 6 large eggs
- Hot pepper sauce, optional

1. In a Dutch oven, cook sausage, onion, yellow pepper and red pepper over medium heat until sausage is no longer pink and vegetables are tender, 6-8 minutes, breaking up sausage into crumbles; drain.

2. Meanwhile, in a large saucepan, bring water to a boil. Slowly stir in grits. Reduce heat to medium-low; cook, covered, until thickened, about 5 minutes, stirring occasionally. Remove from heat. Stir in cheeses, cream, salt and pepper; keep warm.

3. In a large skillet, heat oil over medium-high heat. Break eggs, 1 at a time, into pan; reduce heat to low. Cook until whites are set and yolks begin to thicken, turning once if desired. Divide grits among 6 serving bowls; top with sausage mixture and eggs. If desired, serve with pepper sauce.

1 SERVING: 538 cal., 32g fat (12g sat. fat), 253mg chol., 972mg sod., 38g carb. (5g sugars, 3g fiber), 26g pro.

SPINACH FETA STRATA

My friend shared this recipe with me. My family loved it the
first time I made it, so it will be a regular in our house.
—*Pat Lane, Pullman, WA*

PREP: 10 MIN. + CHILLING • BAKE: 40 MIN. • MAKES: 12 SERVINGS

10 slices French bread
   (1 in. thick) or
   6 croissants, split
6 large eggs, lightly beaten
1½ cups 2% milk
1 pkg. (10 oz.) frozen
   chopped spinach, thawed
   and squeezed dry
½ tsp. salt
¼ tsp. ground nutmeg
¼ tsp. pepper
1½ cups shredded
   Monterey Jack cheese
1 cup crumbled feta cheese

1. In a greased 3-qt. or 13x9-in. baking dish, arrange French bread or croissant halves with sides overlapping.

2. In a large bowl, combine the eggs, milk, spinach, salt, nutmeg and pepper; pour over bread. Sprinkle with cheeses. Cover and refrigerate for 8 hours or overnight.

3. Remove from the refrigerator 30 minutes before baking. Bake, uncovered, at 350° until a knife inserted in the center comes out clean, 40-45 minutes. Let stand for 5 minutes before cutting. Serve warm.

1 SERVING: 190 cal., 10g fat (5g sat. fat), 128mg chol., 443mg sod., 13g carb. (2g sugars, 2g fiber), 12g pro.

WARM GRAPEFRUIT WITH GINGER SUGAR

Sweetly broiled grapefruit is a specialty at my bed-and-breakfast. In addition
to serving it for breakfast or brunch, enjoy it as a light snack or dessert.
—*Stephanie Levy, Lansing, NY*

TAKES: 15 MIN. • MAKES: 2 SERVINGS

1 large red grapefruit
2 to 3 tsp. chopped
   crystallized ginger
2 tsp. sugar

1. Preheat broiler. Cut grapefruit crosswise in half. With a small knife, cut around the membrane in the center of each half and discard. Cut around each section to loosen fruit. Place on a baking sheet, cut side up.

2. Mix ginger and sugar; sprinkle over fruit. Broil 4 in. from heat until sugar is melted, about 4 minutes.

½ GRAPEFRUIT: 85 cal., 0 fat (0 sat. fat), 0 chol., 3mg sod., 22g carb. (17g sugars, 2g fiber), 1g pro. DIABETIC EXCHANGES: 1 fruit, ½ starch.

BASIL VEGETABLE STRATA

I've been cooking this strata for years, and my family just can't get enough!
The fresh basil gives this healthy brunch dish an added flavor boost.
—Jean Ecos, Hartland, WI

PREP: 40 MIN. + CHILLING • BAKE: 1 HOUR + STANDING • MAKES: 8 SERVINGS

3 tsp. canola oil, divided
¾ lb. sliced fresh
    mushrooms
1 cup finely chopped
    sweet onion
1 large sweet red pepper,
    cut into strips
1 large sweet yellow
    pepper, thin strips
1 medium leek (white
    portion only), chopped
½ tsp. salt
½ tsp. pepper
10 slices whole wheat
    bread, cut into 1-in.
    pieces
1½ cups shredded part-skim
    mozzarella cheese
¼ cup grated
    Parmesan cheese
8 large eggs
4 large egg whites
2½ cups fat-free milk
¼ cup chopped fresh basil

1. In a large skillet, heat 1 tsp. oil over medium-high heat. Add mushrooms; cook and stir until tender, 8-10 minutes. Remove from pan.

2. In same pan, heat 1 tsp. oil over medium heat. Add onion; cook and stir until golden brown, 6-8 minutes. Remove from pan and add to the mushrooms.

3. Add remaining oil to pan. Add peppers, leek, salt and pepper; cook and stir until leek is tender, 6-8 minutes. Stir in sauteed mushrooms and onion.

4. In a 13x9-in. baking dish coated with cooking spray, layer half of each of the following: bread pieces, vegetable mixture, mozzarella cheese and Parmesan cheese. Repeat layers. In a large bowl, whisk eggs, egg whites and milk until blended; pour over layers. Sprinkle with basil. Refrigerate, covered, overnight.

5. Preheat oven to 350°. Remove strata from refrigerator while oven heats.

6. Bake, covered, 50 minutes. Bake, uncovered, until strata is lightly browned and a knife inserted in the center comes out clean, 10-15 minutes longer. Let stand 10 minutes before serving.

1 PIECE: 322 cal., 13g fat (5g sat. fat), 201mg chol., 620mg sod., 28g carb. (9g sugars, 4g fiber), 24g pro. DIABETIC EXCHANGES: 2 medium-fat meat, 1½ starch, 1 vegetable, ½ fat.

FROM GRANDMA'S KITCHEN: One of the more popular herbs in the United States, basil has many varieties. Perhaps the most common are sweet (Italian) basil and Thai purple basil. Both are floral and clove-like, with powerful sweetness and a hint of pepper.

TURKEY SWISS QUICHE

Here's a delicious way to put leftover turkey to good use.
My family looks forward to this the morning after Thanksgiving.
—*Lois Forehand, Little River-Academy, TX*

PREP: 25 MIN. • **BAKE:** 30 MIN. + STANDING • **MAKES:** 6 SERVINGS

1 sheet refrigerated pie crust
1½ cups finely chopped cooked turkey
4 large eggs
¾ cup half-and-half cream
2 cups shredded Swiss cheese
4 green onions, finely chopped
2 Tbsp. diced pimientos
1 tsp. dried oregano
1 tsp. dried parsley flakes
Dash salt and pepper
3 slices (¾ oz. each) Swiss cheese, cut into thin strips

1. Preheat oven to 450°. Unroll crust into a 9-in. pie plate; flute edge. Line unpricked crust with a double thickness of heavy-duty foil. Bake 8 minutes. Remove the foil; bake until golden brown, 5-7 minutes longer. Reduce heat to 375°.

2. Sprinkle turkey into crust. In a large bowl, whisk eggs and cream. Stir in the shredded Swiss cheese, onions, pimientos, oregano, parsley, salt and pepper. Pour into crust.

3. Bake 20 minutes. Arrange Swiss cheese strips in a lattice pattern over quiche. Bake until a knife inserted in the center comes out clean, 10-15 minutes longer. Let stand 10 minutes before cutting.

1 PIECE: 489 cal., 31g fat (16g sat. fat), 234mg chol., 334mg sod., 21g carb. (4g sugars, 0 fiber), 30g pro.

BUTTERMILK PANCAKES

You just can't beat a basic buttermilk pancake for a down-home hearty breakfast.
Pair it with sausage and fresh fruit for a mouthwatering morning meal.
—*Betty Abrey, Imperial, SK*

PREP: 10 MIN. • **COOK:** 5 MIN./BATCH • **MAKES:** 2½ DOZEN

4 cups all-purpose flour
¼ cup sugar
2 tsp. baking soda
2 tsp. salt
1½ tsp. baking powder
4 large eggs, room temperature
4 cups buttermilk

1. In a large bowl, combine the flour, sugar, baking soda, salt and baking powder. In another bowl, whisk the eggs and buttermilk until blended; stir into dry ingredients just until moistened.

2. Pour batter by ¼ cupfuls onto a lightly greased hot griddle; turn when bubbles form on top. Cook until the second side of pancake is golden brown.

FREEZE OPTION: Place cooled pancakes between layers of waxed paper in a freezer container. To use, place frozen pancakes on an ungreased baking sheet. Cover with foil and reheat in a preheated 375° oven for 6-10 minutes. Or place a stack of 3 pancakes on a microwave-safe plate and microwave on high until heated through, 45-90 seconds.

3 PANCAKES: 270 cal., 3g fat (1g sat. fat), 89mg chol., 913mg sod., 48g carb. (11g sugars, 1g fiber), 11g pro.

SLOW-COOKER DOUGHNUT BREAKFAST BAKE

This extravagant dish will be the star of the brunch table.
Serve it with sausage, fresh berries and yogurt.
—*Rashanda Cobbins, Milwaukee, WI*

PREP: 15 MIN. • COOK: 4 HOURS + STANDING • MAKES: 12 SERVINGS

24 cake doughnuts, cut into bite-sized pieces
2 apples, peeled and chopped
1 cup heavy whipping cream
4 large eggs
1 Tbsp. vanilla extract
½ cup packed brown sugar
1 tsp. ground cinnamon
Optional: Whipped cream and fresh berries

1. Line inside of 5-qt. slow cooker with a double layer of heavy duty foil; spray insert and foil with cooking spray. Layer half the doughnut pieces in slow cooker; top with half the apples. Repeat with the remaining doughnuts and apples. In large bowl, whisk together cream, eggs and vanilla; pour over doughnut pieces and apples. In a small bowl, mix together brown sugar and cinnamon; sprinkle over doughnut mixture.

2. Cook, covered, on low 4-5 hours or until set. Remove insert. Let stand, uncovered, 20 minutes. If desired, serve with whipped cream and fresh berries.

1 SERVING: 609 cal., 36g fat (17g sat. fat), 95mg chol., 547mg sod., 64g carb. (32g sugars, 2g fiber), 8g pro.

GRANDMA'S SECRET

This recipe is similar to bread pudding, but has an even richer taste and consistency.

AUNT EDITH'S BAKED PANCAKE

My aunt made a mighty breakfast that revolved around "The Big Pancake." I always enjoyed watching as she poured the batter into her huge iron skillet, then baked the confection to perfection in the oven.
—*Marion Kirst, Troy, MI*

PREP: 15 MIN. • **BAKE:** 20 MIN. • **MAKES:** 4 SERVINGS

3   **large eggs, room
    temperature**
½   **tsp. salt**
½   **cup all-purpose flour**
½   **cup 2% milk**
2   **Tbsp. butter, softened
    Confectioners' sugar
    Lemon wedges**

1. In a bowl, beat eggs until very light. Add salt, flour and milk; beat well. Thoroughly rub bottom and sides of a 10-in. cast-iron or other heavy skillet with butter. Pour batter into skillet.

2. Bake at 450° for 15 minutes. Reduce heat to 350° and bake until set, 5 minutes longer. If desired, remove pancake from skillet and place on a large hot platter. Dust with confectioners' sugar and garnish with lemon. Serve immediately.

1 PIECE: 180 cal., 10g fat (5g sat. fat), 158mg chol., 407mg sod., 14g carb. (2g sugars, 0 fiber), 7g pro.

VEGGIE SAUSAGE STRATA

As a retired home economics teacher, I've made quite a few recipes through the years. This hearty breakfast casserole is a favorite in my family.
—*Dorothy Erickson, Blue Eye, MO*

PREP: 15 MIN. + CHILLING • **BAKE:** 1 HOUR 20 MIN. • **MAKES:** 12 SERVINGS

2   **lbs. bulk Italian sausage**
2   **medium green peppers,
    coarsely chopped**
1   **medium onion, chopped**
8   **large eggs**
2   **cups 2% milk**
2   **tsp. salt**
2   **tsp. white pepper**
2   **tsp. ground mustard**
12 **slices bread,
    cut into ½-in. pieces**
1   **pkg. (10 oz.) frozen
    chopped spinach, thawed
    and squeezed dry**
2   **cups shredded
    Swiss cheese**
2   **cups shredded
    cheddar cheese**
1   **medium zucchini,
    cut into ¼-in. slices**

1. In a large skillet, cook the sausage, green peppers and onion over medium heat until meat is no longer pink; drain. Meanwhile, in a large bowl, whisk the eggs, milk, salt, pepper and mustard. Stir in the sausage mixture, bread, spinach, cheeses and zucchini.

2. Transfer mixture to a greased 13x9-in. baking dish. Cover and refrigerate overnight.

3. Remove from the refrigerator 30 minutes before baking. Cover and bake at 350° for 40 minutes. Uncover; bake 40-45 minutes longer or until a knife inserted in the center comes out clean.

1 PIECE: 501 cal., 34g fat (14g sat. fat), 204mg chol., 1236mg sod., 22g carb. (5g sugars, 2g fiber), 27g pro.

AUNT EDITH'S
BAKED PANCAKE

ALL-IN-ONE
SLOW-COOKER BREAKFAST

Let your slow cooker do the work and don't worry about adding sides because this dish already has everything—hash browns, sausage, cheese and eggs. Just cut up some fresh fruit, sip your coffee and breakfast is served.

—Debbie Glasscock, Conway, AR

PREP: 20 MIN. • COOK: 3 HOURS • MAKES: 6 SERVINGS

1 lb. bulk pork sausage
1 small onion, chopped
6 green onions, thinly sliced
1 pkg. (30 oz.) frozen shredded hash brown potatoes, thawed
2 cups shredded sharp cheddar cheese
1 can (10¾ oz.) condensed cream of mushroom soup, undiluted
1 cup sour cream
6 large eggs
¼ tsp. pepper
Chopped fresh parsley
Optional: Salsa and additional sour cream

1. In a large skillet, cook sausage, onion and green onions over medium heat until sausage is no longer pink and onions are tender, 6-8 minutes, breaking up sausage into crumbles; drain. Transfer to a greased 5- or 6-qt. slow cooker. Stir in hash browns, cheese, soup and sour cream until blended.

2. Cook, covered, on high 2½ hours. With the back of a spoon, make 6 wells in potato mixture. Break an egg in each well. Sprinkle eggs with pepper. Cover and cook until egg whites are completely set and yolks begin to thicken but are not hard, 30-35 minutes longer. Sprinkle with parsley. If desired, serve with salsa and additional sour cream.

1 SERVING: 654 cal., 44g fat (19g sat. fat), 276mg chol., 1194mg sod., 36g carb. (5g sugars, 3g fiber), 29g pro.

PIGS IN A POOL

My kids love sausage and pancakes, but making them for breakfast on a
busy weekday is out of the question. My homemade version of pigs in a blanket
is a thrifty alternative to the packaged kind, and they freeze like a dream.
—*Lisa Dodd, Greenville, SC*

PREP: 45 MIN. • **BAKE:** 20 MIN. • **MAKES:** 4 DOZEN

1   **lb. reduced-fat bulk pork
    sausage**
2   **cups all-purpose flour**
¼   **cup sugar**
1   **Tbsp. baking powder**
1   **tsp. salt**
½   **tsp. ground cinnamon**
¼   **tsp. ground nutmeg**
1   **large egg, room
    temperature, lightly
    beaten**
2   **cups fat-free milk**
2   **Tbsp. canola oil**
2   **Tbsp. honey**
    Maple syrup, optional

1. Preheat oven to 350°. Coat 48 mini muffin cups with cooking
spray.

2. Shape sausage into forty-eight ¾-in. balls. Place meatballs on
a rack coated with cooking spray in a shallow baking pan. Bake
until cooked through, 15-20 minutes. Drain on paper towels.

3. In a large bowl, whisk flour, sugar, baking powder, salt and
spices. In another bowl, whisk egg, milk, oil and honey until
blended. Add to flour mixture; stir just until moistened.

4. Place a sausage ball in each mini muffin cup; cover with batter.
Bake until lightly browned, 20-25 minutes. Cool 5 minutes before
removing from pans to wire racks. Serve warm, with maple syrup
if desired.

FREEZE OPTION: Freeze the cooled muffins in airtight freezer
containers. To use, microwave each muffin on high until heated
through, 20-30 seconds.

4 MINI MUFFINS: 234 cal., 10g fat (3g sat. fat), 45mg chol., 560mg
sod., 26g carb. (9g sugars, 1g fiber), 10g pro. **DIABETIC EXCHANGES:**
1½ starch, 1 medium-fat meat, ½ fat.

*"This is my kids' favorite breakfast treat! Make a batch or
two and freeze them. Then 20-30 seconds in the microwave
and they are heated through. Five stars are earned here!"*
—AMANDALINA03, TASTEOFHOME.COM

YANKEE RED FLANNEL HASH

GRANDMA'S SECRET

Don't crack your eggs on the edge of the skillet or you may get pieces of shell in the hash. Gently tap the egg on a countertop, then open it over the skillet. If a bit of shell still sneaks in, use another piece of shell to fish it out.

YANKEE RED FLANNEL HASH

Hash is a classic diner dish. I found that this one with potatoes and pastrami
is easy to make at home. The beets give it fabulous color and flavor.
—*Nancy Mock, Colchester, VT*

TAKES: 30 MIN. • MAKES: 4 SERVINGS

¾ cup half-and-half cream
1 tsp. Louisiana-style
   hot sauce
¼ tsp. salt
¼ tsp. pepper
1 Tbsp. canola oil
1 medium onion, chopped
3 cups frozen cubed hash
   brown potatoes, thawed
½ lb. turkey pastrami, cut
   into ½-in. cubes
1 cup canned diced beets,
   well drained
4 large eggs
1 Tbsp. minced fresh
   parsley

1. In a small bowl, combine cream, hot sauce, salt and pepper. In a large skillet, heat oil over medium heat. Add onion; cook and stir 2-3 minutes or until tender. Add potatoes, pastrami and beets; cook and stir 8-10 minutes or until golden brown. Stir in half-and-half mixture; heat through. Remove from heat.

2. Heat a large skillet coated with cooking spray over medium-high heat. Break eggs, 1 at a time, into pan; reduce heat to low. Cook until desired doneness, turning after whites are set if desired. Serve with hash; sprinkle with parsley.

1 SERVING: 307 cal., 16g fat (6g sat. fat), 247mg chol., 1010mg sod., 19g carb. (7g sugars, 2g fiber), 19g pro.

MUSHROOM-GOUDA QUICHE

For a laid-back Sunday brunch, we make a quiche in no time using refrigerated
pie crust. Load it up with mushrooms, aromatic arugula and creamy Gouda.
—*Thomas Faglon, Somerset, NJ*

PREP: 15 MIN. • BAKE: 30 MIN. + STANDING • MAKES: 6 SERVINGS

1 sheet refrigerated
   pie crust
4 large eggs
1 cup heavy whipping
   cream
¼ tsp. salt
¼ tsp. pepper
2 cups sliced fresh shiitake
   mushrooms (about 4 oz.)
1 cup shredded Gouda or
   Monterey Jack cheese
1 cup chopped arugula or
   fresh baby spinach

1. Preheat oven to 350°. Unroll crust into a 9-in. pie plate; flute edge. Refrigerate while preparing filling.

2. In a large bowl, whisk eggs, cream, salt and pepper until blended. Stir in remaining ingredients. Pour into crust.

3. Bake on a lower oven rack 30-35 minutes or until crust is golden brown and a knife inserted in the center comes out clean. Let stand 10 minutes before cutting.

FREEZE OPTION: Cover and freeze unbaked quiche. To use, remove from freezer 30 minutes before baking (do not thaw). Preheat oven to 350°. Place quiche on a baking sheet; cover edge loosely with foil. Bake as directed, increasing time as necessary for a knife inserted in the center to come out clean.

1 PIECE: 422 cal., 33g fat (18g sat. fat), 207mg chol., 452mg sod., 21g carb. (4g sugars, 1g fiber), 12g pro.

BREAKFAST BREAD BOWLS

These bread bowls are so elegant, tasty and simple, you'll wonder why you haven't been making them for years. My wife loves when I make these for her in the morning.
—Patrick Lavin Jr., Birdsboro, PA

PREP: 20 MIN. • **BAKE:** 20 MIN. • **MAKES:** 4 SERVINGS

½ cup chopped pancetta
4 crusty hard rolls
  (4 in. wide)
½ cup finely chopped fresh
  mushrooms
4 large eggs
⅛ tsp. salt
⅛ tsp. pepper
¼ cup shredded Gruyere or
  fontina cheese

1. Preheat oven to 350°. In a small skillet, cook pancetta over medium heat until browned, stirring occasionally. Remove with a slotted spoon; drain on paper towels.

2. Meanwhile, cut a thin slice off the top of each roll. Hollow out bottom of roll, leaving a ½-in.-thick shell (save removed bread for another use); place shells on an ungreased baking sheet.

3. Add mushrooms and pancetta to bread shells. Carefully break an egg into each; sprinkle eggs with salt and pepper. Sprinkle with cheese. Bake 18-22 minutes or until egg whites are completely set and yolks begin to thicken but are not hard.

1 BREAKFAST BOWL: 256 cal., 13g fat (5g sat. fat), 206mg chol., 658mg sod., 19g carb. (1g sugars, 1g fiber), 14g pro.

CHEESE GRITS & SAUSAGE BREAKFAST CASSEROLE

This recipe brings all my favorites into one dish: creamy grits, tangy cheese, rich eggs and flavorful sausage. It's the perfect alternative to traditional breakfast casseroles.
—Mandy Rivers, Lexington, SC

PREP: 30 MIN. • **BAKE:** 40 MIN. + STANDING • **MAKES:** 12 SERVINGS

2 lbs. bulk Italian sausage
2 cups water
2 cups chicken broth
½ tsp. salt
1¼ cups quick-cooking grits
1 lb. sharp cheddar cheese,
  shredded
1 cup 2% milk
1½ tsp. garlic powder
1 tsp. rubbed sage
6 large eggs, beaten
  Paprika, optional

1. In a large skillet, cook sausage over medium heat until no longer pink; drain.

2. In a large saucepan, bring the water, broth and salt to a boil. Slowly stir in grits. Reduce heat; cook and stir for 5-7 minutes or until thickened. Remove from the heat. Add the cheese, milk, garlic powder and sage, stirring until cheese is melted. Stir in sausage and eggs. Transfer to a greased 13x9-in. baking dish; sprinkle with paprika if desired.

3. Bake, uncovered, at 350° for 40-45 minutes or until a knife inserted in the center comes out clean. Let stand for 10 minutes before serving.

1 PIECE: 496 cal., 35g fat (17g sat. fat), 201mg chol., 1173mg sod., 17g carb. (4g sugars, 1g fiber), 28g pro.

BAKED FRENCH TOAST WITH STRAWBERRIES

French toast is a crowd-pleaser, but it's hard to make and serve to a big group all at once. This overnight recipe with fresh strawberries and a pecan topping fixes everything.
—*David Stelzl, Waxhaw, NC*

> **PREP:** 20 MIN. + CHILLING • **BAKE:** 40 MIN. + STANDING
> **MAKES:** 12 SERVINGS

12 slices day-old French bread (1 in. thick)
6 large eggs
1½ cups 2% milk
1 cup half-and-half cream
2 Tbsp. maple syrup
1 tsp. vanilla extract
½ tsp. ground cinnamon
¼ tsp. ground nutmeg

TOPPING
1 cup packed brown sugar
½ cup butter, melted
2 Tbsp. maple syrup
1 cup chopped pecans
4 cups chopped fresh strawberries
Additional maple syrup

1. Place bread in a single layer in a greased 13x9-in. baking dish. In a large bowl, whisk eggs, milk, cream, syrup, vanilla, cinnamon and nutmeg; pour over bread. For topping, in a small bowl, mix brown sugar, butter and syrup; stir in pecans. Spread over bread. Refrigerate, covered, overnight.

2. Preheat oven to 350°. Remove French toast from refrigerator while oven heats. Bake, uncovered, 40-50 minutes or until a knife inserted in the center comes out clean. Let stand 10 minutes before serving. Serve with strawberries and additional syrup.

1 PIECE: 377 cal., 20g fat (8g sat. fat), 126mg chol., 266mg sod., 42g carb. (27g sugars, 3g fiber), 8g pro.

FROM GRANDMA'S KITCHEN: When it comes to choosing bread for French toast, fresher doesn't always mean better. In fact, the French call this dish "pain perdu," which translates to "lost bread." Use day-old bread that's sturdy and slightly stale. This way it will soak up the liquid egg mixture without becoming soggy.

BREAKFAST BISCUIT CUPS

The first time I made these biscuit cups, my husband and his assistant coach came into the kitchen as I pulled the pan from the oven. They devoured them!

—*Debra Carlson, Columbus Junction, IA*

PREP: 30 MIN. • BAKE: 20 MIN. • MAKES: 8 SERVINGS

⅓ **lb. bulk pork sausage**
1 **Tbsp. all-purpose flour**
⅛ **tsp. salt**
½ **tsp. pepper, divided**
¾ **cup plus 1 Tbsp. 2% milk, divided**
½ **cup frozen cubed hash brown potatoes, thawed**
1 **Tbsp. butter**
2 **large eggs**
⅛ **tsp. garlic salt**
1 **can (16.3 oz.) large refrigerated flaky biscuits**
½ **cup shredded Colby-Monterey Jack cheese**

1. In a large skillet, cook sausage over medium heat until no longer pink; drain. Stir in the flour, salt and ¼ tsp. pepper until blended; gradually add ¾ cup milk. Bring to a boil; cook and stir until thickened, about 2 minutes. Remove from heat and set aside.

2. In another large skillet over medium heat, cook potatoes in butter until tender. Whisk the eggs, garlic salt and remaining milk and pepper; add to skillet. Cook and stir until almost set.

3. One at a time, press biscuits onto the bottom and up the sides of 8 ungreased muffin cups. Spoon the egg mixture, half the Colby Monterey-Jack cheese, and the sausage into cups; sprinkle with remaining cheese.

4. Bake at 375° until golden brown, 18-22 minutes. Cool 5 minutes before removing from pan.

FREEZE OPTION: Freeze cooled biscuit cups in a freezer container, separating layers with waxed paper. To use, microwave 1 frozen biscuit cup on high until heated through, 50-60 seconds.

1 BISCUIT CUP: 303 cal., 18g fat (6g sat. fat), 72mg chol., 774mg sod., 26g carb. (7g sugars, 1g fiber), 9g pro.

"I made these five days before Christmas, and then froze them. Christmas Day, we microwaved them. They were a huge hit. It is now a Christmas morning must-have for breakfast, and if you make them in advance, there is no cooking to do in the morning."
—MBIERI, TASTEOFHOME.COM

BLACK FOREST HAM
ROLL-UPS, PAGE 65

GRANDMA'S FAVORITE
SNACKS

Grandma knew how to get a party on with her best-ever appetizers, dips, spreads, munchies and beverages. Need a platter of hot bites for your game-day gathering or a savory nosh for a holiday bash? Whether the occasion is big or small, it's easy to take your events to new heights with these fun foods.

LEMON SPICED TEA

Adding cinnamon and honey perks up the flavor of basic lemon tea.
The splash of lemon extract takes it delightfully over the top.
—*Adeline Russell, Hartford, WI*

TAKES: 10 MIN. • MAKES: 8 SERVINGS

8   cups water
14 lemon-flavored tea bags
6   cinnamon sticks (3 in.)
½   cup honey
½   to 1 tsp. lemon extract,
    optional
    Lemon slices and
    additional cinnamon
    sticks

1. In a large saucepan, bring water to a boil. Remove from the heat; add tea bags and cinnamon sticks. Cover and steep for 6 minutes.

2. Discard tea bags and cinnamon sticks. Stir in honey and, if desired, extract. Serve warm in mugs. Garnish with lemon slices and cinnamon sticks.

1 CUP: 64 cal., 0 fat (0 sat. fat), 0 chol., 1mg sod., 17g carb. (17g sugars, 0 fiber), 0 pro. **DIABETIC EXCHANGES:** 1 starch.

HERB DIP WITH SPRING VEGETABLES

When you're having a large party and focusing on the entrees, it's smart to have snacks and nibbles ready ahead of time. There's nothing more simple than making dip a day or two ahead and putting it out for guests. I'm a huge fan of ranch, so this is my pick.
—*Michelle Clair, Seattle, WA*

PREP: 10 MIN. + CHILLING • MAKES: 2 CUPS

2   cups sour cream
¼   cup ranch salad
    dressing mix
2   Tbsp. onion soup mix
¼   cup minced fresh parsley
2   Tbsp. chopped fresh
    rosemary
    Fresh rainbow baby
    carrots and watermelon
    (or plain) radishes

Stir together first 5 ingredients; refrigerate, covered, overnight. Sprinkle with additional parsley and rosemary before serving with rainbow carrots and assorted radishes.

2 TBSP. DIP: 76 cal., 6g fat (4g sat. fat), 7mg chol., 559mg sod., 5g carb. (1g sugars, 0 fiber), 1g pro.

LEMON SPICED TEA

SAUSAGE & KRAUT BUNS

This recipe has become a regular at our church potlucks.
Let's just say I'm in trouble if I show up at a get-together
and they don't appear!

—Patsy Unruh, Perryton, TX

PREP: 20 MIN. • COOK: 4 HOURS • MAKES: 12 SERVINGS

- 2 cans (14½ oz. each) no-salt-added diced tomatoes, drained
- 2 cans (14 oz. each) sauerkraut, rinsed and drained
- ½ lb. sliced fresh mushrooms
- 1 large sweet pepper, thinly sliced
- 1 large onion, halved and thinly sliced
- 2 Tbsp. brown sugar
- ½ tsp. pepper
- 2 pkg. (14 oz. each) smoked sausage, sliced
- 12 pretzel sausage buns, warmed and split partway

1. In a 5- or 6-qt. slow cooker, combine first 7 ingredients. In a large skillet, saute the sausage over medium-high heat until lightly browned. Stir into tomato mixture.

2. Cook, covered, on low 4-5 hours or until vegetables are tender. Serve in buns.

1 SANDWICH: 468 cal., 23g fat (8g sat. fat), 44mg chol., 1491mg sod., 51g carb. (12g sugars, 4g fiber), 17g pro.

GRANDMA'S SECRET

Turn this hearty sausage and sauerkraut appetizer into a German beer hall supper by serving it alongside German potato dumplings with a classic apfelkuchen (apple cake) for dessert.

MINI BLT APPETIZERS

A few simple ingredients are all you need to wow friends and family with
a tasty appetizer. I love to make these as much as I love to share them.
—*Nick Berg, Milwaukee, WI*

TAKES: 30 MIN. • MAKES: ABOUT 2½ DOZEN

30 **cherry tomatoes**
¾ **cup reduced-fat mayonnaise**
2 **Bibb or Boston lettuce leaves, torn into 1-in. pieces**
¼ **cup salad croutons, broken into pieces**
3 **bacon strips, cooked and crumbled**
Coarsely ground pepper

1. Cut a thin slice off the top of each tomato. Scoop out and discard pulp; invert tomatoes on paper towels to drain. Pipe mayonnaise into tomatoes.

2. Roll lettuce pieces and insert into tomato centers. Repeat with croutons and bacon. Sprinkle with pepper. Cover and refrigerate up to 1 hour.

1 APPETIZER: 27 cal., 2g fat (0 sat. fat), 3mg chol., 55mg sod., 1g carb. (1g sugars, 0 fiber), 0 pro.

PARTY SPINACH SPREAD

This appetizer is delicious, easy and pretty, too! The spread keeps for several days,
so it's ideal for making ahead. But once you put it out, it won't last long!
—*Maire Macy, Fort Collins, CO*

TAKES: 10 MIN. • MAKES: 15 CUPS

1 **pkg. (10 oz.) frozen chopped spinach, about ⅔ cup**
⅓ **cup fresh parsley, stems trimmed and discarded**
2 **Tbsp. chopped onion**
1 **tsp. salt**
1 **tsp. ground black pepper**
½ **cup mayonnaise**
Assorted crackers

Thaw spinach and drain thoroughly, squeezing out extra liquid. Wash parsley; pat dry on paper toweling. In food processor, chop parsley using steel blade. Add spinach and remaining ingredients; pulse until combined. Store in airtight container in refrigerator. Serve with crackers.

2 TBSP.: 74 cal., 7g fat (1g sat. fat), 3mg chol., 265mg sod., 1g carb. (0 sugars, 1g fiber), 1g pro.

SICILIAN NACHOS

Crispy bread replaces the classic tortilla chips and a savory meat sauce tops things off.
This hearty appetizer easily doubles as a main dish. Add a salad and you have dinner.
—*Sonya Labbe, West Hollywood, CA*

PREP: 20 MIN. • COOK: 35 MIN. • MAKES: 12 SERVINGS

1 lb. ground beef
1 small red onion, finely chopped
1 small carrot, finely chopped
4 garlic cloves, minced
¾ tsp. crushed red pepper flakes
½ cup dry red wine or beef broth
1 can (15 oz.) crushed tomatoes, undrained
1 can (8 oz.) tomato sauce
½ cup vegetable broth
1 bay leaf
¼ tsp. salt
¼ tsp. pepper
2 Tbsp. minced fresh basil or 2 tsp. dried basil
48 slices French bread baguette (¼ in. thick)
2 garlic cloves, halved
⅓ cup olive oil
1 cup shaved Parmesan cheese

1. In a large skillet, cook the first 5 ingredients over medium heat until beef is no longer pink; drain. Add red wine, stirring to loosen browned bits from pan.

2. Stir in the tomatoes, tomato sauce, broth, bay leaf, salt and pepper. Bring to a boil. Reduce heat; simmer, uncovered, until thickened, 20-25 minutes. Discard bay leaf. Stir in basil.

3. Rub baguette slices with garlic halves; place on ungreased baking sheets. Brush lightly with oil. Bake at 400° until lightly browned, 3-5 minutes.

4. Arrange toasts on serving platters; top with beef mixture and cheese. Serve immediately.

1 SERVING: 212 cal., 12g fat (4g sat. fat), 28mg chol., 455mg sod., 14g carb. (1g sugars, 1g fiber), 10g pro.

ROASTED CHEDDAR HERB ALMONDS

I prepared these one Christmas for my son, who was on a low-carb diet. I was afraid he'd be disappointed because he couldn't eat holiday cookies, but these made up for it— he loved them! Save a handful to chop and sprinkle over a green salad or pasta.
—*Mary Bilyeu, Ann Arbor, MI*

PREP: 10 MIN. • BAKE: 20 MIN. + COOLING • MAKES: 2 CUPS

1 **egg yolk**
2 **cups unblanched almonds**
¾ **cup finely shredded sharp cheddar cheese**
1 **tsp. salt-free herb seasoning blend**
¾ **tsp. salt**
½ **tsp. garlic powder**

1. Preheat oven to 325°. In a large bowl, whisk egg yolk; stir in almonds. In a small bowl, toss cheese with seasonings. Add to the almond mixture; toss to combine. Transfer mixture to a greased 15x10x1-in. baking pan.

2. Bake 20-25 minutes or until cheese is golden brown, stirring occasionally. Cool completely.

¼ CUP: 264 cal., 23g fat (4g sat. fat), 34mg chol., 298mg sod., 7g carb. (2g sugars, 4g fiber), 11g pro.

TOMATO-BACON DIP WITH FOCACCIA

For a spread with BLT flavor, mix mayo and sour cream, then add bacon and tomato. We enjoy it as both a dip and a zesty sandwich spread.
—*Marsha Postar, Lubbock, TX*

PREP: 20 MIN. + CHILLING • MAKES: 12 SERVINGS

1 **cup mayonnaise**
1 **cup sour cream**
½ **lb. bacon strips, cooked and crumbled**
1 **large tomato, seeded and finely chopped**
½ **small onion, finely chopped**
Crumbled cooked bacon and minced fresh parsley, optional
Focaccia bread, sliced and lightly toasted

1. In a small bowl, mix mayonnaise and sour cream. Stir in bacon, tomato and onion. Refrigerate until cold, about 1 hour.

2. If desired, sprinkle with bacon and parsley; serve with focaccia.

¼ CUP DIP: 211 cal., 21g fat (5g sat. fat), 27mg chol., 228mg sod., 2g carb. (1g sugars, 0 fiber), 3g pro.

SWEET ONION PIMIENTO CHEESE DEVILED EGGS

For my mother's 92nd birthday, we had deviled eggs topped with pimientos as part of the spread. They're timeless and always in good taste.
—*Linda Foreman, Locust Grove, OK*

TAKES: 15 MIN. • **MAKES:** 1 DOZEN

- 6 hard-boiled large eggs
- ¼ cup finely shredded sharp cheddar cheese
- 2 Tbsp. mayonnaise
- 4 tsp. diced pimientos, drained
- 2 tsp. finely chopped sweet onion
- 1 tsp. Dijon mustard
- 1 small garlic clove, minced
- ¼ tsp. salt
- ⅛ tsp. pepper
- Additional diced pimientos and finely shredded sharp cheddar cheese

Cut eggs lengthwise in half. Remove yolks, reserving whites. In a bowl, mash yolks. Stir in cheese, mayonnaise, pimientos, onion, mustard, garlic, salt and pepper. Spoon or pipe mixture into egg whites. Sprinkle with additional diced pimientos and cheddar cheese. Refrigerate, covered, until serving.

1 STUFFED EGG HALF: 67 cal., 5g fat (2g sat. fat), 96mg chol., 128mg sod., 1g carb. (0 sugars, 0 fiber), 4g pro.

GRANDMA'S SECRET

Older eggs are best for hard-boiling. Eggs that are close to their best-by date will peel much easier than fresh eggs. The shells of fresh eggs will chip much more than eggs that have been in your fridge for a few days.

SMOKED TROUT PATE

This tasty spread is easy to make in a food processor, and it's a guaranteed winner at any party.
The recipe is versatile, so feel free to substitute other favorite smoked fish.
—*Judy Walle, Toledo, OH*

TAKES: 15 MIN. • MAKES: 2⅔ CUPS

1 **lb. flaked smoked trout**
3 **oz. reduced-fat cream cheese**
½ **cup half-and-half cream**
1 **Tbsp. horseradish sauce**
1 **Tbsp. lemon juice**
⅛ **tsp. pepper**
2 **tsp. minced fresh parsley**
Cucumber slices
Assorted crackers

Pulse the first 7 ingredients in a food processor until blended. Refrigerate, covered, until serving. Serve with cucumber slices and assorted crackers.

2 TBSP.: 55 cal., 3g fat (1g sat. fat), 16mg chol., 174mg sod., 1g carb. (1g sugars, 0 fiber), 5g pro.

HOT SPICED CIDER

Next time you're entertaining, stir up a batch of this nicely spiced cider.
The wonderful aroma will make your guests feel welcome on a chilly day.
—*Kimberly Wallace, Dennison, OH*

TAKES: 20 MIN. • MAKES: 4½ QT.

1 **gallon apple cider or apple juice**
1 **cup orange juice**
¼ **cup maple syrup**
½ **tsp. orange extract**
½ **tsp. lemon extract**
4 **cinnamon sticks**
2 **tsp. whole cloves**
1 **tsp. whole allspice**

In a Dutch oven, combine the first five ingredients. Place the cinnamon sticks, cloves and allspice on a double thickness of cheesecloth; bring up corners of cloth and tie with string to form a bag. Add to the pan. Cook, uncovered, over medium heat for 10-15 minutes or until flavors are blended (do not boil). Discard the spice bag.

1 CUP: 113 cal., 0 fat (0 sat. fat), 0 chol., 20mg sod., 28g carb. (24g sugars, 0 fiber), 0 pro.

SMOKED TROUT PATE

THREE CHEESE ARTICHOKE
& SPINACH DIP

Grated Parmesan, shredded mozzarella, cream cheese, mayo and butter make this dip as decadent as it gets. The pull-apart bread bites make it even more fun and indulgent.

—Rashanda Cobbins, Milwaukee, WI

PREP: 30 MIN. + RISING • **BAKE:** 25 MIN. • **MAKES:** 16 SERVINGS (4 CUPS DIP)

SNACKS

1 pkg. (16 oz.) frozen bread dough dinner rolls (12 rolls), thawed
6 Tbsp. butter
½ tsp. garlic powder
¼ tsp. crushed red pepper flakes

DIP
1 Tbsp. butter
1 cup chopped fresh mushrooms
2 garlic cloves, minced
1½ cups mayonnaise
1 pkg. (8 oz.) cream cheese, softened
1 cup shredded part-skim mozzarella cheese, divided
½ cup plus 2 Tbsp. grated Parmesan cheese, divided
1 can (14 oz.) water-packed artichoke hearts, rinsed, drained and chopped
1 pkg. (10 oz.) frozen chopped spinach, thawed and squeezed dry
¼ cup chopped sweet red pepper

1. Place a 6-in. cake pan or small ovenproof saucepan in the center of a 10-in. cast-iron skillet. Cut each roll into thirds; roll each piece into a ball. Place along the outer edge of skillet. Gently stack remaining balls on top of bottom layer, leaving a small amount of space between them. Cover and let rise until almost doubled, about 30 minutes.

2. Preheat the oven to 400°. Microwave butter, garlic powder and red pepper flakes, covered, until butter is melted. Brush half of butter mixture over dough. Reserve remaining butter mixture.

3. Bake until the dough balls are set and beginning to brown, 15-18 minutes. Remove cake pan from skillet. Meanwhile, in a small skillet, heat 1 Tbsp. butter over medium-high heat. Add mushrooms; cook and stir until tender, 5-7 minutes. Add garlic; cook 1 minute longer.

4. In a large bowl, combine the mayonnaise, cream cheese, ¾ cup mozzarella cheese and ½ cup Parmesan cheese. Add mushroom mixture, artichokes and spinach.

5. Spoon dip into center of skillet; sprinkle with red pepper and remaining ¼ cup mozzarella. Brush rolls with remaining butter mixture; sprinkle with remaining 2 Tbsp. Parmesan. Bake until dip is heated through and rolls are golden brown, 10-15 minutes. If desired, sprinkle with additional red pepper flakes.

¼ CUP WITH ABOUT 2 ROLL PIECES: 359 cal., 29g fat (10g sat. fat), 36mg chol., 526mg sod., 19g carb. (2g sugars, 2g fiber), 8g pro.

SO-EASY SNACK MIX

I eat this tasty treat just as much as (if not more than) the kids! Have fun with it by adding other goodies into the mix, like nuts, cereal, pretzels and more.
—*Jeff King, Duluth, MN*

TAKES: 5 MIN. • **MAKES:** 4 QT.

4 **cups Goldfish cheddar crackers**	2 **cups yogurt-covered raisins**
4 **cups golden raisins**	2 **cups miniature pretzels**
4 **cups dried cherries**	

Place all ingredients in a large bowl; toss to combine. Store in airtight containers.

½ **CUP:** 195 cal., 3g fat (1g sat. fat), 1mg chol., 104mg sod., 42g carb. (29g sugars, 2g fiber), 2g pro.

AUNT FRANCES' LEMONADE

Every summer, my sister and I spent a week with our Aunt Frances, who always had this thirst-quenching lemonade in a stoneware crock in her refrigerator. It was so refreshing after running around on a hot day.
—*Debbie Reinhart, New Cumberland, PA*

TAKES: 15 MIN. • **MAKES:** 16 SERVINGS (4 QT.)

5 **lemons**
5 **limes**
5 **oranges**
3 **qt. water**
1½ **to 2 cups sugar**

1. Squeeze the juice from 4 each of the lemons, limes and oranges; pour into a gallon container.

2. Thinly slice the remaining fruit and set aside for garnish. Add water and sugar to the juice mixture; mix well. Store in the refrigerator. Serve over ice with fruit slices.

1 **CUP:** 92 cal., 0 fat (0 sat. fat), 0 chol., 1mg sod., 24g carb. (21g sugars, 1g fiber), 0 pro.

VIDALIA ONION
SWISS DIP

VIDALIA ONION SWISS DIP

I've got one of those sweet, creamy dips you can't resist. Bake it in the oven,
or use the slow cooker to make it ooey-gooey marvelous.
—*Judy Batson, Tampa, FL*

PREP: 10 MIN. • COOK: 25 MIN. • MAKES: 20 SERVINGS

3 cups chopped Vidalia
or other sweet onion
(about 1 large)
2 cups shredded Swiss
cheese
2 cups mayonnaise
¼ cup prepared
horseradish
1 tsp. hot pepper sauce
Fresh coarsely ground
pepper, optional
Assorted crackers or
fresh vegetables

1. Preheat oven to 375°. In a large bowl, mix the first
5 ingredients. Transfer to a deep-dish pie plate.

2. Bake, uncovered, until edges are golden brown and onion is
tender, 25-30 minutes. If desired, sprinkle with pepper. Serve
warm with crackers.

¼ CUP: 212 cal., 21g fat (4g sat. fat), 18mg chol., 143mg sod.,
3g carb. (1g sugars, 1g fiber), 3g pro.

BLUEBERRY ORANGE BLAST

Blueberries are loaded with antioxidants. I developed this healthy smoothie after
our annual blueberry-picking trip. Adding tofu in smoothies boosts the protein,
and the frozen banana acts just like ice cream.
—*Diane Neibling, Overland Park, KS*

TAKES: 5 MIN. • MAKES: 4 SERVINGS

1 cup orange juice
1 cup vanilla yogurt
1 medium banana, sliced
and frozen
1 cup frozen unsweetened
blueberries
½ cup silken firm tofu

In a blender, combine all ingredients; cover and process until
smooth. Pour into chilled glasses; serve immediately.

¾ CUP: 140 cal., 2g fat (1g sat. fat), 3mg chol., 49mg sod., 27g carb.
(22g sugars, 2g fiber), 5g pro. DIABETIC EXCHANGES: 1 starch,
1 fruit.

BARBECUE SAUSAGE BITES

This irresistible appetizer pairs tangy pineapple with sweet barbecue sauce and three kinds of sausage. It'll tide over even the biggest appetites until dinner.
—*Rebekah Randolph, Greer, SC*

PREP: 10 MIN. • COOK: 2½ HOURS • MAKES: 14 SERVINGS

1 pkg. (16 oz.) miniature smoked sausages
¾ lb. fully cooked bratwurst links, cut into ½-in. slices
¾ lb. smoked kielbasa or Polish sausage, cut into ½-in. slices
1 bottle (18 oz.) barbecue sauce
⅔ cup orange marmalade
½ tsp. ground mustard
⅛ tsp. ground allspice
1 can (20 oz.) pineapple chunks, drained

1. In a 3-qt. slow cooker, combine the sausages. In a small bowl, whisk the barbecue sauce, marmalade, mustard and allspice. Pour over sausage mixture; stir to coat.

2. Cover and cook on high until heated through, 2½-3 hours. Stir in pineapple. Serve with toothpicks.

1 SERVING: 327 cal., 22g fat (8g sat. fat), 53mg chol., 980mg sod., 20g carb. (19g sugars, 1g fiber), 11g pro.

AVOCADO QUESADILLAS

Avocado slices give quesadillas a nutritional boost and, fortunately, my son likes them, too. Add chicken or beef for extra protein.
—*Debbie Limas, North Andover, MA*

TAKES: 20 MIN. • MAKES: 4 SERVINGS

1 Tbsp. canola oil
16 corn tortillas (6 in.)
2 cups shredded Mexican cheese blend
1 cup pico de gallo
1 large ripe avocado, peeled and thinly sliced
3 Tbsp. minced fresh cilantro
Additional pico de gallo

1. Grease a griddle with oil; heat over medium heat. Lightly sprinkle tortillas with water to moisten.

2. Place 8 tortillas on griddle; sprinkle with cheese. After cheese has melted slightly, top with 1 cup pico de gallo, avocado and cilantro. Top with remaining tortillas.

3. Cook until tortillas are lightly browned and cheese is melted, 3-4 minutes on each side. Serve with additional pico de gallo.

2 QUESADILLAS: 611 cal., 37g fat (15g sat. fat), 50mg chol., 455mg sod., 54g carb. (2g sugars, 12g fiber), 20g pro.

SUN-DRIED TOMATO GOAT CHEESE EMPANADAS

I created this appetizer because I entertain a lot and wanted something simple but special. The flaky crust gives way to creamy goat cheese and tangy sun-dried tomatoes.
—*Lynn Scully, Rancho Santa Fe, CA*

PREP: 1 HOUR • BAKE: 15 MIN. • MAKES: ABOUT 1½ DOZEN

- 1 Tbsp. olive oil
- 1 medium sweet onion, halved and thinly sliced
- 1 log (4 oz.) fresh goat cheese, crumbled
- ¼ cup finely chopped oil-packed sun-dried tomatoes, drained
- Pastry for a single-crust pie (9 in.) or 1 sheet refrigerated pie crust

1. In a large skillet, heat oil over medium heat. Add onion; cook and stir until softened, 4-5 minutes. Reduce heat to medium-low; cook, stirring occasionally, until onions are deep golden brown, 30-40 minutes. Remove from heat. Let cool slightly. Gently stir in goat cheese and tomatoes.

2. Preheat oven to 400°. On a lightly floured surface, roll dough to ¼-in. thickness. Cut with a floured 3-in. round biscuit cutter. Place circles 2 in. apart on baking sheets. Place 1 heaping tsp. of filling on 1 side of each circle. Brush edges of pastry with water; fold circles in half. With a fork, press edges to seal. Bake until golden brown, 15-20 minutes.

1 EMPANADA: 99 cal., 7g fat (4g sat. fat), 18mg chol., 98mg sod., 8g carb. (0 sugars, 0 fiber), 2g pro.

GRANDMA'S SECRET

These empanadas are perfect for making ahead, because they can easily be frozen and stored for later.

9-LAYER GREEK DIP

Instead of serving the same taco or veggie dip seen at every family event or potluck, try this light, cool and refreshing Greek dip. It looks and tastes healthy—and it is.
—*Shawn Barto, Palmetto, FL*

TAKES: 20 MIN. • **MAKES:** 5½ CUPS

1 carton (10 oz.) hummus
1 cup refrigerated tzatziki sauce
½ cup chopped green pepper
½ cup chopped sweet red pepper
½ cup chopped peeled cucumber
½ cup chopped water-packed artichoke hearts, drained
½ cup chopped pitted Greek olives, optional
¼ cup chopped pepperoncini
1 cup crumbled feta cheese
Baked pita chips

In a 9-in. deep-dish pie plate, layer first 6 ingredients; top with olives, if desired, and pepperoncini. Sprinkle with feta cheese. Refrigerate until serving. Serve with pita chips.

¼ CUP: 60 cal., 4g fat (1g sat. fat), 5mg chol., 210mg sod., 4g carb. (1g sugars, 1g fiber), 3g pro. **DIABETIC EXCHANGES:** ½ starch, ½ fat.

FROM GRANDMA'S KITCHEN: Make your own tzatziki sauce by combining ½ cup peeled, seeded and finely chopped cucumber with ½ cup plain Greek yogurt, 4 tsp. lemon juice, 1 Tbsp. chopped dill, 1 minced garlic clove, and salt and pepper to taste. Refrigerate.

HONEY SPICED LATTE

Combine rich molasses, golden honey and a host of spices to create this warm and comforting beverage. It's divine on a cool day or as part of a holiday spread.
—Taste of Home *Test Kitchen*

TAKES: 20 MIN. • **MAKES:** 4 SERVINGS

½ cup ground coffee
1½ cups cold water
1⅓ cups milk
2 Tbsp. honey
2 Tbsp. molasses
4 tsp. sugar
¼ tsp. ground ginger
¼ tsp. ground cinnamon
⅛ tsp. ground nutmeg
⅛ tsp. ground cloves
Whipped cream, optional

1. Place ground coffee in the filter of a drip coffeemaker. Add water; brew according to manufacturer's instructions.

2. In a small saucepan, combine the milk, honey, molasses, sugar and spices. Cook and stir over medium heat until steaming. Remove from the heat. Transfer to a blender; cover and process for 15 seconds or until foamy.

3. Divide among 4 mugs; add the coffee. Garnish with whipped cream if desired.

¾ CUP: 134 cal., 3g fat (2g sat. fat), 8mg chol., 44mg sod., 26g carb. (22g sugars, 0 fiber), 3g pro. **DIABETIC EXCHANGES:** 1½ starch, ½ fat.

9-LAYER GREEK DIP

PEACHY BUTTERMILK SHAKES

My husband and grandkids enjoy the tang of buttermilk blended with sweet peaches in these delightful shakes.
—Anna Mayer, Fort Branch, IN

TAKES: 10 MIN. • MAKES: 3 SERVINGS

1 cup buttermilk
3 cups fresh or frozen unsweetened sliced peaches, thawed
1 cup vanilla ice cream, softened
¼ cup sugar
¾ tsp. ground cinnamon
Optional: Whipped cream and additional sliced peaches

Place the first 5 ingredients in a blender; cover and process until smooth. Pour into chilled glasses; serve immediately. If desired, top with whipped cream and additional sliced peaches.

1 CUP: 250 cal., 6g fat (3g sat. fat), 23mg chol., 191mg sod., 46g carb. (42g sugars, 3g fiber), 6g pro.

BACON NACHOS

Topped with kid-friendly ingredients like ground beef, bacon bits and cheddar cheese, these crispy nachos are a big hit in our house. My older kids like that they can microwave them themselves.
—Ruth Ann Bott, Lake Wales, FL

TAKES: 20 MIN. • MAKES: 6 SERVINGS

½ lb. ground beef
4 cups tortilla chips
¼ cup bacon bits
2 cups shredded cheddar cheese
½ cup guacamole dip
½ cup sour cream
Optional: Chopped tomatoes and sliced green onions

1. In a small skillet, cook beef over medium heat until no longer pink; drain. Place tortilla chips on a microwave-safe serving plate. Layer with the beef, bacon and cheese.

2. Microwave, uncovered, on high for 1-2 minutes or until cheese is melted. Top with guacamole and sour cream. Sprinkle with tomatoes and onions if desired.

1 CUP: 404 cal., 29g fat (15g sat. fat), 89mg chol., 594mg sod., 13g carb. (1g sugars, 1g fiber), 20g pro.

BEEF WELLINGTON APPETIZERS

Flaky puff pastry, savory beef tenderloin and tangy horseradish cream
easily come together for a positively holiday-worthy hors d'oeuvre.
—*Joan Cooper, Sussex, WI*

PREP: 45 MIN. • **BAKE:** 15 MIN. • **MAKES:** 16 APPETIZERS (1½ CUPS SAUCE)

2   beef tenderloin steaks
    (8 oz. each), cut into ½-in.
    cubes
2   Tbsp. olive oil, divided
1¼ cups chopped fresh
    mushrooms
2   shallots, chopped
2   garlic cloves, minced
⅓   cup sherry or chicken
    broth
⅓   cup heavy whipping
    cream
½   tsp. salt
⅛   tsp. pepper
1   Tbsp. minced fresh
    parsley
1   pkg. (17.3 oz.) frozen puff
    pastry, thawed
1   large egg, beaten

HORSERADISH CREAM
1   cup sour cream
½   cup mayonnaise
2   Tbsp. prepared
    horseradish
1   Tbsp. minced chives
¼   tsp. pepper
    Additional minced chives,
    optional

1. In a large skillet, brown beef in 1 Tbsp. oil. Remove and keep warm.

2. In same skillet, saute mushrooms and shallots in remaining oil until tender. Add garlic; cook 1 minute longer. Add sherry, stirring to loosen browned bits from pan. Stir in cream, salt and pepper. Bring to a boil; cook until the liquid is almost evaporated, about 7 minutes. Stir in beef and parsley; set aside and keep warm.

3. Preheat oven to 400°. On a lightly floured surface, unfold the puff pastry. Roll each sheet into a 12-in. square. Cut each into 16 squares.

4. Place 2 tablespoonfuls of beef mixture in center of half of squares. Top with remaining squares; press edges with a fork to seal. Place on parchment-lined baking sheets. Cut slits in top; brush with egg. Bake until golden brown, 14-16 minutes.

5. In a small bowl, combine horseradish cream ingredients; serve with appetizers. Garnish with additional chives if desired.

1 APPETIZER WITH ABOUT 2 TSP. SAUCE: 315 cal., 22g fat (6g sat. fat), 45mg chol., 231mg sod., 19g carb. (1g sugars, 2g fiber), 10g pro.

HONEY
HORSERADISH DIP

HONEY HORSERADISH DIP

We love having appetizers on Friday night instead of a meal, and during the summer we enjoy cooler foods. This dip has just the right amount of zing.
—*Ann Marie Eberhart, Gig Harbor, WA*

PREP: 10 MIN. + CHILLING • MAKES: 1 CUP

½ cup fat-free plain Greek yogurt
¼ cup stone-ground mustard
¼ cup honey
2 Tbsp. prepared horseradish
Cold cooked shrimp and fresh sugar snap peas

Combine yogurt, mustard, honey and horseradish; refrigerate 1 hour. Serve with shrimp and snap peas.

2 TBSP.: 54 cal., 1g fat (0 sat. fat), 0 chol., 177mg sod., 11g carb. (10g sugars, 0 fiber), 2g pro. **DIABETIC EXCHANGES:** 1 starch.

BACON-PECAN STUFFED MUSHROOMS

I lost the recipe for these mushrooms during a kitchen remodel. Luckily, I'd shared it so many times I had no trouble finding someone to lend it back to me!
—*Beverly Pierce, Indianola, MS*

TAKES: 30 MIN. • MAKES: 1 DOZEN

4 Tbsp. butter, divided
2 Tbsp. canola oil
12 large fresh mushrooms (about 1 lb.), stems removed
¼ tsp. salt
2 Tbsp. finely chopped onion
1 cup soft bread crumbs
6 bacon strips, cooked and crumbled
2 Tbsp. chopped pecans
2 Tbsp. sherry or beef broth
2 Tbsp. sour cream
2 Tbsp. minced fresh chives

1. Preheat broiler. In a large skillet, heat 2 Tbsp. butter and oil over medium-high heat. Add mushroom caps; cook 2 minutes on each side. Sprinkle with salt. Remove with tongs; drain on paper towels, stem side down.

2. In same pan, heat remaining butter over medium-high heat. Add onion; cook and stir until tender. Remove from heat; stir in remaining ingredients. Spoon into mushroom caps.

3. Place on a broiler pan. Broil 5 in. from heat 2-3 minutes or until filling is browned.

NOTE: To make soft bread crumbs, tear bread into pieces and place in a food processor or blender. Cover and pulse until crumbs form. One slice of bread yields ½-¾ cup crumbs.

1 STUFFED MUSHROOM: 184 cal., 16g fat (6g sat. fat), 25mg chol., 277mg sod., 7g carb. (2g sugars, 1g fiber), 5g pro.

PARTY CRAB PUFFS

I received this recipe years ago from my grandmother, who encouraged me to be creative and experiment in the kitchen. My friends request these little puffs at every gathering.
—*Jean Bevilacqua, Rhododendron, OR*

PREP: 45 MIN. • **BAKE:** 20 MIN./BATCH • **MAKES:** 8 DOZEN

1 cup water
½ cup butter, cubed
¼ tsp. salt
1 cup all-purpose flour
4 large eggs, room temperature

FILLING

4 hard-boiled large eggs, finely chopped
1 can (6 oz.) lump crabmeat, drained
4 oz. cream cheese, softened
¼ cup mayonnaise
2 Tbsp. finely chopped onion
2 Tbsp. prepared horseradish, drained
Minced fresh parsley, optional

1. Preheat oven to 400°. In a large saucepan, bring the water, butter and salt to a boil. Add the flour all at once and stir until a smooth ball forms. Remove from heat; let stand 5 minutes. Add eggs, 1 at a time, beating well after each addition. Continue beating until mixture is smooth and shiny.

2. Drop by teaspoonfuls 2 in. apart onto greased baking sheets. Bake until golden brown, 18-22 minutes. Remove to a wire rack. Immediately split puffs open; remove tops and set aside. Discard soft dough from inside. Cool puffs.

3. In a large bowl, combine filling ingredients. Just before serving, spoon 1 teaspoonful filling into each puff; sprinkle with parsley if desired. Replace tops.

1 SERVING: 30 cal., 2g fat (1g sat. fat), 23mg chol., 32mg sod., 1g carb. (0 sugars, 0 fiber), 1g pro.

GRANDMA'S SECRET

The filling for these party puffs can harbor harmful bacteria if left out at room temperature for longer than 2 hours. If you're including these on a buffet, place the serving container in a larger pan filled with ice to keep them cold.

SPICED PUMPKIN WARM-UP

Make this drink your own! You can add coffee or even alcohol if you want an extra kick. I've also chilled this mixture and blended it with vanilla ice cream to make it a pumpkin shake.
—*Andrea Heyart, Aubrey, TX*

TAKES: 10 MIN. • **MAKES:** 2 SERVINGS

2 cups half-and-half cream
3 Tbsp. sugar
2 Tbsp. canned pumpkin
1 tsp. pumpkin pie spice

¼ tsp. vanilla extract
    Whipped cream and
    additional pumpkin pie
    spice

In a small saucepan, combine cream, sugar, pumpkin and pie spice; cook and stir over medium heat until blended and heated through. Remove from heat; stir in vanilla. Top servings with whipped cream and additional pie spice.

1 CUP: 402 cal., 24g fat (16g sat. fat), 120mg chol., 121mg sod., 28g carb. (27g sugars, 1g fiber), 8g pro.

ORANGE FRUIT DIP

Served with fresh fruit, this dip makes a delicious appetizer that won't spoil appetites.
—*Vicki Eatwell, Eau Claire, WI*

TAKES: 5 MIN. • **MAKES:** 16 SERVINGS

1 pkg. (8 oz.) cream cheese, softened
1 cup marshmallow creme
4 tsp. grated orange zest (about 1 orange)
    Assorted fresh fruit

In a large bowl, beat cream cheese, marshmallow creme and orange zest until smooth. Cover and refrigerate until serving. Serve with fresh fruit.

2 TBSP.: 70 cal., 5g fat (3g sat. fat), 16mg chol., 47mg sod., 6g carb. (4g sugars, 0 fiber), 1g pro.

SLOW-COOKER SPICED MIXED NUTS

What slow cookers do for soups and stews, they'll also do for mixed nuts.
The scent of spices is delightful, and the nuts are delicious.
—*Stephanie Loaiza, Layton, UT*

PREP: 15 MIN. • COOK: 1 HOUR 50 MIN. + COOLING • MAKES: 6 CUPS

1   large egg white
2   tsp. vanilla extract
1   cup unblanched almonds
1   cup pecan halves
1   cup shelled walnuts
1   cup unsalted cashews
1   cup sugar
1   cup packed brown sugar
4   tsp. ground cinnamon
2   tsp. ground ginger
1   tsp. ground nutmeg
½   tsp. ground cloves
⅛   tsp. salt
2   Tbsp. water

1. In a large bowl, whisk egg white and vanilla until blended; stir in nuts. In a small bowl, mix sugars, spices and salt. Add to nut mixture and toss to coat.

2. Transfer to a greased 3-qt. slow cooker. Cook, covered, on high 1½ hours, stirring every 15 minutes. Gradually stir in water. Cook, covered, on low 20 minutes.

3. Spread onto waxed paper; cool completely. Store in airtight containers up to 1 week.

⅓ CUP: 261 cal., 15g fat (2g sat. fat), 0 chol., 26mg sod., 30g carb. (24g sugars, 2g fiber), 5g pro.

BACON ROLL-UPS

This family recipe dates back to the 1930s, when my grandmother started making these hearty rolls. Serve them as appetizers for game-day parties or brunch gatherings.
—*Janet Abate, North Brunswick, NJ*

PREP: 25 MIN. • COOK: 20 MIN. • MAKES: 10 ROLL-UPS

⅓   cup finely chopped onion
1   Tbsp. butter
3   cups cubed day-old bread
¼   tsp. celery salt
¼   tsp. garlic powder
⅛   tsp. salt
⅛   tsp. pepper
1   large egg, lightly beaten
10 bacon strips

1. In a small skillet, saute onion in butter until tender. In a large bowl, combine the bread cubes, celery salt, garlic powder, salt, pepper and onion mixture; toss to mix evenly. Add egg; toss to coat bread cubes. Roll into ten 1¼-in. balls. Wrap a bacon strip around each ball. Secure each ball with a toothpick.

2. In a large skillet, cook bacon roll-ups on all sides over medium heat for 18 minutes or until bacon is crisp and a thermometer inserted into stuffing reads at least 160°. Drain on paper towels.

2 ROLL-UPS: 348 cal., 30g fat (11g sat. fat), 79mg chol., 613mg sod., 12g carb. (2g sugars, 1g fiber), 7g pro.

SLOW-COOKER
SPICED MIXED NUTS

STRAWBERRY SPRITZER

Three simple ingredients are all you need to
create this fresh and fruity beverage. It's great all year
long, but especially refreshing on warm summer days.
—*Krista Collins, Concord, NC*

TAKES: 10 MIN. • MAKES: 2½ QT.

1 pkg. (10 oz.) frozen
  sweetened sliced
  strawberries, thawed

2 liters lemon-lime soda,
  chilled
1 can (12 oz.) frozen pink
  lemonade concentrate,
  thawed

Place the strawberries in a blender; cover and process until
pureed. Pour into a large pitcher; stir in the soda and lemonade
concentrate. Serve immediately.

1¼ CUPS: 215 cal., 0 fat (0 sat. fat), 0 chol., 31mg sod., 56g carb.
(53g sugars, 1g fiber), 0 pro.

HORSERADISH CHEESE SPREAD

A friend gave me the recipe for this creamy dip. It makes a delicious party starter
or a great snack whenever you're craving something with a little zip.
—*Connie Simon, Jensen Beach, FL*

PREP: 15 MIN. + CHILLING • MAKES: 4 CUPS

2 lbs. Velveeta, cubed
½ cup prepared
  horseradish
⅓ cup mayonnaise
1 tsp. hot pepper sauce
¼ tsp. garlic salt
¼ tsp. Worcestershire
  sauce
  Assorted crackers or
  raw vegetables

Melt Velveeta in the top of a double boiler over simmering water
until smooth. Stir in horseradish, mayonnaise, hot pepper sauce,
garlic salt and Worcestershire sauce until blended. Transfer to
storage containers. Cover and refrigerate until chilled. Serve with
crackers or raw vegetables.

2 TBSP.: 112 cal., 9g fat (5g sat. fat), 19mg chol., 377mg sod.,
3g carb. (2g sugars, 0 fiber), 6g pro.

CRESCENT SAMOSAS

Tender buttery crescents are filled with a delicious filling, making these appetizers a real standout. No one will guess that they're light!
—*Jennifer Kemp, Grosse Pointe Park, MI*

PREP: 25 MIN. • BAKE: 10 MIN. • MAKES: 16 APPETIZERS (¾ CUP SAUCE)

¾ cup reduced-fat plain yogurt
2 Tbsp. minced fresh cilantro
1 garlic clove, minced
½ tsp. ground cumin
Dash pepper

SAMOSAS
1 Tbsp. olive oil
1 can (14½ oz.) diced new potatoes, well drained, or 1¾ cups diced cooked red potatoes
¼ cup canned chopped green chiles
1 garlic clove, minced
1 tsp. curry powder
Dash pepper
1½ tsp. lemon juice
1 cup frozen peas, thawed
2 tubes (8 oz. each) refrigerated reduced-fat crescent rolls

1. Preheat oven to 375°. For sauce, mix first 5 ingredients; refrigerate until serving.

2. In a large nonstick skillet, heat oil over medium-high heat; saute potatoes until lightly browned. Add chiles, garlic, curry powder and pepper; cook and stir 1 minute. Transfer to a bowl; add lemon juice and coarsely mash. Stir in peas.

3. Unroll crescent dough and separate into 16 triangles. Place 1 Tbsp. potato mixture on the wide end of each triangle; roll up from wide end. Place 2 in. apart on ungreased baking sheets, point side down; curve to form crescents.

4. Bake until golden brown, 10-12 minutes. Serve with sauce.

1 APPETIZER WITH 2 TSP. SAUCE: 130 cal., 6g fat (2g sat. fat), 1mg chol., 305mg sod., 18g carb. (3g sugars, 1g fiber), 4g pro.

FROM GRANDMA'S KITCHEN: Samosas are savory fried pastries traditionally stuffed with spices, potatoes and other vegetables. (For other variations, you can also fill them with Paneer, an unaged Indian cheese, and jalapenos.) They're a common street food in northern and western India. Serve samosas with a dipping sauce like green mint chutney or sweet tamarind chutney.

BLACK FOREST HAM
ROLL-UPS

BLACK FOREST HAM ROLL-UPS

We love to entertain. Ham and cheese rolled in tortillas make a quick and easy appetizer.
—*Susan Zugehoer, Hebron, KY*

PREP: 25 MIN. + CHILLING • MAKES: ABOUT 6½ DOZEN

1 pkg. (8 oz.) cream cheese, softened
2 tsp. minced fresh parsley
2 tsp. dried celery flakes
2 tsp. Dijon mustard
1 tsp. lemon juice
⅛ tsp. salt
⅛ tsp. pepper
½ cup dried cranberries, chopped
2 green onions, chopped
5 flour tortillas (10 in.), room temperature
½ lb. thinly sliced Black Forest deli ham
½ lb. thinly sliced Swiss cheese

1. In a small bowl, mix the first 7 ingredients until blended. Stir in cranberries and green onions; spread over tortillas. Layer with ham and cheese. Roll up tightly; wrap and refrigerate for at least 1 hour.

2. Just before serving, unwrap and cut each tortilla crosswise into 16 slices.

1 APPETIZER: 42 cal., 2g fat (1g sat. fat), 7mg chol., 83mg sod., 3g carb. (1g sugars, 0g fiber), 2g pro.

TUNA DILL SPREAD

Slather this tasty tuna spread on crackers. I love that it can be made in a jiffy.
—*Geraldine Grisdale, Mount Pleasant, MI*

TAKES: 10 MIN. • MAKES: 5 SERVINGS

1 can (6 oz.) tuna, drained and flaked
3 oz. cream cheese, softened
⅓ cup finely chopped seeded cucumber
2 Tbsp. lemon juice
1 to 2 Tbsp. minced fresh dill
½ tsp. salt
¼ tsp. pepper

In a bowl, combine all ingredients; mix well. Use as sandwich filling or spread on crackers.

¼ CUP: 102 cal., 6g fat (4g sat. fat), 29mg chol., 402mg sod., 1g carb. (1g sugars, 0 fiber), 10g pro.

CRANBERRY ORANGE ALMOND
QUICK BREAD, PAGE 79

GRANDMA'S FAVORITE

BREADS, ROLLS & MORE

Dinner rolls and quick breads, sweet muffins and
herb loaves—let the aroma of these freshly baked
delights usher in heartwarming memories of
Grandma's kitchen and the amazing, magical treats
she pulled from her oven.

AMISH ONION CAKE

This rich, moist bread with an onion-poppy seed topping is a wonderful break from your everyday bread routine. It's a nice sidekick to soup or salad and goes well with any entree.

—Mitzi Sentiff, Annapolis, MD

PREP: 25 MIN. • **BAKE:** 35 MIN. • **MAKES:** 12 SERVINGS

3 to 4 medium onions, chopped
2 cups cold butter, divided
1 Tbsp. poppy seeds
1½ tsp. salt
1½ tsp. paprika
1 tsp. coarsely ground pepper
4 cups all-purpose flour
½ cup cornstarch
1 Tbsp. baking powder
1 Tbsp. sugar
1 Tbsp. brown sugar
5 large eggs, room temperature
¾ cup 2% milk
¾ cup sour cream

1. In a large skillet, cook onions in ½ cup butter over low heat for 10 minutes. Stir in the poppy seeds, salt, paprika and pepper; cook until onions are golden brown, stirring occasionally. Remove from the heat; set aside.

2. In a large bowl, combine the flour, cornstarch, baking powder and sugars. Cut in 1¼ cups butter until mixture resembles coarse crumbs. Melt the remaining butter. In a small bowl, whisk the eggs, milk, sour cream and melted butter. Make a well in dry ingredients; stir in egg mixture just until moistened.

3. Spread into a greased 10-in. cast-iron skillet or springform pan. Spoon onion mixture over the batter. Place pan on a baking sheet. Bake at 350° until a toothpick inserted in the center comes out clean, 35-40 minutes. Serve warm.

1 PIECE: 539 cal., 36g fat (22g sat. fat), 182mg chol., 748mg sod., 44g carb. (7g sugars, 2g fiber), 9g pro.

GRANDMA'S SECRET

Is your brown sugar rock-solid? Try this easy trick to make it soft. Place a small piece of bread or apple in the bag with the sugar and let it sit for a little while. When you come back, the sugar will be soft again.

SWEET POTATO & PESTO SLOW-COOKER BREAD

I love to bake fresh bread, both as a way to offer my family a delicious dinner accompaniment and just because I enjoy the process. Baking bread in the slow cooker allows me to achieve a tender, perfectly baked loaf without turning on the oven, which is especially helpful in summer. Baking bread this way also eliminates the need for a second rise, which is a nice timesaver. This beautiful loaf is one of my favorite recipes.
—*Shauna Havey, Roy, UT*

PREP: 45 MIN. + RISING • **COOK:** 3 HOURS + COOLING
MAKES: 1 LOAF (12 PIECES)

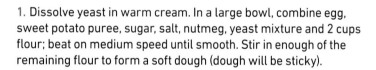

- 1 pkg. (¼ oz.) active dry yeast
- ⅔ cup warm half-and-half cream (110° to 115°)
- 1 large egg, room temperature
- 1 cup canned sweet potato puree or canned pumpkin
- 1 tsp. sugar
- 1 tsp. kosher salt
- ¼ tsp. ground nutmeg
- 3½ to 4 cups bread flour
- 1 container (7 oz.) refrigerated prepared pesto
- ½ cup plus 2 Tbsp. grated Parmesan cheese, divided

1. Dissolve yeast in warm cream. In a large bowl, combine egg, sweet potato puree, sugar, salt, nutmeg, yeast mixture and 2 cups flour; beat on medium speed until smooth. Stir in enough of the remaining flour to form a soft dough (dough will be sticky).

2. Turn onto a lightly floured surface; knead until smooth and elastic, 6-8 minutes. Place in a greased bowl, turning once to grease the top. Cover and let rise in a warm place until doubled, about 1 hour.

3. Punch down dough. Turn onto a lightly floured surface; roll into a 18x9-in. rectangle. Spread the pesto to within 1 in. of edges; sprinkle with ½ cup Parmesan. Roll up jelly-roll style, starting with a long side; pinch seam and ends to seal.

4. Using a sharp knife, cut roll lengthwise in half; carefully turn each half cut side up. Loosely twist strips around each other, keeping cut surfaces facing up. Shape into a coil; place on parchment. Transfer to a 6-qt. slow cooker; sprinkle with remaining 2 Tbsp. Parmesan. Let rise until doubled, about 1 hour.

5. Cook, covered, on low 3-3½ hours or until bread is lightly browned. Remove bread from slow cooker and cool slightly before slicing.

1 PIECE: 271 cal., 10g fat (3g sat. fat), 26mg chol., 464mg sod., 36g carb. (3g sugars, 2g fiber), 8g pro.

UPSIDE-DOWN BANANA MONKEY BREAD

Everyone digs in to monkey bread thanks to its pull-apart shape. We add bananas and pecans in this scrumptious showpiece for a brunch or family gathering.

—Donna-Marie Ryan, Topsfield, MA

PREP: 45 MIN. + RISING • BAKE: 25 MIN. • MAKES: 24 SERVINGS

2 tsp. active dry yeast

1 Tbsp. plus ½ cup packed brown sugar, divided

1 cup warm 2% milk (110° to 115°)

1 cup mashed ripe bananas (about 2 large)

1 large egg, room temperature

2 Tbsp. butter, melted

1 tsp. salt

1 tsp. ground cinnamon

5¼ to 5¾ cups all-purpose flour

2 tsp. banana extract, optional

GLAZE

⅔ cup packed brown sugar

½ cup half-and-half cream

6 Tbsp. butter, cubed

COATING

¾ cup chopped pecans, toasted

6 Tbsp. butter, melted

1¼ cups sugar

2½ tsp. ground cinnamon

1 large banana, sliced

1. In a small bowl, dissolve yeast and 1 Tbsp. brown sugar in warm milk. In a large bowl, combine bananas, egg, butter, yeast mixture, salt, cinnamon, 1½ cups flour and remaining ½ cup brown sugar; if desired, add extract. Beat on medium speed 2 minutes. Stir in enough remaining flour to form a soft dough (dough will be sticky).

2. Turn dough onto a floured surface; knead until smooth and elastic, 6-8 minutes. Place in a greased bowl, turning once to grease the top. Cover and let rise in a warm place until doubled, about 1 hour.

3. In a small saucepan, combine glaze ingredients; bring just to a boil, stirring constantly. Reserve ¼ cup for topping. Pour the remaining glaze into a greased 13x9-in. baking pan; sprinkle with toasted pecans.

4. Pour melted butter into a shallow bowl. In another shallow bowl, mix sugar and cinnamon. Punch down dough. Turn onto a lightly floured surface; divide and shape into 48 balls.

5. Dip the dough balls in butter, roll in sugar mixture and place in prepared pan. Cover with a kitchen towel; let rise in a warm place until almost doubled, about 30 minutes. Preheat oven to 375°.

6. Bake 25-30 minutes or until golden brown. Cool in pan for 5 minutes before inverting onto a serving plate. Top with sliced banana; drizzle with reserved glaze. Serve warm.

NOTE: To toast nuts, bake in a shallow pan in a 350° oven for 5-10 minutes or cook in a skillet over low heat until lightly browned, stirring occasionally.

2 PIECES: 296 cal., 10g fat (5g sat. fat), 29mg chol., 166mg sod., 47g carb. (24g sugars, 2g fiber), 4g pro.

BRAIDED EGG BREAD

For Rosh Hashana, we bake loaves of braided bread—commonly called challah—to symbolize continuity. Since I first made this bread some years ago, it has become a much-requested recipe.
—*Marlene Jeffery, Holland, MB*

PREP: 30 MIN. + RISING • **BAKE:** 25 MIN. + COOLING • **MAKES:** 1 LOAF (16 PIECES)

3¼ to 3¾ cups all-purpose
    flour
1 **Tbsp. sugar**
1 **pkg. (¼ oz.) active
    dry yeast**
¾ **tsp. salt**
¾ **cup water**
3 **Tbsp. canola oil**
2 **large eggs, room
    temperature**

TOPPING
1 **large egg**
1 **tsp. water**
½ **tsp. poppy seeds**

1. In a large bowl, combine 2½ cups flour, sugar, yeast and salt. In a small saucepan, heat water and oil to 120°-130°. Add to the dry ingredients along with the eggs. Beat on medium speed for 3 minutes. Stir in enough remaining flour to form a soft dough.

2. Turn onto a lightly floured surface; knead until smooth and elastic, 6-8 minutes. Place in a greased bowl, turning once to grease top. Cover and let rise in a warm place until doubled, about 1½ hours.

3. Punch dough down. Turn onto a lightly floured surface. Set a third of the dough aside. Divide remaining dough into 3 pieces. Shape each into a 13-in. rope. Place ropes on a greased baking sheet and braid; pinch ends to seal and tuck under.

4. Divide reserved dough into 3 equal pieces; shape each into a 14-in. rope. Braid ropes. Center 14-in. braid on top of the shorter braid. Pinch ends to seal and tuck under. Cover and let rise until doubled, about 30 minutes.

5. Preheat oven to 375°. In a small bowl, beat egg and water; brush over dough. Sprinkle with poppy seeds. Bake until golden brown, 25-30 minutes. Cover with foil during the last 15 minutes of baking. Remove from pan to a wire rack to cool.

1 PIECE: 134 cal., 4g fat (1g sat. fat), 40mg chol., 123mg sod., 20g carb. (1g sugars, 1g fiber), 4g pro.

FROM GRANDMA'S KITCHEN: Challah, a braided bread, is made with a simple dough of eggs, water, flour, yeast and salt. The bread is typically pale yellow in color because so many eggs are used, and it has a delectable rich flavor. Some challah recipes call for inclusions like raisins, honey or seeds. It all depends on the celebration and your preferences.

GRANDMA'S FAVORITE HOT CROSS BUNS

My husband's grandma used to make these every year for Good Friday, and I carry on the tradition with my own version of her recipe. I make six dozen every year, and they all disappear.

—Jill Evely, Wilmore, KY

PREP: 45 MIN. + RISING • **BAKE:** 15 MIN./BATCH • **MAKES:** 6 DOZEN

4 pkg. (¼ oz. each) active dry yeast
3 cups warm 2% milk (110° to 115°)
2 cups canola oil
8 large eggs, room temperature
4 large eggs, room temperature, separated
1⅓ cups sugar
4 tsp. ground cinnamon
3 tsp. salt
2 tsp. ground cardamom
13 to 15 cups all-purpose flour
2⅔ cups raisins
2 tsp. water

ICING
3 cups confectioners' sugar
2 Tbsp. butter, melted
4 to 5 Tbsp. 2% milk

1. In a very large bowl, dissolve yeast in warm milk. Add oil, eggs, egg yolks, sugar, cinnamon, salt, cardamom, yeast mixture and 10 cups flour. Beat until smooth. Stir in enough remaining flour to form a firm dough. Stir in raisins.

2. Turn onto a floured surface; knead until smooth and elastic, 6-8 minutes. Place in a greased bowl, turning once to grease top. Cover and let rise in a warm place until doubled, about 1¼ hours.

3. Punch dough down. Turn onto a lightly floured surface. Cover and let rest 10 minutes. Divide into 72 pieces; shape each into a ball. Place 2 in. apart in 4 greased 15x10x1-in. baking pans. Cover and let rise in a warm place until doubled, about 40 minutes.

4. Preheat oven to 375°. Combine egg whites and water; brush over tops. Bake 12-15 minutes or until golden brown. Remove from pans to wire racks to cool. For icing, combine confectioners' sugar, butter and enough milk to achieve desired consistency. Pipe a cross on top of each bun.

1 BUN: 219 cal., 8g fat (1g sat. fat), 37mg chol., 120mg sod., 32g carb. (12g sugars, 2g fiber), 5g pro.

GRANDMA'S SECRET
The icing will thin a little when it comes in contact with the warm buns. So keep it on the thicker side.

CAPE COD BAY BROWN BREAD

This reminds me of the brown bread my grandmother made whenever we would visit her out East. The aroma evokes fond memories of her New England home during the peak of fall. I use blackstrap molasses and agave nectar to make mine a little different without sacrificing flavor. Cranberries are another special touch, but this would also taste delicious with raisins.

—Kellie Foglio, Salem, WI

PREP: 40 MIN. + RISING • BAKE: 30 MIN. + COOLING
MAKES: 2 LOAVES (12 PIECES EACH)

2 pkg. (¼ oz. each) active dry yeast
3 Tbsp. molasses
2 tsp. agave nectar or honey
2⅔ cups warm water (110° to 115°)
½ cup dried cranberries

2 Tbsp. wheat bran
1 tsp. salt
6 to 7 cups whole wheat flour

TOPPING
1 Tbsp. 2% milk
1 Tbsp. old-fashioned oats

1. In a small bowl, dissolve the yeast, molasses and agave nectar in ⅔ cup warm water. In a large bowl, combine the cranberries, wheat bran, salt, yeast mixture, 4 cups flour and remaining water; beat on medium speed until smooth, about 3 minutes. Stir in enough of the remaining flour to form a soft dough (dough will be sticky).

2. Turn dough onto a floured surface; knead until smooth and elastic, 6-8 minutes. Place in a greased bowl, turning once to grease the top. Cover and let rise in a warm place until doubled, about 1 hour.

3. Turn onto a lightly floured surface; divide in half. Shape into loaves. Place in 2 greased 8x4-in. loaf pans. Cover; let rise in a warm place until almost doubled, about 1 hour. Preheat the oven to 400°.

4. Brush tops with milk. Sprinkle with oats. Bake until golden brown, 30-40 minutes. Remove from pans to wire racks; cool completely.

1 PIECE: 125 cal., 1g fat (0 sat. fat), 0 chol., 101mg sod., 27g carb. (5g sugars, 4g fiber), 4g pro.

CAST-IRON APPLE NUTMEG COFFEE CAKE

In an effort to practice my baking, I used up the morning's last bit of coffee to make a coffee cake. It's super moist and crumbly and tastes like you dunked your cake right into a cup of hot joe. You can add pecans to the apples if you want some crunch.
—*Darla Andrews, Boerne, TX*

PREP: 25 MIN. • **BAKE:** 20 MIN. + COOLING • **MAKES:** 8 SERVINGS

3 Tbsp. butter, cubed
2 cups chopped peeled Gala apple
½ cup packed brown sugar, divided
¼ cup brewed coffee
⅔ cup canola oil
½ cup sugar
1 large egg plus 1 large egg white, room temperature
2 tsp. vanilla extract
1½ cups all-purpose flour
2 tsp. ground cinnamon
½ tsp. salt
½ tsp. baking soda
¼ tsp. ground nutmeg

DRIZZLE

⅓ cup brewed coffee
¼ cup heavy whipping cream
1½ cups confectioners' sugar

1. Preheat oven to 375°. In a 10-in. cast-iron or other ovenproof skillet, melt butter over low heat. Add apple and ¼ cup brown sugar. Cook and stir until crisp-tender, about 5 minutes. Stir in coffee; remove from heat.

2. In a large bowl, beat the oil, sugar, egg, egg white, vanilla and remaining ¼ cup brown sugar until well blended. In another bowl, whisk flour, cinnamon, salt, baking soda and nutmeg; gradually beat into oil mixture. Gently spread over apple mixture.

3. Bake until a toothpick inserted in the center comes out clean, 18-22 minutes. Cool on a wire rack 10 minutes.

4. Meanwhile, for drizzle, in a small saucepan, bring the coffee and whipping cream to a boil; cook until the liquid is reduced to ¼ cup, 10-12 minutes. Remove from heat; stir in confectioners' sugar. Let stand 10 minutes. Drizzle over cake.

1 PIECE: 532 cal., 27g fat (6g sat. fat), 43mg chol., 284mg sod., 71g carb. (51g sugars, 1g fiber), 4g pro.

"My daughter had a blast helping make this with my wife. Turned out great and I heard them giggling the whole time making it. Thanks for a great treat!"
—MIKE, TASTEOFHOME.COM

VEGGIE PULL-APART BREAD

A bread machine hurries along the dough-making process, but chopped vegetables, bacon and cheese make this buttery wreath unforgettable.
—*Christi Ross, Guthrie, TX*

PREP: 35 MIN. + RISING • **BAKE:** 40 MIN. + COOLING • **MAKES:** 12 SERVINGS

½ cup water
½ cup sour cream
1 Tbsp. butter
3 Tbsp. sugar
1½ tsp. salt
3 cups all-purpose flour
1½ tsp. active dry yeast

VEGETABLE MIXTURE
½ cup butter, cubed
1 cup chopped celery

1 cup chopped green pepper
1 cup chopped green onions
6 bacon strips, cooked and crumbled
1 cup shredded cheddar cheese
Ranch salad dressing, optional

1. In bread machine pan, place the first 7 ingredients in order suggested by the manufacturer. Select dough setting. Check the dough after 5 minutes of mixing; add 1-2 Tbsp. additional water or flour if needed.

2. When cycle is completed, punch down dough and let rest, covered, 10 minutes. Meanwhile, in a large skillet, heat butter over medium-high heat. Add celery and pepper; cook and stir until crisp-tender. Stir in green onions. Transfer to a bowl; cool slightly. Stir in bacon and cheese.

3. Divide and shape dough into 24 balls; roll in vegetable mixture and place in a greased 10-in. fluted tube pan.

4. Cover with a kitchen towel; let rise in a warm place until doubled, about 45 minutes. Preheat oven to 350°.

5. Bake until golden brown, 40-45 minutes. Cool in the pan for 5 minutes before inverting onto a serving plate. If desired, serve with ranch dressing.

2 PIECES: 289 cal., 15g fat (9g sat. fat), 44mg chol., 507mg sod., 29g carb. (4g sugars, 2g fiber), 8g pro.

GOLDEN CRESCENTS

When my grandchildren take one of these slightly sweet, tender rolls out of the basket, they say, "Grandma, you're the world's best cook." There's no better compliment for a grandmother!
—*Bertha Johnson, Indianapolis, IN*

PREP: 25 MIN. + RISING • **BAKE:** 10 MIN. • **MAKES:** 2 DOZEN

2 pkg. (¼ oz. each) active dry yeast
¾ cup warm water (110° to 115°)
½ cup sugar
2 large eggs, room temperature
¼ cup butter, softened
2 Tbsp. shortening
1 tsp. salt
4 to 4½ cups all-purpose flour
2 Tbsp. melted butter plus additional as needed, divided

1. In a large bowl, dissolve yeast in warm water. Add the sugar, eggs, softened butter, shortening, salt and 2 cups flour; beat until smooth. Add enough of the remaining flour to form a soft dough. Turn dough onto a floured surface; knead until smooth and elastic, 6-8 minutes.

2. Place in a greased bowl, turning once to grease the top. Cover and let rise in a warm place until doubled, about 1½ hours.

3. Punch dough down; divide in half. Roll each portion into a 12-in. circle. Brush each with 1 Tbsp. melted butter, and cut into 12 wedges. Roll up wedges from the wide end and place point side down 2 in. apart on greased baking sheets. Curve ends to form crescents. Cover and let rise until doubled, 45 minutes.

4. Bake at 375° until golden, 8-10 minutes. Brush with additional melted butter if desired.

1 ROLL: 133 cal., 4g fat (2g sat. fat), 25mg chol., 133mg sod., 20g carb. (4g sugars, 1g fiber), 3g pro.

CRANBERRY ORANGE ALMOND QUICK BREAD
PICTURED ON PAGE 66

The beauty of this bread is that you can customize it to your family's specific tastes. Try dried apricots and pecans, or dried blueberries and hazelnuts.
—Taste of Home *Test Kitchen*

PREP: 15 MIN. • **BAKE:** 40 MIN. + COOLING • **MAKES:** 1 LOAF (12 PIECES)

3 cups all-purpose flour
3 Tbsp. sugar
1 Tbsp. baking powder
½ tsp. salt
1 cup dried cranberries
½ cup sliced almonds, toasted
1 large egg, room temperature
1 cup fat-free milk
⅓ cup canola oil
¾ tsp. grated orange zest
¾ tsp. almond extract

1. Preheat oven to 350°. In a large bowl, whisk together first 4 ingredients; stir in cranberries and almonds. In another bowl, whisk together egg, milk, oil, zest and extract. Add to the flour mixture; stir just until moistened.

2. Transfer to a 9x5-in. loaf pan coated with cooking spray. Bake until a toothpick inserted in the center of loaf comes out clean, 40-50 minutes. Cool in pan 10 minutes before removing to a wire rack to cool.

1 PIECE: 258 cal., 9g fat (1g sat. fat), 16mg chol., 234mg sod., 40g carb. (14g sugars, 2g fiber), 5g pro.

OMA'S MARZIPAN STOLLEN

My German grandma made this stollen for us when we were young. I love its homey taste and how it reminds me of her and the German food she made. I often freeze this sweet bread once it's shaped into a braid. I can pull it out the night before, let it rise on the counter overnight, and bake it in the morning.
—*Abigail Leszczynski, Beaufort, SC*

PREP: 30 MIN. + RISING • BAKE: 30 MIN. + COOLING • MAKES: 1 LOAF (16 PIECES)

- 3 to 3½ cups all-purpose flour
- ⅓ cup sugar
- 1 pkg. (¼ oz.) active dry yeast
- 1¼ cups 2% milk
- 6 Tbsp. butter, cubed
- 2 tsp. grated lemon zest

FILLING
- 1 can (12½ oz.) almond cake and pastry filling
- 1 cup finely ground almonds
- 1 Tbsp. 2% milk
- 1 tsp. rum extract

GLAZE
- ¼ cup confectioners' sugar
- ½ to 1 tsp. 2% milk

1. In a large bowl, combine 2 cups flour, sugar and yeast. In a small saucepan, heat milk and butter to 120°-130°. Add to dry ingredients; beat just until moistened. Add lemon zest; beat until smooth. Stir in enough remaining flour to form a soft dough (dough will be sticky).

2. Turn onto a floured surface; knead until smooth and elastic, 6-8 minutes. Place in a greased bowl, turning once to grease the top. Cover and let rise in a warm place until doubled, about 1 hour.

3. For filling, in a large bowl, beat almond pastry filling, almonds, milk and extract. Punch dough down; turn onto a floured surface. Divide into thirds. Roll each portion into a 15x6-in. rectangle. Spread each portion with a third of the filling to within ¼ in. of edges. Roll up jelly-roll style, starting with a long slide; pinch seam to seal. Place ropes on a parchment-lined baking sheet. Using a sharp knife, make a ½-in.-deep cut lengthwise down the center of each rope, stopping ½ in. from ends. Keeping cut surfaces facing up, braid ropes. Pinch ends to seal; tuck under.

4. Cover with a kitchen towel; let rise in a warm place until almost doubled, about 30 minutes. Preheat oven to 375°. Bake until golden brown, 30-35 minutes. Remove to a wire rack to cool. Combine the glaze ingredients to desired consistency; drizzle over stollen.

1 PIECE: 270 cal., 10g fat (4g sat. fat), 13mg chol., 73mg sod., 41g carb. (16g sugars, 2g fiber), 5g pro.

DOUBLE CRANBERRY BANANA BREAD

We love quick breads, and I've found they freeze nicely if properly wrapped. This is a scrumptious recipe to make before the holidays and freeze for last-minute guests or gifts.

—Joan Hallford, North Richland Hills, TX

PREP: 25 MIN. • BAKE: 50 MIN. + COOLING • MAKES: 1 LOAF (12 PIECES)

⅓ cup shortening
⅔ cup sugar
2 large eggs, room temperature
1 cup mashed ripe banana
1 tsp. vanilla extract
1¾ cups all-purpose flour
2 tsp. baking powder
½ tsp. salt
¼ tsp. baking soda
1 cup whole-berry cranberry sauce
¾ cup chopped pecans, divided
½ cup dried cranberries

1. Preheat oven to 350°. In a large bowl, cream shortening and sugar until light and crumbly. Beat in eggs, banana and vanilla. In another bowl, whisk flour, baking powder, salt and baking soda; gradually beat into creamed mixture. Stir in the cranberry sauce, ½ cup pecans and dried cranberries.

2. Transfer to a greased 8x4-in. loaf pan. Sprinkle with remaining pecans. Bake until a toothpick inserted in center comes out clean, 50-60 minutes. Cool in pan 10 minutes before removing to a wire rack to cool completely.

FREEZE OPTION: Securely wrap cooled loaf in foil, then freeze. To use, thaw at room temperature.

1 PIECE: 289 cal., 11g fat (2g sat. fat), 31mg chol., 229mg sod., 45g carb. (24g sugars, 2g fiber), 4g pro.

GRANDMA'S APPLE BREAD

The heavenly aroma of apples, cinnamon and nuts baking in the bread will make anyone's mouth water. This recipe will earn a place in your keeper files.

—Sheila Bradshaw, Powell, OH

PREP: 20 MIN. • BAKE: 35 MIN. + COOLING • MAKES: 2 LOAVES (12 PIECES EACH)

1⅓ cups all-purpose flour
⅔ cup rye flour
½ cup sugar
2 tsp. baking powder
1½ tsp. ground cinnamon
½ tsp. baking soda
½ tsp. salt
1 large egg, room temperature
¾ cup unsweetened apple juice
¾ cup sweetened applesauce
⅓ cup canola oil
½ cup chopped pecans

1. In a large bowl, combine the flours, sugar, baking powder, cinnamon, baking soda and salt. In another bowl, whisk the egg, apple juice, applesauce and oil until smooth. Stir into the dry ingredients just until moistened. Fold in pecans.

2. Pour into 2 greased 8x4-in. loaf pans. Bake at 350° until a toothpick inserted in the center comes out clean, 35-40 minutes. Cool for 10 minutes before removing from pans to wire racks.

1 PIECE: 108 cal., 5g fat (1g sat. fat), 9mg chol., 112mg sod., 15g carb. (7g sugars, 1g fiber), 1g pro.

SOUR CREAM ROLLS
WITH WALNUT FILLING

My grandmother taught me how to make these rolls when I was
a young girl. I remember feeling so special when we served them.
If you have never worked with yeast, this is the recipe for you.
—*Nadine Mesch, Mount Healthy, OH*

PREP: 1 HOUR + RISING • BAKE: 20 MIN. • MAKES: 8 LOAVES (6 PIECES EACH)

4 cups ground walnuts
(about 14 oz.)
1 cup sugar
¾ cup butter, melted
½ cup 2% milk
⅓ cup honey

DOUGH
2 pkg. (¼ oz. each) active
dry yeast

1 tsp. plus ⅓ cup sugar,
divided
½ cup warm 2% milk
(110° to 115°)
1 cup butter, melted
1 cup sour cream
4 large eggs, room
temperature, divided use
1 tsp. salt
5¼ to 5¾ cups all-purpose
flour

1. In a large bowl, mix the first 5 ingredients until blended. In
a small bowl, dissolve yeast and 1 tsp. sugar in warm milk; let
stand 15 minutes. In a large bowl, combine melted butter, sour
cream, 3 eggs, salt, remaining sugar, yeast mixture and 2 cups
flour; beat on medium speed 3 minutes. Stir in enough remaining
flour to form a soft dough (dough will be sticky).

2. Turn dough onto a floured surface; knead until smooth and
elastic, 6-8 minutes. Place in a greased bowl, turning once to
grease the top. Cover and let rise in a warm place until doubled,
about 1 hour.

3. Punch down dough. Turn onto a lightly floured surface; divide
and shape into 8 portions. Roll each into a 12x8-in. rectangle
(dough will be very thin). Spread each with ½ cup walnut mixture
to within ¾ in. of edges. Carefully roll up jelly-roll style, starting
with a long side; pinch seam and ends to seal.

4. Place rolls 2 in. apart on parchment-lined baking sheets, seam
side down. Prick tops with a fork. Cover; let rise in a warm place
until almost doubled, about 1 hour. Preheat oven to 350°.

5. Lightly beat remaining egg; brush over rolls. Bake until golden
brown, 20-25 minutes, switching position of pans halfway through
baking (filling may leak during baking). Remove loaves to wire
racks to cool. To serve, cut into slices.

1 PIECE: 201 cal., 13g fat (5g sat. fat), 37mg chol., 113mg sod., 20g
carb. (8g sugars, 1g fiber), 3g pro.

TRIPLE CITRUS SCONES

I love the bright and buttery flavor of these tender scones.
Serve them with a yummy jam, or try them as a base for strawberry shortcake.
—*Angela Lemoine, Howell, NJ*

PREP: 20 MIN. • **BAKE:** 15 MIN. • **MAKES:** 8 SCONES

2¼ cups all-purpose flour
¼ cup plus 1 Tbsp. sugar, divided
4 tsp. grated orange zest
2 tsp. grated lemon zest
1½ tsp. grated lime zest
3 tsp. baking powder
½ tsp. salt
6 Tbsp. cold butter, cubed
1 large egg, room temperature
¼ cup orange juice
¼ cup buttermilk
1 Tbsp. butter, melted

GLAZE

¼ cup confectioners' sugar
1½ tsp. grated lime zest
1 Tbsp. lime juice
1 Tbsp. orange juice

1. Preheat oven to 400°. Place flour, ¼ cup sugar, citrus zests, baking powder and salt in a food processor; pulse until blended. Add cold butter; pulse until butter is the size of peas. Transfer to a large bowl. In a small bowl, whisk the egg, orange juice and buttermilk until blended; stir into the crumb mixture just until moistened.

2. Turn onto a lightly floured surface; knead gently 6-8 times. Pat dough into a 6-in. circle. Cut into 8 wedges. Place the wedges on a parchment-lined baking sheet. Brush with melted butter; sprinkle with remaining sugar.

3. Bake 14-18 minutes or until golden brown. Meanwhile, in a small bowl, mix glaze ingredients until smooth. Remove scones from oven; immediately brush with glaze. Serve warm.

1 SCONE: 281 cal., 11g fat (7g sat. fat), 50mg chol., 403mg sod., 41g carb. (13g sugars, 1g fiber), 5g pro.

GRANDMA'S SECRET

Scones are generally patted into a circle and cut into wedges. If the wedges are separated, the scones will have a crisper crust. If the wedges are cut but not fully separated, the scones will have a softer crust.

CINNAMON CHOCOLATE CHIP ROLLS

I started adding chocolate chips to my cinnamon rolls because several children didn't like the raisins in them. The chocolate and cinnamon are a fun flavor combination. My family loves them, and so does my Sunday school class.

—Patty Wynn, Pardeeville, WI

PREP: 45 MIN. + RISING • **BAKE:** 25 MIN./BATCH • **MAKES:** 4 DOZEN

4 pkg. (¼ oz. each) active
  dry yeast
2½ cups warm water
  (110° to 115°)
3 cups warm 2% milk
  (110° to 115°)
½ cup butter, softened
2 large eggs, room
  temperature
¾ cup honey
4 tsp. salt
14 cups all-purpose flour

FILLING
6 Tbsp. butter, softened
2¼ cups packed brown sugar
1 pkg. (10 oz.) miniature
  semisweet chocolate
  chips
3 tsp. ground cinnamon

GLAZE
3 cups confectioners' sugar
6 Tbsp. butter, softened
1 tsp. vanilla extract
6 to 8 Tbsp. 2% milk

1. In a large bowl, dissolve the yeast in warm water; let stand for 5 minutes. Add the milk, butter, eggs, honey, salt and 3 cups flour; beat on low for 3 minutes. Stir in enough remaining flour to form a soft dough.

2. Turn onto a floured surface; knead until smooth and elastic, 6-8 minutes. Place in a large greased bowl, turning once. Cover and let rise in a warm place until doubled, about 1 hour.

3. Punch dough down. Turn onto a floured surface; divide into 4 pieces. Roll each into a 14x8-in. rectangle; spread with butter. Combine the brown sugar, chips and cinnamon; sprinkle over dough to within ½ in. of edges and press into dough.

4. Roll up jelly-roll style, starting with a long side; pinch seam to seal. Cut each into 12 slices. Place cut side down in 4 greased 13x9-in. baking dishes. Cover and let rise until doubled, about 30 minutes.

5. Bake at 350° until golden brown, 25-30 minutes. Cool for 5 minutes; remove from pans to wire racks.

6. For glaze, in a large bowl, combine the confectioners' sugar, butter, vanilla and enough milk to reach desired consistency; drizzle over warm rolls.

1 ROLL: 308 cal., 8g fat (5g sat. fat), 22mg chol., 251mg sod., 56g carb. (27g sugars, 2g fiber), 5g pro.

SAVORY BISCUIT-BREADSTICKS

I love to experiment in the kitchen with simple ingredients like refrigerated biscuits. The results are usually a big hit. These super fast and yummy breadsticks are one of my best creations!
—*Billy Hensley, Mount Carmel, TN*

TAKES: 20 MIN. • MAKES: 10 BREADSTICKS

½ cup grated Parmesan cheese
2 tsp. dried minced garlic
¼ tsp. crushed red pepper flakes
1 tube (12 oz.) refrigerated buttermilk biscuits
2 Tbsp. olive oil

Preheat oven to 400°. In a shallow bowl, mix cheese, garlic and pepper flakes. Roll each biscuit into a 6-in. rope. Brush lightly with oil; roll in cheese mixture. Place on a greased baking sheet. Bake until golden brown, 8-10 minutes.

1 BREADSTICK: 142 cal., 8g fat (2g sat. fat), 3mg chol., 353mg sod., 16g carb. (2g sugars, 0 fiber), 3g pro.

OLIVE & ONION QUICK BREAD

I've been baking for over 50 years and I never get tired of trying new recipes for my family, friends and co-workers. Baking actually relaxes me. I feel like an artist creating a masterpiece of love. This savory loaf makes a great gift.
—*Paula Marchesi, Lenhartsville, PA*

PREP: 15 MIN. • BAKE: 45 MIN. + COOLING • MAKES: 1 LOAF (12 PIECES)

1 Tbsp. canola oil
1 medium onion, finely chopped
2 cups all-purpose flour
1 Tbsp. minced fresh rosemary
1 tsp. baking soda
½ tsp. salt
2 large eggs, room temperature
1 cup buttermilk
2 Tbsp. butter, melted
¼ cup plus 2 Tbsp. shredded sharp cheddar cheese, divided
¼ cup each chopped pitted green and ripe olives

1. Preheat oven to 350°. In a skillet, heat oil over medium-high heat. Add onion; cook and stir until tender, 2-3 minutes. Remove from heat.

2. In a large bowl, whisk flour, rosemary, baking soda and salt. In another bowl, whisk eggs, buttermilk and melted butter until blended. Add to flour mixture; stir just until moistened. Fold in ¼ cup cheese, olives and onion.

3. Transfer to a greased 8x4-in. loaf pan. Bake 40 minutes. Sprinkle remaining cheese over top. Bake until a toothpick inserted in center comes out clean, 5-10 minutes longer. Cool in pan 10 minutes before removing to a wire rack to cool.

1 PIECE: 150 cal., 6g fat (2g sat. fat), 41mg chol., 373mg sod., 18g carb. (1g sugars, 1g fiber), 5g pro.

SPICED APPLE
CORNBREAD

SPICED APPLE CORNBREAD

There's nothing better than a big piece of cornbread to serve alongside fried chicken,
pork chops or baked ham. I sweetened my recipe by adding a little apple and spice.
Everyone raves over this tender, moist and delicious cornbread.
—*Kelly Williams, Forked River, NJ*

PREP: 15 MIN. • BAKE: 40 MIN. • MAKES: 12 SERVINGS

2 cups all-purpose flour
2 cups yellow cornmeal
1 Tbsp. baking powder
1 tsp. salt
½ tsp. ground cinnamon
½ tsp. pumpkin pie spice
½ cup butter, softened
1½ cups sugar
½ tsp. vanilla extract
4 large eggs, room
temperature
2 cups water
1 cup shredded peeled
apple

1. Preheat oven to 400°. Whisk together first 6 ingredients. In a large bowl, beat butter and sugar until blended. Add vanilla; add eggs, 1 at a time, beating well after each addition. Stir in the flour mixture alternately with water, adding water slowly (mixture may appear slightly curdled). Stir in apple.

2. Transfer to a greased 10-in. cast-iron skillet (pan will be very full). Bake on a lower oven rack until a toothpick inserted in center comes out clean, 40-50 minutes. Serve warm.

1 PIECE: 371 cal., 10g fat (5g sat. fat), 82mg chol., 404mg sod., 64g carb. (27g sugars, 2g fiber), 6g pro.

GRANDMA'S HONEY MUFFINS

I remember my Grandma Wheeler making these delicious muffins—she'd serve them warm,
fresh from the oven. She was a "pinch of this and handful of that" kind of cook, so getting the exact
ingredient measurements for the recipe was a challenge. Now it's a family treasure!
—*Darlis Wilfer, West Bend, WI*

TAKES: 30 MIN. • MAKES: 1 DOZEN

2 cups all-purpose flour
½ cup sugar
3 tsp. baking powder
½ tsp. salt
1 large egg, room
temperature
1 cup 2% milk
¼ cup butter, melted
¼ cup honey

1. Preheat oven to 400°. In a large bowl, combine the flour, sugar, baking powder and salt. In a small bowl, combine egg, milk, butter and honey. Stir into dry ingredients just until moistened.

2. Fill greased or paper-lined muffin cups three-fourths full. Bake until a toothpick inserted in the center comes out clean, 15-18 minutes. Cool 5 minutes before removing from pan to a wire rack. Serve warm.

FREEZE OPTION: Freeze cooled muffins in freezer containers. To use, thaw at room temperature or, if desired, microwave each muffin on high until heated through, 20-30 seconds.

1 MUFFIN: 179 cal., 5g fat (3g sat. fat), 29mg chol., 242mg sod., 31g carb. (15g sugars, 1g fiber), 3g pro.

GOLDEN HONEY PAN ROLLS

A cousin in North Carolina gave me the recipe for these delicious
honey-glazed rolls. Using my bread machine to make the dough saves me about
two hours compared to the traditional method. The rich buttery taste is so popular
with family and friends that I usually make two batches so I have enough!

—*Sara Wing, Philadelphia, PA*

PREP: 35 MIN. + RISING • **BAKE:** 20 MIN. • **MAKES:** 2 DOZEN

1 cup warm 2% milk
(70° to 80°)
1 large egg, room
temperature
1 large egg yolk, room
temperature
½ cup canola oil
2 Tbsp. honey
1½ tsp. salt
3½ cups bread flour
2¼ tsp. active dry yeast

GLAZE
⅓ cup sugar
2 Tbsp. butter, melted
1 Tbsp. honey
1 large egg white
Additional honey,
optional

1. In bread machine pan, place the first 8 ingredients in order suggested by manufacturer. Select the dough setting (check dough after 5 minutes of mixing; add 1 to 2 Tbsp. of water or flour if needed).

2. When cycle is completed, turn the dough onto a lightly floured surface. Punch down; cover and let rest for 10 minutes. Divide into 24 pieces; shape each into a ball. Place 12 balls each in 2 greased 8-in. square baking pans. Cover and let rise in a warm place until doubled, about 30 minutes.

3. For glaze, combine the sugar, butter, honey and egg white; drizzle over dough. Bake at 350° until golden brown, 20-25 minutes. Brush with additional honey if desired.

NOTE: We don't recommend using the bread machine's time-delay feature for this recipe.

1 ROLL: 139 cal., 6g fat (2g sat. fat), 22mg chol., 168mg sod., 18g carb. (5g sugars, 1g fiber), 3g pro.

GRANDMA'S SECRET

To allow for good air circulation while baking, leave at least 1 in. of space between the square baking pans and between pans and the sides of the oven.

DATE PECAN TEA BREAD

Packed with dates and pecans, this moist
sweet bread is excellent on its own and even better
topped with the chunky cream cheese spread.
—*Carole Resnick, Cleveland, OH*

PREP: 20 MIN. • **BAKE:** 65 MIN. + COOLING
MAKES: 1 LOAF (16 PIECES) AND ½ CUP SPREAD

2½ cups chopped dates
1½ cups boiling water
1½ tsp. baking soda
1¾ cups all-purpose flour
¼ tsp. each ground cloves,
cinnamon, ginger and
nutmeg
2 Tbsp. butter, softened
1¼ cups sugar
1 large egg, room
temperature

2 tsp. vanilla extract
1½ cups coarsely chopped
pecans

SPREAD
3 oz. cream cheese,
softened
2 Tbsp. chopped dates
2 Tbsp. coarsely chopped
pecans
1 Tbsp. 2% milk

1. Place dates in a large bowl. Combine boiling water and baking soda; pour over dates. In a small bowl, combine the flour, cloves, cinnamon, ginger and nutmeg; set aside.

2. In another large bowl, beat butter and sugar until crumbly. Beat in egg and vanilla. Add the flour mixture alternately with the date mixture. Stir in pecans.

3. Pour into a greased and floured 9x5-in. loaf pan. Bake at 350° for 65-75 minutes or until a toothpick inserted in the center comes out clean. Cool for 10 minutes before removing from pan to wire rack to cool completely.

4. In a small bowl, combine the spread ingredients. Cover and refrigerate for 1 hour. Serve with bread.

1 SLICE WITH 1½ TSP. SPREAD: 312 cal., 13g fat (3g sat. fat), 23mg chol., 154mg sod., 50g carb. (35g sugars, 4g fiber), 4g pro.

CHEDDAR/SQUASH CLOVERLEAF ROLLS

My rolls started out as a basic bread recipe that I adapted to suit our tastes.
They're great with a meal any time of year, but especially in fall.
Our son-in-law doesn't care for squash—he loves these, though!
—DeDe Waldmann, Monona, WI

PREP: 25 MIN. + RISING • **BAKE:** 20 MIN. • **MAKES:** 2 DOZEN

2 Tbsp. sugar
¼ cup warm water
  (110° to 115°)
1 pkg. (¼ oz.) active dry
  yeast
1 cup warm 2% milk
  (110° to 115°)
4 Tbsp. butter, melted,
  divided
1 tsp. salt
1 cup mashed cooked
  winter squash
¾ cup shredded cheddar
  cheese
4 to 4½ cups all-purpose
  flour
  Sesame seeds, optional

1. In a large bowl, dissolve sugar in water. Sprinkle the yeast over the water and stir gently. Let stand until light and foamy. Stir in the milk, 3 Tbsp. butter, salt, squash and cheese. Add enough flour to form a soft dough.

2. Turn out onto a lightly floured surface; knead until the dough is no longer sticky, about 5 minutes. Form into a ball and place in a greased bowl, turning once to grease the top. Cover and let rise in a warm place until doubled, about 1 hour.

3. Meanwhile, lightly grease 24 muffin cups. Punch down dough. Break off small portions and roll into 1-in. balls. Put 3 balls into each cup. Cover and let rise in a warm place until doubled, about 30 minutes.

4. Brush tops of rolls with remaining butter; sprinkle with sesame seeds if desired. Bake at 375° for 16-18 minutes or until golden. Serve warm.

1 ROLL: 120 cal., 3g fat (2g sat. fat), 10mg chol., 145mg sod., 19g carb. (2g sugars, 1g fiber), 3g pro.

FROM GRANDMA'S KITCHEN: Always let the dough rise in a warm (80°-85°) draft-free area. Proper rising helps in the development of the rolls' texture.

GARLIC-DILL SODA BREAD

It's true. You can bake bread in a slow cooker! Let the inviting aroma of dill and cheese fill your kitchen. Who knew it could be so simple?
—*Melissa Hansen, Ellison Bay, WI*

PREP: 15 MIN. • COOK: 1½ HOURS • MAKES: 1 LOAF (12 PIECES)

- 4 cups all-purpose flour
- 2 Tbsp. dried parsley flakes
- 1 Tbsp. dried minced onion
- 2 tsp. garlic powder
- 1½ tsp. dill weed
- 1 tsp. salt
- 1 tsp. baking soda
- 1 tsp. ground mustard
- 1¾ cups buttermilk
- 1 cup shredded sharp cheddar cheese

1. In a large bowl, whisk the first 8 ingredients. Add buttermilk and cheese; stir just until moistened. Turn onto a lightly floured surface; knead gently 6-8 times or just until the dough comes together. Shape dough into a 6-in. round loaf. Using a sharp knife, score surface with 1-in.-deep cuts in a crisscross pattern. Place in a greased 5-qt. slow cooker.

2. Cook, covered, on high 1½-2 hours or until a thermometer reads 190°-200°.

3. Preheat broiler. Remove bread; place on a baking sheet. Broil 6-8 in. from heat 2-3 minutes or until golden brown. Remove to a wire rack to cool completely.

1 WEDGE: 209 cal., 4g fat (2g sat. fat), 11mg chol., 434mg sod., 35g carb. (2g sugars, 1g fiber), 8g pro.

FROM GRANDMA'S KITCHEN: Be sure to keep the bread in the slow cooker for the recipe's recommended baking time so that it cooks all the way through and you don't end up with an undercooked, gummy interior. The good news is you save a little time baking in the slow cooker because the dough doesn't need to rise first. The bread will rise and bake at the same time.

CORNMEAL PARKER HOUSE ROLLS

My mom deserves the credit for making this recipe a family tradition. These sweet, tender rolls have been on every holiday table at her house for as long as I can remember.
—*Lisa Brenner, Harrisburg, NE*

PREP: 40 MIN. + RISING • **BAKE:** 15 MIN. • **MAKES:** 2½ DOZEN

½ cup butter, cubed
½ cup sugar
⅓ cup cornmeal
1 tsp. salt
2 cups 2% milk
1 pkg. (¼ oz.) active dry yeast
½ cup warm water (110° to 115°)
2 large eggs, room temperature
4½ to 5½ cups all-purpose flour
3 Tbsp. butter, melted
Optional: Olive oil and balsamic vinegar

1. In a small saucepan, melt butter. Stir in the sugar, cornmeal and salt. Gradually add milk. Bring to a boil over medium-high heat, stirring constantly. Reduce heat; cook and stir until thickened, 5-10 minutes. Cool to 110°-115°.

2. In a large bowl, dissolve yeast in warm water. Add eggs and cornmeal mixture. Beat in enough flour to form a soft dough. Turn onto a floured surface; knead dough until smooth and elastic, 6-8 minutes. Place in a greased bowl, turning once to grease top. Cover and let rise in a warm place until doubled, about 1 hour.

3. Punch dough down. Turn onto a lightly floured surface; roll out to ½-in. thickness. Cut with a floured 2½-in. biscuit cutter. Brush with melted butter.

4. Using the dull edge of a table knife, make an off-center crease in each roll. Fold along crease so the large half is on top; press along folded edge. Place 2 in. apart on greased baking sheets. Cover and let rise until nearly doubled, about 30 minutes.

5. Bake at 375° until golden brown, 15-20 minutes. Brush with melted butter. Remove from pans to wire racks. If desired, serve with olive oil and balsamic vinegar.

1 SERVING: 137 cal., 5g fat (3g sat. fat), 26mg chol., 122mg sod., 20g carb. (4g sugars, 1g fiber), 3g pro.

SUGAR PLUM
BREAD

SUGAR PLUM BREAD

I grew up with my Grandma Mitchell's irresistible plum bread. We slathered it with butter and ate it with cottage cheese and fresh fruit for a simple breakfast. And it always makes an appearance at the holidays!
—*Emily Tyra, Lake Ann, MI*

PREP: 15 MIN. + STANDING • BAKE: 40 MIN. + COOLING • MAKES: 1 LOAF (12 PIECES)

1 cup pitted dried plums (prunes), coarsely chopped
¾ cup water
2 Tbsp. plus ¾ cup sugar, divided
2 Tbsp. shortening
1 large egg, room temperature
2 cups all-purpose flour
2 tsp. baking powder
1 tsp. baking soda
½ tsp. salt
2 Tbsp. coarse sugar

1. Preheat oven to 350°. In a small saucepan, combine dried plums, water and 2 Tbsp. sugar. Bring to a simmer over medium heat for 1 minute. Remove from the heat; let stand until plumped, about 10 minutes. Drain the plums, reserving the fruit and liquid. Measure liquid, adding enough water to yield ½ cup.

2. Cream shortening and remaining sugar until light and fluffy, 5-7 minutes. Beat in egg. In another bowl, whisk together flour, baking powder, baking soda and salt. Add to creamed mixture alternately with reserved cooking liquid; fold in cooled dried plums (batter will be thick).

3. Transfer batter to a greased 8x4-in. loaf pan. Sprinkle with coarse sugar. Bake until a toothpick inserted in center comes out with moist crumbs, 40-45 minutes. Cool in pan 10 minutes before removing to a wire rack to cool completely.

1 PIECE: 202 cal., 3g fat (1g sat. fat), 16mg chol., 291mg sod., 41g carb. (21g sugars, 1g fiber), 3g pro.

AUNT BETTY'S BLUEBERRY MUFFINS

My Aunt Betty bakes many items each Christmas,
but I look forward to these mouthwatering muffins the most.
—*Sheila Raleigh, Kechi, KS*

PREP: 15 MIN. • BAKE: 20 MIN. • MAKES: ABOUT 1 DOZEN

½ cup old-fashioned oats
½ cup orange juice
1 large egg, room temperature
½ cup canola oil
½ cup sugar
1½ cups all-purpose flour
1¼ tsp. baking powder
½ tsp. salt
¼ tsp. baking soda
1 cup fresh or frozen blueberries

TOPPING
2 Tbsp. sugar
½ tsp. ground cinnamon

1. In a large bowl, combine oats and orange juice; let stand for 5 minutes. Beat in the egg, oil and sugar until blended. Combine the flour, baking powder, salt and baking soda; stir into the oat mixture just until moistened. Fold in blueberries.

2. Fill greased or paper-lined muffin cups about two-thirds full. Combine the topping ingredients; sprinkle over batter. Bake at 400° until a toothpick inserted in the center comes out clean, 20-25 minutes. Cool for 5 minutes before removing from pan to a wire rack. Serve warm.

NOTE: If using frozen blueberries, use without thawing to avoid discoloring the batter.

1 MUFFIN: 208 cal., 10g fat (1g sat. fat), 18mg chol., 172mg sod., 28g carb. (13g sugars, 1g fiber), 3g pro.

BACON-WRAPPED
TURKEY, PAGE 111

MAIN COURSES

Heavenly roasts, comforting stews and creamy pastas were all staples on Grandma's kitchen table. Re-create some of her nostalgic dishes with these soul-warming dinner recipes that the whole family will love.

COUNTRY CASSOULET

This bean stew is great with fresh dinner rolls and your favorite green salad.
It's a hearty meal that's perfect after a long day in the garden.
—*Suzanne McKinley, Lyons, GA*

PREP: 20 MIN. + STANDING • COOK: 6 HOURS • MAKES: 10 SERVINGS

1 lb. dried great northern beans
2 uncooked garlic-flavored pork sausage links
3 bacon strips, diced
1½ lbs. boneless pork, cut into 1-in. cubes
1 lb. boneless lamb, cut into 1-in. cubes
1½ cups chopped onion
3 garlic cloves, minced
2 tsp. salt
1 tsp. dried thyme
4 whole cloves
2 bay leaves
2½ cups chicken broth
1 can (8 oz.) tomato sauce

1. Rinse and sort beans; soak according to package directions. Drain and rinse beans, discarding liquid.

2. In a large skillet over medium-high heat, brown sausage links; transfer to a 5-qt. slow cooker. Add bacon to skillet; cook until crisp. Remove with a slotted spoon to slow cooker.

3. In bacon drippings, cook pork and lamb until browned on all sides. Place in the slow cooker. Stir in the beans and remaining ingredients.

4. Cover and cook on low for 6-8 hours or until beans are tender. Discard cloves and bay leaves. Remove sausage and cut into ¼-in. slices; return to slow cooker and stir gently.

1 CUP: 375 cal., 12g fat (4g sat. fat), 74mg chol., 950mg sod., 32g carb. (5g sugars, 10g fiber), 35g pro.

SPINACH & GOUDA STUFFED PORK CUTLETS

This started as a restaurant copycat dish I tried at home.
Melty cheese oozes out of the center, and mustard lends a lot of flavor.
—*Joan Oakland, Troy, MT*

TAKES: 30 MIN. • MAKES: 2 SERVINGS

3 Tbsp. dry bread crumbs
2 Tbsp. grated Parmesan cheese
2 pork sirloin cutlets (3 oz. each)
¼ tsp. salt
⅛ tsp. pepper
2 slices smoked Gouda cheese (about 2 oz.)
2 cups fresh baby spinach
2 Tbsp. horseradish mustard

1. Preheat oven to 400°. In a shallow bowl, mix bread crumbs and Parmesan cheese.

2. Sprinkle tops of cutlets with salt and pepper. Layer end of each with Gouda cheese and spinach. Fold cutlets in half, enclosing filling; secure with toothpicks. Brush mustard over outsides of pork; dip in bread crumb mixture, patting to help coating adhere.

3. Place on a greased foil-lined baking sheet. Bake until breading is golden brown and pork is tender, 12-15 minutes. Discard toothpicks before serving.

1 STUFFED CUTLET: 299 cal., 16g fat (7g sat. fat), 91mg chol., 898mg sod., 10g carb. (2g sugars, 2g fiber), 30g pro.

COUNTRY
CASSOULET

CORNISH PASTIES

My Great-Aunt Gladys was from a small mining town in England where pasties were popular. I loved to watch her craft each Cornish pasty, as she made them in different sizes depending on who was eating. Serve with a green salad to make a wonderful meal.

—*Verna Hainer, Pueblo, CO*

PREP: 30 MIN. + CHILLING • BAKE: 50 MIN. • MAKES: 8 SERVINGS

3 cups all-purpose flour
1½ tsp. salt
¾ tsp. baking powder
1 cup shortening
8 to 10 Tbsp. ice water

FILLING
1 lb. beef top round steak, cut into ½-in. pieces
1½ cups finely chopped onion
1½ cups cubed peeled potatoes (½-in. cubes)
1½ cups chopped peeled turnips (½-in. cubes)
1 tsp. salt
¼ tsp. pepper
4 Tbsp. butter
½ cup evaporated milk, optional
Ketchup

1. In a large bowl, mix flour, salt and baking powder; cut in the shortening until crumbly. Gradually add water, tossing with a fork until dough forms a ball. Cover and refrigerate for 30 minutes.

2. Preheat oven to 375°. In another large bowl, combine beef, onion, potatoes, turnips, salt and pepper. Divide the dough into 4 equal portions. On a lightly floured surface, roll 1 portion into a 9-in. circle. Mound 1½ cups filling on half of circle; dot with 1 Tbsp. butter. Moisten edges with water; fold the dough over filling and press edges with a fork to seal. Place on a parchment-lined rimmed 15x10x1-in. baking pan. Repeat with remaining dough, filling and butter. Cut slits in tops of pasties. Bake 50-60 minutes or until golden brown. (If desired, pour milk into slits halfway through baking time.) Serve with ketchup.

FREEZE OPTION: Freeze cooled pasties in a freezer container. To use, reheat pasties on a parchment-lined baking sheet in a preheated 375° oven until heated through.

½ PASTY: 556 cal., 32g fat (10g sat. fat), 47mg chol., 864mg sod., 46g carb. (3g sugars, 3g fiber), 19g pro.

PRETZEL-CRUSTED CATFISH

I'm not a big fish lover, so any concoction that has me enjoying fish is a keeper in my book.
This combination of flavors works for me. It's delicious served with corn muffins, butter and honey.
—*Kelly Williams, Forked River, NJ*

TAKES: 30 MIN. • **MAKES:** 4 SERVINGS

4 catfish fillets (6 oz. each)
½ tsp. salt
½ tsp. pepper
2 large eggs
⅓ cup Dijon mustard
2 Tbsp. 2% milk
½ cup all-purpose flour
4 cups honey mustard
   miniature pretzels,
   coarsely crushed
   Oil for frying
   Lemon slices, optional

1. Sprinkle catfish with salt and pepper. Whisk the eggs, mustard and milk in a shallow bowl. Place flour and pretzels in separate shallow bowls. Coat fillets with flour, then dip in egg mixture and coat with pretzels.

2. Heat ¼ in. oil to 375° in an electric skillet. Fry fillets, a few at a time, until fish flakes easily with a fork, 3-4 minutes on each side. Drain on paper towels. Serve with lemon slices if desired.

1 FILLET: 610 cal., 31g fat (4g sat. fat), 164mg chol., 1579mg sod., 44g carb. (2g sugars, 2g fiber), 33g pro.

SLOW-COOKED BEEF TIPS

This dish reminds me of a childhood favorite. I cook the beef tips with
mushrooms and serve over brown rice, noodles or mashed potatoes.
—*Amy Lents, Grand Forks, ND*

PREP: 25 MIN. • **COOK:** 6¼ HOURS • **MAKES:** 2 SERVINGS

¼ lb. sliced baby portobello
   mushrooms
½ small onion, sliced
1 beef top sirloin steak
   (½ lb.), cubed
¼ tsp. salt
⅛ tsp. pepper
1 tsp. olive oil
3 Tbsp. dry red wine
   or beef broth
1 cup beef broth
1½ tsp. Worcestershire
   sauce
1 Tbsp. cornstarch
2 Tbsp. water
   Hot cooked mashed
   potatoes

1. Place mushrooms and onion in a 3-qt. slow cooker. Sprinkle beef with salt and pepper. In a large skillet, heat 1 tsp. oil over medium-high heat; brown meat in batches, adding additional oil as needed. Transfer meat to slow cooker.

2. Add wine to skillet, stirring to loosen browned bits from pan. Stir in broth and Worcestershire sauce; pour over meat. Cook, covered, on low 6-8 hours or until meat is tender.

3. In a small bowl, mix the cornstarch and cold water until smooth; gradually stir into slow cooker. Cook, covered, on high for 15-30 minutes or until the gravy is thickened. Serve with mashed potatoes.

1 CUP: 213 cal., 7g fat (2g sat. fat), 46mg chol., 836mg sod., 8g carb. (2g sugars, 1g fiber), 27g pro. **DIABETIC EXCHANGES:** 3 lean meat, 1½ fat, ½ starch.

BEST-EVER
LAMB CHOPS

BEST-EVER LAMB CHOPS

My mom just loved a good lamb chop, and this easy recipe was her
favorite way to have them. I've also grilled these chops with great results.
—*Kim Mundy, Visalia, CA*

PREP: 10 MIN. + CHILLING • **BROIL:** 10 MIN. • **MAKES:** 4 SERVINGS

1 tsp. each dried basil,
   marjoram and thyme
½ tsp. salt
8 lamb loin chops
   (3 oz. each)
   Mint jelly, optional

1. Combine herbs and salt; rub over lamb chops. Cover and refrigerate for 1 hour.

2. Broil 4-6 in. from the heat until meat reaches desired doneness, 5-8 minutes on each side (for medium-rare, a thermometer should read 135°; medium, 140°; medium-well, 145°). Serve with mint jelly if desired.

2 LAMB CHOPS: 157 cal., 7g fat (2g sat. fat), 68mg chol., 355mg sod., 0 carb. (0 sugars, 0 fiber), 22g pro. **DIABETIC EXCHANGES:** 3 lean meat.

SOY-GINGER POT ROAST

My husband loves roast beef, and I love my slow cooker. I incorporated
Asian influences for a melt-in-your mouth pot roast with some oomph.
—*Lisa Varner, El Paso, TX*

PREP: 25 MIN. • **COOK:** 7 HOURS • **MAKES:** 6 SERVINGS

1 boneless beef chuck
   roast (3 to 4 lbs.)
1 tsp. salt
½ tsp. pepper
1 Tbsp. canola oil
1½ cups water
½ cup reduced-sodium
   soy sauce
¼ cup honey
3 Tbsp. cider vinegar
3 garlic cloves, minced
2 tsp. ground ginger
1 tsp. ground mustard
1 large onion, halved
   and sliced
2 Tbsp. cornstarch
2 Tbsp. cold water

1. Sprinkle roast with salt and pepper. In a large skillet, heat oil over medium-high heat. Brown roast on all sides. Transfer meat to a 5- or 6-qt. slow cooker. In a small bowl, mix water, soy sauce, honey, vinegar, garlic, ginger and mustard; pour over meat. Top with onion. Cook, covered, on low 7-9 hours, until meat is tender.

2. Remove roast and onion to a serving platter; keep warm. Transfer cooking juices to a large saucepan; skim fat. Bring cooking juices to a boil. In a small bowl, mix cornstarch and cold water until smooth; stir into cooking juices. Return to a boil; cook and stir until thickened, 1-2 minutes. Serve with roast.

6 OZ. COOKED BEEF WITH ½ CUP GRAVY: 489 cal., 24g fat (9g sat. fat), 147mg chol., 1256mg sod., 19g carb. (13g sugars, 1g fiber), 46g pro.

PRESSURE-COOKER SPICED SHORT RIBS

This recipe is ideal for busy nights when your family wants a comforting dinner but you are limited on time. The ribs are tender and feature the perfect amount of sweet and sour. Feel free to use red wine instead of chicken stock. And instead of butter, add more olive oil.

—*Shanon Tranchina, Massapequa Park, NY*

PREP: 20 MIN. • **COOK:** 40 MIN. • **MAKES:** 12 SERVINGS

1 **Tbsp. olive oil**
6 **lbs. bone-in beef short ribs**
2 **Tbsp. butter**
1 **medium leek (white portion only), finely chopped**
1 **garlic clove, minced**
1 **cup chicken stock**
1 **can (6 oz.) tomato paste**
2 **Tbsp. ground mustard**
2 **Tbsp. red wine vinegar**
2 **Tbsp. Worcestershire sauce**
2 **tsp. paprika**
2 **tsp. celery salt**
1 **tsp. ground cinnamon**
½ **tsp. pepper**

1. Select saute or browning setting on a 6-qt. electric pressure cooker. Adjust for medium heat; add oil. When oil is hot, brown ribs in batches; set aside.

2. Add butter to pressure cooker. When melted, add leek. Cook and stir leek until tender, 2-3 minutes. Add garlic; cook 1 minute longer. Add stock to pressure cooker. Cook 1 minute, stirring to loosen browned bits from pan. Press cancel.

3. In a small bowl, combine the remaining ingredients; spread over ribs. Return ribs to pressure cooker. Lock lid; close the pressure-release valve. Adjust to pressure-cook on high for 40 minutes. Let pressure release naturally.

1 SERVING: 232 cal., 14g fat (6g sat. fat), 60mg chol., 324mg sod., 5g carb. (2g sugars, 1g fiber), 20g pro.

GRANDMA'S SECRET

Store short ribs in an airtight container in the refrigerator for 3-4 days. You can freeze cooked short ribs in a freezer container or storage bag for up to 2 months.

PERFECT FOUR-CHEESE LASAGNA

Lasagna is one of my favorite meals, and this is the recipe I've been making since I was a teenager. It's a tantalizing combo of pasta, meat sauce, cheese and more cheese. It definitely lives up to its name!

—*Lauren Delaney-Wallace, Glen Carbon, IL*

PREP: 25 MIN. • BAKE: 50 MIN. + STANDING • MAKES: 12 SERVINGS

1 lb. ground beef
1 medium onion, chopped
2 garlic cloves, minced
1 tsp. dried oregano
1 tsp. dried basil
2 cans (15 oz. each) tomato sauce
2 large eggs, lightly beaten
2 cups 4% cottage cheese
⅔ cup grated Parmesan cheese
¼ cup shredded cheddar cheese
1½ cups shredded part-skim mozzarella cheese, divided
12 no-cook lasagna noodles (about 7 oz.)
1 tsp. Italian seasoning

1. Preheat oven to 350°. In a large skillet, cook and crumble ground beef with onion and garlic over medium-high heat until browned, 5-7 minutes; drain. Stir in herbs and tomato sauce. In a bowl, mix the eggs, cottage cheese, Parmesan cheese, cheddar cheese and ½ cup mozzarella cheese.

2. Spread 1 cup meat sauce into a greased 13x9-in. baking dish; layer with 4 lasagna noodles, the cottage cheese mixture, an additional 4 noodles and half the remaining meat sauce. Repeat last 2 layers. Sprinkle with Italian seasoning and the remaining mozzarella cheese.

3. Cover dish with greased foil; bake until the cheese is melted, 50-55 minutes. Let stand 10 minutes before serving.

FREEZE OPTION: Cover and freeze unbaked lasagna. To use, partially thaw in refrigerator overnight. Remove from refrigerator 30 minutes before baking. Preheat oven to 350°. Bake lasagna as directed until heated through and a thermometer inserted in center reads 165°, increasing time to 1-1½ hours.

1 PIECE: 279 cal., 13g fat (6g sat. fat), 72mg chol., 662mg sod., 22g carb. (4g sugars, 2g fiber), 20g pro.

SALMON WITH BROWN SUGAR GLAZE

Need a simple way to serve a whole salmon fillet to a group of friends?
Here's the easy recipe that finally made me a fan of this fish.
—*Rachel Garcia, Honolulu, HI*

PREP: 15 MIN. • BAKE: 20 MIN. • MAKES: 8 SERVINGS

1 Tbsp. brown sugar
2 tsp. butter
1 tsp. honey
1 Tbsp. olive oil
1 Tbsp. Dijon mustard
1 Tbsp. reduced-sodium soy sauce
½ to ¾ tsp. salt
¼ tsp. pepper
1 salmon fillet (2½ lbs.)

1. In a small saucepan over medium heat, cook and stir the brown sugar, butter and honey until melted. Remove from the heat; whisk in the oil, mustard, soy sauce, salt and pepper. Cool for 5 minutes.

2. Place salmon in a large foil-lined baking pan; spoon brown sugar mixture over top. Bake at 350° for 20-25 minutes or until fish flakes easily with a fork.

1 SERVING: 295 cal., 18g fat (3g sat. fat), 84mg chol., 403mg sod., 3g carb. (2g sugars, 0 fiber), 28g pro.

CREAMY GREEN CHILE CHICKEN COBBLER

Biscuity crumbs take this family-friendly combo of rotisserie chicken and cheesy, creamy green enchilada sauce over the top.
—*Johnna Johnson, Scottsdale, AZ*

PREP: 30 MIN. • BAKE: 35 MIN. • MAKES: 8 SERVINGS

2 cups all-purpose flour
½ cup grated Parmesan cheese
2 tsp. baking powder
6 Tbsp. cold butter, cubed
¾ cup plus 2 Tbsp. heavy whipping cream
3 oz. cream cheese, softened
½ cup sour cream
1 can (10½ oz.) condensed cream of chicken soup, undiluted
1 can (10 oz.) green enchilada sauce
2 cans (4 oz. each) chopped green chiles
2½ cups shredded rotisserie chicken (about 10 oz.)
1½ cups shredded Colby-Monterey Jack cheese

1. Preheat oven to 450°. For crumb topping, whisk together flour, cheese and baking powder. Cut in butter until mixture resembles coarse crumbs. Add cream; stir just until moistened. On a lightly greased 15x10x1-in. pan, crumble mixture into ½- to 1-in. pieces.

2. Bake topping on an upper oven rack until light golden brown, 8-10 minutes. Reduce oven setting to 350°.

3. In a large bowl, mix the cream cheese and sour cream until smooth. Stir in soup, enchilada sauce, green chiles and chicken. Transfer to an 11x7-in. baking dish; sprinkle with cheese. Add crumb topping (dish will be full).

4. Place dish on a baking sheet. Bake, uncovered, on a lower oven rack until the topping is deep golden brown and filling is bubbly, 35-40 minutes.

1¼ CUPS: 581 cal., 39g fat (22g sat. fat), 132mg chol., 1076mg sod., 33g carb. (3g sugars, 2g fiber), 25g pro.

SALMON WITH
BROWN SUGAR
GLAZE

SQUASH & LENTIL LAMB STEW

My family lived in New Zealand many years ago.
Every Sunday my mother made a lamb stew—it was
Dad's favorite! I changed the recipe to suit my family's more
modern palates, but it seems just as exotic and delicious.
—*Nancy Heishman, Las Vegas, NV*

PREP: 30 MIN. • COOK: 6 HOURS • MAKES: 8 SERVINGS (2½ QT.)

- 1 can (13.66 oz.) coconut milk
- ½ cup creamy peanut butter
- 2 Tbsp. red curry paste
- 1 Tbsp. hoisin sauce
- 1 tsp. salt
- ½ tsp. pepper
- 1 can (14½ oz.) chicken broth
- 3 tsp. olive oil, divided
- 1 lb. lamb or beef stew meat (1½-in. pieces)
- 2 small onions, chopped
- 1 Tbsp. minced fresh gingerroot
- 3 garlic cloves, minced
- 1 cup dried brown lentils, rinsed
- 4 cups cubed peeled butternut squash (about 1 lb.)
- 2 cups chopped fresh spinach
- ¼ cup minced fresh cilantro
- ¼ cup lime juice

1. In a 5- or 6-qt. slow cooker, whisk together first 7 ingredients. In a large skillet, heat 2 tsp. oil over medium heat; brown lamb in batches. Add to slow cooker.

2. In same skillet, saute onions in remaining oil over medium heat until tender, 4-5 minutes. Add ginger and garlic; cook and stir 1 minute. Add to slow cooker. Stir in lentils and squash.

3. Cook, covered, on low 6-8 hours, until meat and lentils are tender. Stir in spinach until wilted. Stir in cilantro and lime juice.

FREEZE OPTION: Freeze cooled stew in freezer containers. To use, partially thaw in refrigerator overnight. Heat through in a saucepan, stirring occasionally; add broth if necessary.

1¼ CUPS: 411 cal., 21g fat (11g sat. fat), 38mg chol., 777mg sod., 34g carb. (7g sugars, 6g fiber), 23g pro.

GRANDMA'S SECRET

With a thick outer skin, butternut squash can be tough to slice. Microwaving the squash for 4-5 minutes can help soften it, making it easier to cut into.

BACON-WRAPPED TURKEY

PICTURED ON PAGE 98

Everything's better with bacon, including turkey! This impressive take on a holiday favorite is covered in bacon, which not only adds flavor, but helps keep the bird juicy. The best part? It's easier than it looks!
—Taste of Home *Test Kitchen*

PREP: 10 MIN. • BAKE: 3½ HOURS + STANDING • MAKES: 18 SERVINGS

1 turkey (14 to 16 lbs.)
¼ cup butter, softened
2 tsp. dried thyme
1 tsp. salt
1 tsp. dried rosemary, crushed
1 tsp. rubbed sage
½ tsp. poultry seasoning
½ tsp. pepper
1½ lbs. thick-sliced bacon strips (about 20-24 strips)

1. Preheat oven to 475°. Place turkey on a rack in a shallow roasting pan, breast side up. In a small bowl, combine butter, thyme, salt, rosemary, sage, poultry seasoning and pepper; spread over outside of turkey breast and legs. Add 2 cups water to pan.

2. Wrap turkey legs in a single layer of bacon strips, trimming to fit (about 6 slices total). Tie drumsticks together. On parchment or waxed paper, arrange 8 bacon strips side by side. Weave 8 slices bacon perpendicular to first 8 strips, making a lattice. Adjust lattice so it is tightly woven. Transfer lattice to turkey breast by flipping parchment over the turkey; carefully peel off parchment. Adjust lattice to cover turkey breast and trim edges of bacon to fit. Secure with toothpicks, if needed.

3. Roast, uncovered, until bacon is lightly browned, 25-30 minutes. Reduce oven setting to 350°. Bake until a thermometer inserted in thickest part of thigh reads 170°-175°, about 90 minutes longer. Cover loosely with foil if bacon browns too quickly.

4. Remove from oven. Cover and let stand for 15 minutes before carving.

7 OZ. COOKED TURKEY: 496 cal., 27g fat (9g sat. fat), 208mg chol., 536mg sod., 0 carb. (0 sugars, 0 fiber), 60g pro.

FROM GRANDMA'S KITCHEN: Use thick-cut bacon for this recipe. Thicker bacon will cover the whole bird and create a tight lattice. It also will hold its shape during cooking.

NEW ZEALAND ROSEMARY LAMB SHANKS

When I was young, my family lived in New Zealand for two years after World War II.
Some things were in short supply, but one item that was always available was lamb shanks.
Mother cooked them all the time with root vegetables, and to this day I love lamb!

—*Nancy Heishman, Las Vegas, NV*

PREP: 25 MIN. • COOK: 6 HOURS • MAKES: 8 SERVINGS

1   **tsp. salt**
¾ **tsp. pepper**
4   **lamb shanks**
    (about 20 oz. each)
1   **Tbsp. butter**
½ **cup white wine**
3   **medium parsnips, peeled**
    and cut into 1-in. chunks
2   **large carrots, peeled and**
    cut into 1-in. chunks
2   **medium turnips, peeled**
    and cut into 1-in. chunks
2   **large tomatoes, chopped**
1   **large onion, chopped**
4   **garlic cloves, minced**
2   **cups beef broth**
1   **pkg. (10 oz.) frozen peas,**
    thawed
⅓ **cup chopped fresh**
    parsley
2   **Tbsp. minced fresh**
    rosemary

1. Rub salt and pepper over lamb. In a large skillet, heat butter over medium-high heat; brown meat. Transfer meat to a 6- or 7-qt. slow cooker. Add wine to skillet; cook and stir 1 minute to loosen brown bits. Pour over lamb. Add the parsnips, carrots, turnips, tomatoes, onion, garlic and broth. Cook, covered, on low 6-8 hours or until meat is tender.

2. Remove lamb; keep warm. Stir in peas, parsley and rosemary; heat through. Serve lamb with vegetables.

½ LAMB SHANK WITH 1 CUP VEGETABLES: 350 cal., 15g fat (6g sat. fat), 103mg chol., 668mg sod., 22g carb. (8g sugars, 6g fiber), 31g pro. DIABETIC EXCHANGES: 4 lean meat, 1 starch, 1 vegetable, ½ fat.

FROM GRANDMA'S KITCHEN: Lamb shanks are a tough cut of meat. The secret to achieving meat that is fall-off-the bone tender is to cook the shanks low and slow, which is why slow-cooking is an ideal cooking method.

PICNIC FRIED CHICKEN

In our family, it's not a picnic unless there's fried chicken! Chicken, deviled eggs and potato salad are all musts for a picnic as far as my husband is concerned. This recipe is a "golden oldie"—I've used it many times.
—*Edna Hoffman, Hebron, IN*

PREP: 30 MIN. + MARINATING • COOK: 40 MIN. • MAKES: 6 SERVINGS

1 broiler/fryer chicken (3 lbs.), cut up
¾ to 1 cup buttermilk

COATING
1½ to 2 cups all-purpose flour
1½ tsp. salt
½ tsp. pepper
½ tsp. garlic powder
½ tsp. onion powder
1 Tbsp. paprika
¼ tsp. ground sage
¼ tsp. ground thyme
⅛ tsp. baking powder
Oil for frying

1. Pat chicken pieces with paper towels; place in large flat dish. Pour buttermilk over chicken; cover and refrigerate for at least 1 hour or overnight.

2. Combine coating ingredients in large shallow dish. Add chicken pieces, 1 at a time, and turn to coat. Lay coated pieces on waxed paper for 15 minutes to allow the coating to dry (this will help it cling better during frying).

3. In a Dutch oven or other deep skillet, heat ½ in. oil over medium heat to 350°. Fry chicken, uncovered, turning occasionally, until coating is dark golden brown and meat is no longer pink, 7-8 minutes per side. Drain on paper towels.

5 OZ. COOKED CHICKEN: 623 cal., 40g fat (7g sat. fat), 106mg chol., 748mg sod., 26g carb. (2g sugars, 1g fiber), 38g pro.

PIZZA MACARONI & CHEESE

My grandma made this for us once during a visit and I never forgot how good it was. Since my kids love anything with pepperoni and cheese, I bake it so they can enjoy it as much as I did.
—*Juli Meyers, Hinesville, GA*

PREP: 30 MIN. • BAKE: 25 MIN. • MAKES: 12 SERVINGS

2 pkg. (14 oz. each) deluxe macaroni and cheese dinner mix
½ cup sour cream
1 can (14½ oz.) petite diced tomatoes, drained
1 can (15 oz.) pizza sauce
1 small green pepper, chopped
1 small sweet red pepper, chopped
2 cups shredded Italian cheese blend
2 oz. sliced pepperoni

1. Preheat oven to 350°. Cook macaroni according to package directions for al dente. Drain; return to pan. Stir in contents of cheese packets and sour cream. Transfer to a greased 13x9-in. baking dish.

2. In a small bowl, combine tomatoes and pizza sauce; drop by spoonfuls over macaroni. Top with peppers, cheese and pepperoni. Bake, uncovered, until bubbly, 25-30 minutes.

1 CUP: 340 cal., 14g fat (7g sat. fat), 37mg chol., 927mg sod., 37g carb. (5g sugars, 3g fiber), 14g pro.

SLOW-COOKED HAM WITH PINEAPPLE SAUCE

We serve this dish during the holidays because everyone is crazy about it. But we also enjoy it all year long because it's so simple to prepare.
—*Terry Roberts, Yorktown, VA*

PREP: 10 MIN. • COOK: 6 HOURS • MAKES: 12 SERVINGS

1 fully cooked boneless ham (4 to 5 lbs.)
1 Tbsp. cornstarch
2 Tbsp. lemon juice
1 cup packed brown sugar
1 Tbsp. yellow mustard
¼ tsp. salt
1 can (20 oz.) unsweetened crushed pineapple, undrained

1. Place ham in a 5-qt. slow cooker. In a small saucepan, mix cornstarch and lemon juice until smooth. Stir in the remaining ingredients; bring to a boil, stirring occasionally. Pour over ham, covering completely.

2. Cook, covered, on low 6-8 hours (a thermometer inserted in ham should read at least 140°).

4 OZ. HAM WITH ¼ CUP SAUCE: 262 cal., 6g fat (2g sat. fat), 77mg chol., 1638mg sod., 27g carb. (25g sugars, 0 fiber), 28g pro.

PRESSURE-COOKER SWISS STEAK

Swiss steak has a been a standby for family cooks for decades, and this no-fuss way to cook it promises to keep the entree popular for years to come. Best of all, it's low in calories and fat.
—*Sarah Burks, Wathena, KS*

PREP: 10 MIN. • COOK: 20 MIN. + RELEASING • MAKES: 6 SERVINGS

1½ lbs. beef round steak, cut into 6 pieces
½ tsp. salt
¼ tsp. pepper
1 medium onion, cut into ¼-in. slices
1 celery rib, cut into ½-in. slices
2 cans (8 oz. each) tomato sauce

Sprinkle steak with salt and pepper. Place onion in a 6-qt. electric pressure cooker. Top with celery, tomato sauce and steak. Lock lid; close pressure-release valve. Adjust to pressure-cook on high for 20 minutes. Let the pressure release naturally for 5 minutes; quick-release any remaining pressure. A thermometer inserted in steak should read at least 145°.

1 SERVING: 167 cal., 4g fat (1g sat. fat), 63mg chol., 581mg sod., 6g carb. (2g sugars, 2g fiber), 27g pro. **DIABETIC EXCHANGES:** 3 lean meat, 1 vegetable.

PUFF PASTRY CHICKEN POTPIE

When my wife is craving comfort food, I whip up my chicken potpie.
It's easy to make, sticks to your ribs and delivers soul-satisfying flavor.
—*Nick Iverson, Denver, CO*

PREP: 45 MIN. • **BAKE:** 45 MIN. + STANDING • **MAKES:** 8 SERVINGS

1 pkg. (17.3 oz.) frozen puff
  pastry, thawed
2 lbs. boneless skinless
  chicken breasts, cut into
  1-in. pieces
1 tsp. salt, divided
1 tsp. pepper, divided
4 Tbsp. butter, divided
1 large onion, chopped
2 garlic cloves, minced
1 tsp. minced fresh thyme
  or ¼ tsp. dried thyme
1 tsp. minced fresh sage
  or ¼ tsp. rubbed sage
½ cup all-purpose flour
1½ cups chicken broth
1 cup plus 1 Tbsp. half-
  and-half cream, divided
2 cups frozen mixed
  vegetables (about 10 oz.)
1 Tbsp. lemon juice
1 large egg yolk

1. Preheat oven to 400°. On a lightly floured surface, roll each pastry sheet into a 12x10-in. rectangle. Cut 1 sheet crosswise into six 2-in. strips; cut remaining sheet lengthwise into five 2-in. strips. On a baking sheet, closely weave strips to make a 12x10-in. lattice. Freeze while making filling.

2. Toss chicken with ½ tsp. each salt and pepper. In a large skillet, heat 1 Tbsp. butter over medium-high heat; saute chicken until browned, 5-7 minutes. Remove from pan.

3. In same skillet, heat remaining butter over medium-high heat; saute onion until tender, 5-7 minutes. Stir in garlic and herbs; cook 1 minute. Stir in the flour until blended; cook and stir 1 minute. Gradually stir in broth and 1 cup cream. Bring to a boil, stirring constantly; cook and stir until thickened, about 2 minutes.

4. Stir in vegetables, lemon juice, chicken and the remaining salt and pepper; return to a boil. Transfer to a greased 2½-qt. oblong baking dish. Top with lattice, trimming to fit.

5. Whisk together egg yolk and remaining cream; brush over pastry. Bake, uncovered, until filling is bubbly and pastry is golden brown, 45-55 minutes. Cover loosely with foil if pastry starts getting too dark. Let stand 15 minutes before serving.

1 SERVING: 523 cal., 25g fat (10g sat. fat), 118mg chol., 768mg sod., 42g carb. (4g sugars, 6g fiber), 30g pro.

"My family has always loved chicken potpies. This one got rave reviews last night at dinnertime. They want to know when I will make it again. Definitely a keeper in my meal rotation."
—HARLEEN, TASTEOFHOME.COM

GRANDMA EDNA'S CAJUN PORK

My grandma used to make this every year as part of our Christmas dinner. These days, I make it for my family at the holidays. We love to carry on the delicious tradition of Grandma's Cajun pork.

—*Tonya Cline, Greenville, OH*

PREP: 35 MIN. • **COOK:** 6 HOURS • **MAKES:** 12 SERVINGS (2¼ CUPS GRAVY)

1 small onion	½ tsp. each salt, white pepper and pepper
1 celery rib	
1 small green pepper	½ tsp. ground mustard
3 Tbsp. butter	½ tsp. hot pepper sauce
3 garlic cloves, minced	1 boneless pork loin roast (4 lbs.)
2 tsp. dried thyme	
1 tsp. paprika	2 Tbsp. cornstarch
	2 Tbsp. cold water

1. Finely chop vegetables. In a large skillet, saute vegetables in butter until tender. Add garlic; cook 1 minute longer. Stir in the seasonings and pepper sauce.

2. Cut several slits in roast to within ½ in. of bottom. Place in a 5-qt. slow cooker. Spoon onion mixture between slits and over the top of meat. Cover and cook on low for 6-8 hours or until pork is tender.

3. Transfer roast to a serving platter; keep warm. Strain cooking juices and pour into a small saucepan. Combine cornstarch and water until smooth; stir into the pan. Bring to a boil; cook and stir until thickened, about 2 minutes. Serve with roast.

4 OZ. COOKED PORK WITH 3 TBSP. GRAVY: 225 cal., 10g fat (4g sat. fat), 83mg chol., 167mg sod., 3g carb. (0 sugars, 1g fiber), 29g pro. **DIABETIC EXCHANGES:** 4 lean meat, ½ fat.

AUTUMN APPLE CHICKEN

I went apple picking and wanted to bake something new with the bounty. Slow-cooking chicken with apples and barbecue sauce filled my whole house with the most heavenly aroma. We couldn't wait to eat.
—*Caitlyn Hauser, Brookline, NH*

PREP: 20 MIN. • **COOK:** 3½ HOURS • **MAKES:** 4 SERVINGS

- 1 Tbsp. canola oil
- 4 bone-in chicken thighs (about 1½ lbs.), skin removed
- ¼ tsp. salt
- ¼ tsp. pepper
- 2 medium Fuji or Gala apples, coarsely chopped
- 1 medium onion, chopped
- 1 garlic clove, minced
- ⅓ cup barbecue sauce
- ¼ cup apple cider or juice
- 1 Tbsp. honey

1. In a large skillet, heat oil over medium heat. Brown chicken thighs on both sides; sprinkle with salt and pepper. Transfer to a 3-qt. slow cooker; top with apples.

2. Add onion to same skillet; cook and stir over medium heat 2-3 minutes or until tender. Add garlic; cook 1 minute longer. Stir in barbecue sauce, apple cider and honey; increase the heat to medium-high. Cook 1 minute, stirring to loosen browned bits from pan. Pour over chicken and apples. Cook, covered, on low 3½-4½ hours, until chicken is tender.

FREEZE OPTION: Freeze cooled chicken mixture in freezer containers. To use, partially thaw in refrigerator overnight. Heat through in a covered saucepan, stirring occasionally.

1 CHICKEN THIGH WITH ½ CUP APPLE MIXTURE: 333 cal., 13g fat (3g sat. fat), 87mg chol., 456mg sod., 29g carb. (22g sugars, 3g fiber), 25g pro. **DIABETIC EXCHANGES:** 4 lean meat, 1½ starch, ½ fruit.

MOM'S MEAT LOAF FOR 2

If you're looking for a small but mighty meal, here's a great fit. You'll love the old-fashioned flavor and scrumptious sauce. The recipe is easy to double for sandwiches the next day.
—*Michelle Beran, Claflin, KS*

PREP: 15 MIN. • **BAKE:** 40 MIN. • **MAKES:** 2 MINI MEAT LOAVES

- 1 large egg
- ¼ cup 2% milk
- ⅓ cup crushed saltines
- 3 Tbsp. chopped onion
- ¼ tsp. salt
- ⅛ tsp. rubbed sage
   Dash pepper
- ½ lb. lean ground beef (90% lean)
- ¼ cup ketchup
- 2 Tbsp. brown sugar
- ¼ tsp. Worcestershire sauce

1. Preheat oven to 350°. In a large bowl, beat egg. Add the milk, cracker crumbs, onion, salt, sage and pepper. Crumble beef over mixture and mix well. Shape into 2 loaves; place in a shallow baking dish coated with cooking spray.

2. Combine the ketchup, brown sugar and Worcestershire sauce; spoon over meat loaves. Bake until meat is no longer pink and a thermometer reads 160°, 40-45 minutes.

1 SERVING: 337 cal., 12g fat (4g sat. fat), 162mg chol., 898mg sod., 31g carb. (18g sugars, 1g fiber), 27g pro. **DIABETIC EXCHANGES:** 3 lean meat, 2 starch.

HERB-GLAZED
TURKEY

HERB-GLAZED TURKEY

Honey and corn syrup blend with savoy herbs and seasonings to give my turkey a slightly sweet flavor. My tried-and-true recipe never fails to win compliments.
—*Charlene Melenka, Vegreville, AB*

PREP: 10 MIN. • BAKE: 3½ HOURS + STANDING • MAKES: 18 SERVINGS

1 turkey (14 to 16 lbs.)
¼ cup olive oil
2 tsp. dried thyme
1½ tsp. salt, divided
1¼ tsp. pepper, divided
1 cup honey
1 cup corn syrup
¼ cup butter, melted
2 tsp. dried rosemary, crushed
1 tsp. rubbed sage
1 tsp. dried basil

1. Brush turkey with oil; tie drumsticks together. Place turkey breast side up on a rack in a roasting pan. Combine thyme, 1 tsp. salt and 1 tsp. pepper; sprinkle evenly over turkey. Bake, uncovered, at 325° for 2 hours.

2. In a small bowl, combine honey, corn syrup, butter, rosemary, sage, basil and the remaining salt and pepper. Brush over turkey. Bake until a thermometer inserted in thickest part of thigh reads 170°-175°, about 90 minutes longer, basting frequently with pan drippings. Cover loosely with foil if turkey browns too quickly.

3. Remove from oven. Cover and let turkey stand for 15 minutes before carving.

7 OZ. COOKED TURKEY: 570 cal., 25g fat (8g sat. fat), 197mg chol., 380mg sod., 30g carb. (24g sugars, 0 fiber), 56g pro.

GROUND BEEF SPAGHETTI SKILLET

I remember my grandma making this stovetop supper many times—we always loved Granny's spaghetti! Now my husband and I enjoy making it. You can easily use ground turkey instead of ground beef if that's what you have on hand.
—*Jill Thomas, Washington, IN*

TAKES: 30 MIN. • MAKES: 4 SERVINGS

1 lb. ground beef
1 medium green pepper, chopped
1 small onion, chopped
2 garlic cloves, minced
1½ cups water
1 can (14½ oz.) diced tomatoes, undrained
1 can (8 oz.) tomato sauce
1 Tbsp. chili powder
1 Tbsp. grape jelly
½ tsp. salt
6 oz. uncooked thin spaghetti, halved

1. In a Dutch oven, cook beef, green pepper, onion and garlic over medium heat, breaking beef into crumbles, until meat is no longer pink and vegetables are tender, 8-10 minutes; drain.

2. Add water, tomatoes, tomato sauce, chili powder, jelly and salt. Bring to a boil. Stir in spaghetti. Reduce heat; simmer, covered, until spaghetti is tender, 6-8 minutes.

1½ CUPS: 431 cal., 15g fat (5g sat. fat), 70mg chol., 843mg sod., 47g carb. (10g sugars, 5g fiber), 28g pro.

BEEF TENDERLOIN WITH SAUTEED VEGETABLES

This is the most elegant, tender beef. It's made the classic French way—which is so easy!

—*Cleo Gonske, Redding, CA*

PREP: 20 MIN. • BAKE: 50 MIN. + STANDING • MAKES: 12 SERVINGS

1 beef tenderloin (5 lbs.), trimmed
2 tsp. salt
½ tsp. pepper

VEGETABLES

¼ cup butter, cubed
8 medium carrots, julienned
6 celery ribs, julienned
¼ tsp. salt
¼ tsp. pepper
3 cans (14 oz. each) water-packed artichoke hearts, drained and quartered

HOLLANDAISE SAUCE

3 large egg yolks
3 Tbsp. heavy whipping cream
2 tsp. Dijon mustard
¼ tsp. cayenne pepper
1 cup butter, melted
1 Tbsp. lemon juice

1. Preheat oven to 425°. Tuck thin tail end of tenderloin under; tie beef at 2-in. intervals with kitchen string. Sprinkle with salt and pepper.

2. Place tenderloin on a rack in a shallow roasting pan. Roast 50-60 minutes or until meat reaches desired doneness (for medium-rare, a thermometer should read 135°; medium, 140°; medium-well, 145°). Remove tenderloin from oven; tent with foil. Let stand 15 minutes before slicing.

3. In a large skillet, heat butter over medium-high heat. Add carrots; cook and stir 5 minutes. Add celery, salt and pepper; cook and stir 5-7 minutes longer or until the vegetables are crisp-tender. Stir in artichokes.

4. In top of a double boiler or a metal bowl over simmering water, whisk egg yolks, cream, mustard and cayenne until blended; cook until mixture is just thick enough to coat a metal spoon and temperature reaches 160°, whisking constantly. Remove from heat. Very slowly drizzle in warm melted butter, whisking constantly. Whisk in lemon juice.

5. Transfer sauce to a small bowl if necessary. Place bowl in a larger bowl of warm water. Keep warm, stirring sauce occasionally, until ready to serve, up to 30 minutes. Serve with beef and vegetables.

5 OZ. COOKED BEEF WITH ½ CUP VEGETABLES AND ABOUT 1 TBSP. SAUCE: 526 cal., 33g fat (18g sat. fat), 184mg chol., 910mg sod., 11g carb. (2g sugars, 2g fiber), 44g pro.

SKILLET-GRILLED CATFISH

You can use any thick fish fillet for this recipe, but I suggest catfish or haddock. The Cajun flavor is outstanding.
—*Traci Wynne, Denver, PA*

TAKES: 25 MIN. • MAKES: 4 SERVINGS

¼ cup all-purpose flour
¼ cup cornmeal
1 tsp. onion powder
1 tsp. dried basil
½ tsp. garlic salt
½ tsp. dried thyme
¼ to ½ tsp. white pepper
¼ to ½ tsp. cayenne pepper
¼ to ½ tsp. pepper
4 catfish fillets (6 to 8 oz. each)
¼ cup butter

1. In a large shallow dish, combine the first 9 ingredients. Add catfish, 1 fillet at a time, and turn to coat.

2. Place a large cast-iron skillet on a grill rack over medium-high heat. Melt butter in the skillet; add catfish in batches, if necessary. Grill, covered, until the fish just begins to flake easily with a fork, 5-10 minutes on each side.

1 FILLET: 222 cal., 15g fat (8g sat. fat), 51mg chol., 366mg sod., 14g carb. (0 sugars, 1g fiber), 8g pro.

DILLED CHICKEN & ASPARAGUS

If a delicious chicken and rice entree is what you're craving, look no further than this mild herb-flavored rice dish with tender asparagus.
—*Mary Ann Marino, West Pittsburgh, PA*

TAKES: 30 MIN. • MAKES: 2 SERVINGS

½ cup uncooked long grain rice
1 tsp. chicken bouillon granules
1½ cups water, divided
2 Tbsp. minced fresh parsley
1 Tbsp. lemon juice
2 tsp. olive oil
1½ tsp. dill weed
⅛ tsp. salt
9 fresh asparagus spears, cut into 2-in. pieces
½ lb. boneless skinless chicken breasts, cut into 1-in. cubes

1. In a small saucepan, bring the rice, bouillon and 1 cup water to a boil. Reduce heat; cover and simmer for 15-18 minutes or until liquid is absorbed and rice is tender.

2. Meanwhile, combine the parsley, lemon juice, oil, dill and salt; set aside. In a large nonstick skillet, bring remaining water to a boil. Add asparagus; cover and boil for 3 minutes. Drain and immediately place asparagus in ice water. Drain and pat dry.

3. In the same skillet coated with cooking spray, saute chicken until juices run clear; drain. Add the rice, asparagus and lemon mixture; toss to coat.

1¼ CUPS: 356 cal., 8g fat (2g sat. fat), 63mg chol., 371mg sod., 42g carb. (2g sugars, 2g fiber), 28g pro.

PRONTO VEGETARIAN PEPPERS

In the summer, I serve these peppers with a fresh salad and a roll. At the end of summer,
I freeze them for the colder months when produce costs are high. For a hot meal on
a chilly day, I serve them with a side of warm pasta tossed in olive oil.
—Renee Hollobaugh, Altoona, PA

TAKES: 25 MIN. • MAKES: 2 SERVINGS

2 large sweet red peppers
1 cup canned stewed
   tomatoes
⅓ cup instant brown rice
2 Tbsp. hot water
¾ cup canned kidney beans,
   rinsed and drained
½ cup frozen corn, thawed
2 green onions, thinly
   sliced
⅛ tsp. crushed red pepper
   flakes
½ cup shredded part-skim
   mozzarella cheese
1 Tbsp. grated Parmesan
   cheese

1. Cut peppers in half lengthwise; remove seeds. Place the peppers in an ungreased shallow microwave-safe dish. Cover and microwave on high until tender, 3-4 minutes.

2. Combine the stewed tomatoes, rice and water in a small microwave-safe bowl. Cover and microwave on high until rice is tender, 5-6 minutes. Stir in the beans, corn, onions and pepper flakes; spoon into peppers.

3. Sprinkle with cheeses. Microwave, uncovered, until heated through, 3-4 minutes.

2 STUFFED PEPPER HALVES: 341 cal., 7g fat (3g sat. fat), 19mg chol., 556mg sod., 56g carb. (16g sugars, 11g fiber), 19g pro.

CRAB-TOPPED FISH FILLETS

These fillets are elegant enough for company but no trouble to make. Fish is abundant here
in South Florida, and we like to get together with friends in the afternoon, so I often need to
whip up a quick dinner when we get home. This special dish is one of my husband's favorites.
—Mary Tuthill, Fort Myers Beach, FL

TAKES: 30 MIN. • MAKES: 4 SERVINGS

4 sole or cod fillets, or fish
   fillets of your choice
   (6 oz. each)
1 can (6 oz.) crabmeat,
   drained and flaked,
   or 1 cup imitation
   crabmeat, chopped
½ cup grated Parmesan
   cheese
½ cup mayonnaise
1 tsp. lemon juice
⅓ cup slivered almonds,
   toasted
   Paprika, optional

1. Preheat oven to 350°. Place fish fillets in a greased 13x9-in. baking pan. Bake, uncovered, until fish flakes easily with a fork, 18-22 minutes. Meanwhile, in a large bowl, combine the crab, cheese, mayonnaise and lemon juice.

2. Drain cooking juices from baking dish; spoon crab mixture over fillets. Broil 4-5 in. from the heat until topping is lightly browned, about 5 minutes. Sprinkle with almonds and, if desired, paprika.

1 FILLET: 429 cal., 31g fat (6g sat. fat), 128mg chol., 1063mg sod., 3g carb. (0 sugars, 1g fiber), 33g pro.

PRONTO VEGETARIAN PEPPERS

ONE-POT SALSA CHICKEN

Here's a colorful and healthy main dish that can be on the table
in just over an hour. The subtle sweet-spicy flavor is a nice surprise.
—*Ann Sheehy, Lawrence, MA*

PREP: 20 MIN. • **COOK:** 45 MIN. • **MAKES:** 6 SERVINGS

- 2 Tbsp. canola oil
- 2 lbs. boneless skinless
  chicken thighs, cut into
  1-in. pieces
- 1 tsp. pepper
- ½ tsp. salt
- 2 medium sweet potatoes,
  peeled and chopped
- 1 jar (16 oz.) medium salsa
- 2 medium nectarines,
  peeled and sliced
- 2 Tbsp. Tajin seasoning
- 1 cup uncooked instant
  brown rice
- 1 cup water
- ¼ cup minced fresh parsley
  Minced fresh chives

1. In a Dutch oven, heat oil over medium-high heat. Sprinkle the chicken with pepper and salt. Brown chicken in batches; return all to pan. Add the sweet potatoes, salsa, nectarines and seasoning. Bring to a boil; reduce heat. Cover and simmer until potatoes are almost tender, about 15 minutes.

2. Stir in rice and water; bring to a boil. Reduce heat. Cover and simmer until the potatoes are tender, about 10 minutes. Stir in parsley. Serve in bowls; sprinkle with chives.

1⅔ **CUPS:** 432 cal., 16g fat (3g sat. fat), 101mg chol., 1254mg sod., 39g carb. (13g sugars, 4g fiber), 31g pro.

GRANDMA'S SECRET
Choose nectarines that are ripe (slightly soft) and free from any blemishes or bruises. A ripe nectarine will separate easily from the pit, making prep easy, too.

SUGAR-GLAZED HAM

This old-fashioned sugar glaze gives your ham a pretty golden brown coating
just like Grandma's. The mustard and vinegar complement the brown sugar
and add tangy flavor. Be prepared to serve seconds!
—*Carol Strong Battle, Heathsville, VA*

PREP: 5 MIN. • BAKE: 1¾ HOURS • MAKES: 14 SERVINGS

1 fully cooked bone-in ham
  (5 to 7 lbs.)
1 cup packed brown sugar
2 tsp. prepared mustard
1 to 2 Tbsp. cider vinegar

1. Preheat oven to 325°. Place ham on a rack in a shallow roasting pan. Using a sharp knife, score surface of ham with ¼-in.-deep cuts in a diamond pattern. Cover and bake until a thermometer reads 130°, 1½-2 hours.

2. Meanwhile, in a small bowl, combine brown sugar, mustard and enough cider vinegar to make a thick paste. Remove ham from oven. Spread the sugar mixture over ham. Bake, uncovered, until a thermometer reads 140°, 15-30 minutes longer.

4 OZ. HAM: 284 cal., 16g fat (6g sat. fat), 57mg chol., 1110mg sod., 15g carb. (15g sugars, 0 fiber), 20g pro.

TAMALE PIE

The amount of spice in this recipe is just right for my family—we prefer things on the mild side.
Make it once with these measurements, then spice it up a little more if you like!
—*Ruth Aden, Polson, MT*

PREP: 35 MIN. • BAKE: 30 MIN. • MAKES: 8 SERVINGS

1½ lbs. ground beef
 2 cans (14½ oz. each)
   stewed tomatoes
 1 medium onion, chopped
 ½ tsp. garlic powder
 ½ tsp. chili powder
 ¼ tsp. salt
 ¼ tsp. pepper
10 flour tortillas (6 in.)
 3 cups (12 oz. each)
   shredded cheddar-
   Monterey Jack cheese
   or Colby-Jack cheese
 1 can (2¼ oz.) sliced ripe
   olives, drained

1. In a skillet, brown ground beef; drain. Add tomatoes, onion and spices. Simmer, uncovered, for 20 minutes.

2. Arrange 5 tortillas in the bottom of a 13x9-in. baking dish, tearing tortillas as needed. Cover with half the meat mixture, then half the cheese. Repeat layers, using remaining tortillas, meat mixture and cheese. Sprinkle with olives.

3. Bake at 350° for 30 minutes or until heated through. Let stand a few minutes before serving.

1 PIECE: 428 cal., 24g fat (13g sat. fat), 79mg chol., 829mg sod., 24g carb. (4g sugars, 1g fiber), 29g pro.

SLOW-COOKER
MILK-CAN SUPPER

SLOW-COOKER MILK-CAN SUPPER

Here's a slow-cooked version of an old campfire classic. Pioneers and cowboys would cook this kind of meal over a milk can on an open fire, letting the flavors and textures blend together beautifully.
—*Nick Iverson, Denver, CO*

PREP: 20 MIN. • COOK: 6 HOURS • MAKES: 8 SERVINGS

1 Tbsp. canola oil
8 uncooked bratwurst links
2 lbs. small Yukon Gold potatoes, quartered
1 small head cabbage, coarsely chopped
2 medium onions, quartered
3 medium carrots, peeled and cut into 2-in. lengths
3 medium parsnips, peeled and cut into 2-in. lengths
6 fresh thyme sprigs
2 garlic cloves, crushed
2 bay leaves
½ tsp. salt
½ tsp. pepper
1 cup light beer
1 cup reduced-sodium chicken broth

1. Heat oil in large skillet over medium heat; add sausages and cook until browned, 3-4 minutes. Remove from heat; set aside.

2. Place potatoes in single layer on the bottom of a 6-qt. slow cooker. Top with cabbage, onions, carrots and parsnips. Add thyme, garlic, bay leaves, salt and pepper. Add sausages; pour beer and chicken broth over top. Cook, covered, 6-8 hours or until vegetables are tender. Remove bay leaves before serving.

1 SERVING: 457 cal., 27g fat (9g sat. fat), 63mg chol., 967mg sod., 37g carb. (6g sugars, 4g fiber), 15g pro.

FROM GRANDMA'S KITCHEN: Parsnips, a white root vegetable, have a creamy texture when cooked. Look for them in the produce section, near the carrots, in your grocery store.

GRANDMA'S SPICED DUCK

When I was growing up, my grandma raised and butchered ducks. She always served duck for the holidays, and for other family events throughout the year. I always thought it was better than turkey! While finding a dressed duck can be difficult, I do occasionally purchase the smaller ducks available in the grocery store, just so my family can enjoy something that was a special part of my past.
—*Sue Gronholz, Beaver Dam, WI*

PREP: 10 MIN. ROAST: 1¾ HOURS + STANDING • MAKES: 4 SERVINGS

1 domestic duck (4 to 5 lbs.)
3 Tbsp. sugar
2 tsp. water
¾ tsp. salt
¼ tsp. ground cloves
¼ tsp. pepper

1. Preheat oven to 325°. Pierce duck skin all over with a fork. Mix remaining ingredients; rub over the outside of duck. Place duck on a rack in a shallow roasting pan; add 1 in. of water.

2. Roast duck, uncovered, until a thermometer inserted in thigh reads 180°, 1½-2 hours. Remove from oven; let stand 15 minutes before carving. If desired, skim fat and thicken pan drippings for gravy. Serve with duck.

6 OZ. COOKED DUCK: 649 cal., 51g fat (18g sat. fat), 152mg chol., 550mg sod., 10g carb. (9g sugars, 0 fiber), 34g pro.

ITALIAN HERB-CRUSTED PORK LOIN

I like to change things up during the holidays by roasting pork loin with my favorite herbs and veggies. This dish is a showpiece that always dazzles my family.
—*Kim Palmer, Kingston, GA*

PREP: 15 MIN. + CHILLING • BAKE: 50 MIN. + STANDING • MAKES: 8 SERVINGS

3 Tbsp. olive oil
5 garlic cloves, minced
1 tsp. salt
1 tsp. each dried basil, thyme and rosemary, crushed
½ tsp. Italian seasoning
½ tsp. pepper
1 boneless pork loin roast (3 to 4 lbs.)
8 medium carrots, halved lengthwise
2 medium onions, quartered

1. In a small bowl, mix oil, garlic and seasonings; rub over roast. Arrange carrots and onions on the bottom of a 13x9-in. baking pan. Place roast over vegetables, fat side up. Refrigerate, covered, 1 hour.

2. Preheat oven to 475°. Roast the pork for 20 minutes.

3. Reduce oven setting to 425°. Roast until a thermometer reads 145° and vegetables are tender, 30-40 minutes longer. Remove roast from oven; tent with foil. Let roast stand for 20 minutes before slicing.

1 SERVING: 295 cal., 13g fat (4g sat. fat), 85mg chol., 388mg sod., 9g carb. (4g sugars, 2g fiber), 34g pro. DIABETIC EXCHANGES: 5 lean meat, 1 vegetable, 1 fat.

CHICKEN & GOAT CHEESE SKILLET

My husband was completely bowled over by this on-a-whim skillet meal. I couldn't wait to make it again!
—*Ericka Barber, Eureka, CA*

TAKES: 20 MIN. • MAKES: 2 SERVINGS

½ lb. boneless skinless chicken breasts, cut into 1-in. pieces
¼ tsp. salt
⅛ tsp. pepper
2 tsp. olive oil
1 cup cut fresh asparagus (1-in. pieces)
1 garlic clove, minced
3 plum tomatoes, chopped
3 Tbsp. 2% milk
2 Tbsp. herbed fresh goat cheese, crumbled
Hot cooked rice or pasta
Additional goat cheese, optional

1. Toss chicken with salt and pepper. In a large skillet, heat oil over medium-high heat; saute chicken until no longer pink, 4-6 minutes. Remove from pan; keep warm.

2. Add asparagus to skillet; cook and stir over medium-high heat 1 minute. Add garlic; cook and stir 30 seconds. Stir in tomatoes, milk and 2 Tbsp. cheese; cook, covered, over medium heat until cheese begins to melt, 2-3 minutes. Stir in chicken. Serve with rice. If desired, top with additional cheese.

1½ CUPS CHICKEN MIXTURE: 251 cal., 11g fat (3g sat. fat), 74mg chol., 447mg sod., 8g carb. (5g sugars, 3g fiber), 29g pro. DIABETIC EXCHANGES: 4 lean meat, 2 fat, 1 vegetable.

SLOW-COOKER CHEESY WHITE LASAGNA

Here's my best version of my favorite food—lasagna!
The recipe is a winner, so it's worth the extra prep. You'll have
plenty of time to make side dishes while the main dish is cooking.

—*Suzanne Smith, Bluffton, IN*

PREP: 30 MIN. • **COOK:** 3 HOURS + STANDING • **MAKES:** 8 SERVINGS

- 1 lb. ground chicken or beef
- 2 tsp. canola oil
- 1¾ cups sliced fresh mushrooms
- 1 medium onion, chopped
- 2 medium carrots, chopped
- 2 garlic cloves, minced
- 2 tsp. Italian seasoning
- ¾ tsp. salt
- ½ tsp. pepper
- ½ cup white wine or chicken broth
- 1 cup half-and-half cream
- 4 oz. cream cheese, softened
- 1 cup shredded white cheddar cheese
- 1 cup shredded Gouda cheese
- 1 large egg, beaten
- 1½ cups 2% cottage cheese
- ¼ cup minced fresh basil or 4 tsp. dried basil
- 9 no-cook lasagna noodles
- 4 cups shredded part-skim mozzarella cheese
  Additional minced fresh basil, optional

1. Fold two 18-in. square pieces of heavy-duty foil into thirds. Crisscross strips and place on bottom and up sides of a 6-qt. slow cooker. Coat strips with cooking spray.

2. In a 6-qt. stockpot, cook chicken over medium heat until no longer pink, 6-8 minutes, breaking into crumbles; drain. Set chicken aside.

3. In same pot, heat oil over medium-high heat. Add mushrooms, onion and carrots; cook and stir just until tender, 6-8 minutes. Add garlic, Italian seasoning, salt and pepper; cook 1 minute longer. Stir in wine. Bring to a boil; cook until liquid is reduced by half, 4-5 minutes. Stir in cream, cream cheese, cheddar and Gouda cheeses. Return chicken to pot. In a large bowl, combine egg, cottage cheese and basil.

4. Spread 1 cup meat mixture into slow cooker. Layer with 3 noodles (breaking noodles as necessary to fit), 1 cup meat mixture, ½ cup cottage cheese mixture and 1 cup mozzarella cheese. Repeat layers twice. Top with remaining meat mixture and cheese. Cook, covered, on low 3-4 hours, until noodles are tender. Remove slow cooker insert and let stand 30 minutes. If desired, sprinkle with additional basil. Using foil strips as handles, remove lasagna to a cutting board or platter.

1 PIECE: 603 cal., 35g fat (19g sat. fat), 165mg chol., 1086mg sod., 28g carb. (7g sugars, 2g fiber), 40g pro.

CHICKEN PAPRIKASH

Some recipes for chicken paprikash include vegetables like bell peppers and celery, but not my grandmother's. Hers was a simple combination of chicken, onions, garlic, paprika and sour cream.

—Lily Julow, Lawrenceville, GA

PREP: 20 MIN. • **COOK:** 45 MIN. • **MAKES:** 12 SERVINGS

2 **broiler/fryer chickens (about 3½ to 4 lbs. each), cut into 8 pieces each**
2 **tsp. kosher salt**
1 **tsp. pepper**
2 **Tbsp. peanut oil or canola oil**
2 **medium onions, halved and sliced**
2 **large garlic cloves, chopped**
3 **Tbsp. all-purpose flour**
1 **Tbsp. sweet Hungarian paprika**
2 **cups hot chicken broth or water**
1 **cup sour cream**
  Optional: Minced fresh parsley and additional sweet Hungarian paprika
  Hot cooked noodles or mashed potatoes

1. Season chicken with kosher salt and pepper. In a Dutch oven, heat peanut oil over medium-high heat. Brown chicken in batches. Remove with a slotted spoon; drain and keep warm.

2. Reduce heat to medium-low. Add the onions; cook, stirring to loosen browned bits from pan, until onions begin to soften, 6-8 minutes. Add garlic; cook 1 minute longer.

3. Stir in flour and paprika; reduce heat to low. Cook until paprika is fragrant, 3-5 minutes. Add broth; cook, stirring constantly, until smooth, 6-8 minutes. Return chicken to pan; simmer, covered, until a thermometer inserted into deepest part of thigh reads 170°, about 30 minutes. Transfer chicken to a serving platter.

4. Skim fat. Stir in sour cream; heat just until warmed through, 3-5 minutes (do not allow to boil). If desired, sprinkle with parsley and additional paprika. Serve with hot cooked noodles or mashed potatoes.

1 SERVING: 422 cal., 26g fat (8g sat. fat), 127mg chol., 596mg sod., 5g carb. (2g sugars, 1g fiber), 40g pro.

GRANDMA'S SECRET

Serve this dish with mashed potatoes, hot cooked noodles of your choice, or traditional Hungarian nokedli, which are egg noodle dumplings similar to German spaetzle.

CREAMY BEEF & POTATOES

One of my husband's favorite childhood memories is eating his Grandma Barney's famous Tater Tot casserole. One day I started preparing it with O'Brien potatoes instead of Tater Tots. Now I always make it this way.
—*Heather Matthews, Keller, TX*

TAKES: 20 MIN. • MAKES: 4 SERVINGS

4 cups frozen O'Brien potatoes
1 Tbsp. water
1 lb. ground beef
½ tsp. salt
¼ tsp. pepper

2 cans (10¾ oz. each) condensed cream of mushroom soup, undiluted
⅔ cup 2% milk
2 cups shredded Colby-Monterey Jack cheese

1. Place frozen potatoes and water in a microwave-safe bowl. Microwave, covered, on high until the potatoes are tender, 8-10 minutes, stirring twice.

2. Meanwhile, in a Dutch oven, cook beef, breaking into crumbles, over medium heat until no longer pink, 6-8 minutes. Stir in salt and pepper. In a small bowl, whisk soup and milk until blended; add to beef. Stir in potatoes. Sprinkle with cheese. Reduce heat to low; cook, covered, until cheese is melted.

1¾ CUPS: 664 cal., 38g fat (19g sat. fat), 130mg chol., 1851mg sod., 40g carb. (5g sugars, 6g fiber), 37g pro.

"Quick, easy and delicious! My husband and I loved it. Will definitely make again and make it often! Might double the recipe next time so I have more leftovers."
—OBSESSEDWITHFOOD, TASTEOFHOME.COM

ROASTED SAGE TURKEY WITH VEGETABLE GRAVY

On Thanksgiving, I fill my bird with fresh sage and thyme sprigs to achieve the same delicious flavors found in many classic dressing/stuffing recipes. A homemade gravy is the crowning touch.
—*Beth Jacobson, Milwaukee, WI*

PREP: 30 MIN. + CHILLING • **BAKE:** 2 HOURS 10 MIN. + STANDING • **MAKES:** 16 SERVINGS (3½ CUPS GRAVY)

1   turkey (14 to 16 lbs.)
1   Tbsp. kosher salt
1   tsp. ground sage
½   tsp. garlic powder
1   large onion, chopped
3   celery ribs, chopped
3   medium carrots, chopped
1¼ cups water, divided
3   Tbsp. canola oil
½   tsp. freshly ground
     pepper
¾   cup white wine
3   fresh sage sprigs
4   fresh thyme sprigs

GRAVY
1   to 1½ cups reduced-
     sodium chicken broth or
     homemade chicken stock
¼   cup all-purpose flour
¼   tsp. minced fresh sage
¼   tsp. freshly ground
     pepper

1. Remove giblets and neck from turkey. Reserve turkey neck; refrigerate, covered, overnight. Place turkey in a 15x10-in. baking pan, breast side up. Secure skin to underside of neck cavity with toothpicks. Mix salt, sage and garlic powder. Tuck wings under turkey; tie drumsticks together. Pat turkey dry. Rub outside of turkey with salt mixture. Refrigerate, loosely covered, overnight.

2. Preheat oven to 475°. Place onion, celery, carrots and reserved neck in bottom of a broiler pan; add ½ cup water. Place broiler pan rack over top; transfer turkey to rack. Rub outside of turkey with oil; sprinkle with pepper. Pour wine and remaining water into turkey cavity; add sage and thyme sprigs.

3. Place turkey in oven, legs facing toward back of oven. Roast, uncovered, 40 minutes.

4. Reduce oven setting to 350°. Cover breast tightly with a double thickness of foil. Roast until a thermometer inserted in thickest part of thigh reads 170°-175° (thermometer should not touch bone or fat), 1½-2 hours longer.

5. Remove turkey from oven. Let stand, uncovered, 20 minutes before carving. Using a turkey baster, remove liquid from turkey cavity to a large measuring cup. Line a strainer or colander with cheesecloth; place over measuring cup. With a slotted spoon, remove the vegetables from bottom of broiler pan, reserving 1¼ cups. Discard the turkey neck. Strain the cooking liquid into measuring cup. Skim fat, reserving ¼ cup fat. Add enough broth to the cooking liquid to measure 2 cups.

6. In a large saucepan, mix flour and reserved fat until smooth; gradually whisk in broth mixture. Bring gravy to a boil over medium-high heat, stirring constantly; cook and stir until thickened, 1-2 minutes. Add half of the reserved vegetables. Puree gravy using an immersion blender; or cool gravy slightly and puree in a blender. Stir in sage, pepper and remaining vegetables; heat through. Serve with turkey.

9 OZ. COOKED TURKEY WITH ABOUT ¼ CUP GRAVY: 514 cal., 24g fat (6g sat. fat), 215mg chol., 562mg sod., 4g carb. (1g sugars, 1g fiber), 64g pro.

COLLARD GREENS
& BEANS, PAGE 138

GRANDMA'S FAVORITE
SIDE DISHES

A memorable menu isn't complete without on-the-side sensations. From dressed-up vegetables and greens to comforting potatoes, Grandma's treasured side dishes have stood the test of time. Try one of her beloved dinner sidekicks to round out your meal.

ROASTED BRUSSELS SPROUTS & CAULIFLOWER

My grandkids aren't huge fans of cauliflower, but toss a little bacon on it and they can't get enough! They like it even more with golden cauliflower instead of white.
—*Patricia Hudson, Riverview, FL*

PREP: 25 MIN. • COOK: 25 MIN. • MAKES: 12 SERVINGS

8 bacon strips, chopped
6 garlic cloves, minced
1 Tbsp. olive oil
1 Tbsp. butter, melted
¼ tsp. kosher salt
¼ tsp. coarsely ground pepper
4 cups Brussels sprouts, halved
4 cups fresh cauliflowerets
¼ cup grated Parmesan cheese
Additional grated Parmesan cheese, optional

1. In a large skillet, cook bacon over medium heat until crisp, stirring occasionally. Remove with a slotted spoon; drain on paper towels. Discard drippings, reserving 1 Tbsp.

2. In a large bowl, mix the garlic, oil, butter, salt, pepper and reserved drippings. Add Brussels sprouts and cauliflower; toss to coat. Transfer to 2 greased 15x10x1-in. baking pans.

3. Bake at 400° for 20-25 minutes. Sprinkle each pan with 2 Tbsp. cheese. Bake 5 minutes longer or until vegetables are tender. Sprinkle with bacon and, if desired, additional cheese.

½ CUP: 137 cal., 11g fat (4g sat. fat), 17mg chol., 221mg sod., 5g carb. (2g sugars, 2g fiber), 5g pro.

COLLARD GREENS & BEANS

PICTURED ON PAGE 136

I didn't eat Southern-style collards until a friend gave me a recipe for greens with bacon and pinto beans. Now I'm delighted to make them.
—*April Burroughs, Vilonia, AR*

PREP: 20 MIN. • COOK: 55 MIN. • MAKES: 8 SERVINGS

2 lbs. collard greens
3 bacon strips, chopped
1 small red onion, chopped
2 garlic cloves, minced
2½ cups water
2 Tbsp. brown sugar
1 Tbsp. cider vinegar
¾ tsp. salt
½ tsp. pepper
1 can (15 oz.) pinto beans, rinsed and drained

1. Remove and discard center ribs and stems from collard greens. Cut leaves into 1-in. pieces. In a Dutch oven, cook bacon over medium heat until crisp, stirring occasionally.

2. Add onion and garlic to bacon and drippings; cook and stir 2 minutes. Add collard greens; cook and stir until they begin to wilt. Stir in water, brown sugar, vinegar, salt and pepper. Bring to a boil. Reduce heat; simmer, covered, 55-65 minutes or until greens are tender, adding beans during the last 15 minutes.

⅔ CUP: 145 cal., 5g fat (1g sat. fat), 7mg chol., 382mg sod., 19g carb. (5g sugars, 7g fiber), 7g pro. **DIABETIC EXCHANGES:** 1 starch, 1 vegetable, 1 fat.

ROASTED BRUSSELS SPROUTS
& CAULIFLOWER

ANNIE'S ORIGINAL SALSA

I spent 5 years working on this recipe. Everyone loves it, and it's one of the few recipes that is actually mine, not inherited from someone else! It's been so popular that a friend canned 4 ounce jars and gave them as wedding favors.

—*Angela Barnes, Big Rapids, MI*

PREP: 45 MIN. • PROCESS: 15 MIN. • MAKES: 7 PINTS

- 2 cups tomato sauce
- 2 cups tomato paste
- 2 cups chopped onions
- 1 cup chopped green pepper
- 3 to 5 chopped jalapeno peppers, seeded
- ½ cup chopped fresh cilantro
- 6 garlic cloves, minced
- ⅔ cup white vinegar
- ⅓ cup sugar
- 2 Tbsp. canning salt
- 2 tsp. ground cumin
- 2 tsp. pepper
- 8 cups chopped peeled tomatoes, drained (about 5 lbs. medium tomatoes)

1. In a stockpot, combine the first 12 ingredients. Stir in tomatoes. Bring to a boil over medium-high heat. Reduce the heat; simmer, uncovered, vegetables are tender, about 20 min.

2. Ladle hot mixture into hot 1-pint jars, leaving ½-in. headspace. Remove air bubbles and adjust headspace, if necessary, by adding hot mixture. Wipe rims. Center lids on jars; screw on bands until fingertip tight.

3. Place jars into canner with simmering water, ensuring that they are completely covered with water. Bring to a boil; process for 15 minutes. Remove jars and cool.

NOTE: The processing time listed is for altitudes of 1,000 feet or less. For altitudes up to 3,000 feet, add 5 minutes; 6,000 feet, add 10 minutes; 8,000 feet, add 15 minutes; 10,000 feet, add 20 minutes.

¼ CUP: 24 cal., 0 fat (0 sat. fat), 0 chol., 300mg sod., 5g carb. (3g sugars, 1g fiber), 1g pro.

GRANDMA'S SECRET

Only use a boiling water bath canner or a pressure canner. Open-kettle canning or the use of a dishwasher, oven or microwave for processing is not recommended.

WINTER BEET SALAD

To save a little time, you can use packaged salad greens in this recipe.
The simple dressing is easy to assemble.
—Taste of Home *Test Kitchen*

PREP: 20 MIN. • BAKE: 1 HOUR + COOLING • MAKES: 4 SERVINGS

2 medium fresh beets
1 pkg. (5 oz.) mixed
   salad greens
2 medium navel oranges,
   peeled and sliced
1 small fennel bulb,
   halved and thinly sliced
¼ cup chopped hazelnuts,
   toasted

DRESSING
3 Tbsp. olive oil
2 Tbsp. orange juice
1 Tbsp. balsamic vinegar
2 tsp. grated orange zest
¼ tsp. onion powder

Preheat oven to 425°. Cut slits in beets; place on a baking sheet. Bake until tender, about 1 hour. When cool enough to handle, peel beets and cut into wedges. Divide greens among 4 salad plates; top with the beets, oranges, fennel and hazelnuts. Combine the dressing ingredients in a jar with a tight-fitting lid; shake well. Drizzle over salads.

NOTE: To toast the nuts, bake in a shallow pan in a 350° oven for 5-10 minutes or cook in a skillet over low heat until lightly browned, stirring occasionally.

1 SERVING: 213 cal., 15g fat (2g sat. fat), 0 chol., 80mg sod., 21g carb. (12g sugars, 6g fiber), 4g pro. DIABETIC EXCHANGES: 3 fat, 2 vegetable, ½ starch.

SPICY FRIED OKRA

This fried veggie is a southern delicacy that's sure to add excitement to any meal.
—Rashanda Cobbins, Milwaukee, WI

TAKES: 30 MIN. • MAKES: 4 SERVINGS

3 cups sliced fresh or
   frozen okra, thawed
6 Tbsp. buttermilk
2 tsp. Louisiana-style
   hot sauce
¼ cup all-purpose flour
¼ cup cornmeal
½ tsp. seasoned salt
¼ tsp. cayenne pepper
   Oil for deep-fat frying
   Additional salt and
   pepper, optional

1. Pat okra dry with paper towels. Place buttermilk and hot sauce in a shallow bowl. In another shallow bowl, combine the flour, cornmeal, salt and pepper. Dip okra in buttermilk mixture, then roll in cornmeal mixture.

2. In a cast-iron or other heavy skillet, heat 1 in. of oil to 375°. Fry okra, a few pieces at a time, until golden brown, 1½ to 2½ minutes on each side. Drain on paper towels. If desired, season okra with additional salt and pepper.

¾ CUP: 237 cal., 16g fat (1g sat. fat), 1mg chol., 326mg sod., 20g carb. (4g sugars, 3g fiber), 5g pro.

CHIP-CRUSTED
GRILLED CORN

CHIP-CRUSTED GRILLED CORN

For my version of Mexican street corn, I roll the ears in crushed chips.
For extra pizazz, try different chip flavors like ranch or jalapeno.
—Crystal Schlueter, Northglenn, CO

TAKES: 30 MIN. • MAKES: 6 SERVINGS

¾ cup mayonnaise
¼ cup sour cream
2 Tbsp. minced fresh
   cilantro
½ tsp. salt
¼ tsp. cayenne pepper
¼ tsp. pepper
1 cup crushed tortilla chips
6 medium ears sweet corn,
   husks removed
   Lime wedges

1. In a small bowl, combine the first 6 ingredients. Refrigerate, covered, until serving. Place crushed tortilla chips in a shallow bowl. Grill corn, covered, over medium heat until tender, turning occasionally, 15-20 minutes.

2. When cool enough to handle, spread corn with mayonnaise mixture; roll in chips. Grill corn, covered, until lightly browned, 1-2 minutes longer. Serve with lime wedges.

1 EAR OF CORN: 355 cal., 27g fat (5g sat. fat), 17mg chol., 405mg sod., 26g carb. (7g sugars, 2g fiber), 4g pro.

ROASTED RED POTATO SALAD

I got this recipe from my sister-in-law and I've made it numerous times at the request of friends and co-workers. It's quick and easy, which is just what I need in my busy life. I learned how to cook from the two best cooks I know—my mom, Arline, and my Grandma Etta.
—Ginger Cusano, Sandusky, OH

PREP: 40 MIN. + CHILLING • MAKES: 8 SERVINGS

2 lbs. red potatoes,
   cut into 1-in. cubes
1 medium onion, chopped
4 hard-boiled large eggs,
   sliced
6 bacon strips,
   cooked and crumbled
1 cup mayonnaise
½ tsp. salt
¼ tsp. pepper
   Paprika and minced fresh
   parsley, optional

1. Place the potatoes in a greased 15x10x1-in. baking pan. Bake, uncovered, at 400° until potatoes are tender and golden brown, stirring occasionally, 25-30 minutes. Cool for 15 minutes.

2. Transfer to a large bowl; add onion, eggs, bacon, mayonnaise, salt and pepper. Toss to coat. Cover and refrigerate for several hours or overnight. If desired, sprinkle with paprika and parsley.

¾ CUP: 355 cal., 27g fat (5g sat. fat), 120mg chol., 412mg sod., 20g carb. (3g sugars, 2g fiber), 7g pro.

SCALLOPED POTATOES WITH MUSHROOMS

Potatoes and mushrooms make a one-dish meal I absolutely love. Give it a try and you'll see what I mean!
—*Courtney Stultz, Weir, KS*

PREP: 40 MIN. • BAKE: 15 MIN. + STANDING • MAKES: 8 SERVINGS

2 lbs. potatoes (about 4 medium), peeled and sliced
1 Tbsp. butter
½ lb. sliced fresh mushrooms
1 small onion, chopped
1 garlic clove, minced
¼ cup all-purpose flour
1 cup chicken broth
1 tsp. salt
½ tsp. dried oregano
½ tsp. pepper
1 cup sour cream
1 cup coarsely chopped fresh spinach
2 cups shredded Swiss cheese

1. Preheat oven to 375°. Place potatoes in a large saucepan; add water to cover. Bring to a boil. Reduce heat; cook, uncovered, until tender, 8-12 minutes. Drain.

2. Meanwhile, in another saucepan, heat butter over medium-high heat. Add mushrooms and onion; cook and stir 6-8 minutes or until tender. Stir in garlic; cook 1 minute longer.

3. In a small bowl, whisk flour, broth and seasonings until smooth; stir into mushroom mixture. Bring to a boil, stirring constantly; cook and stir until sauce is thickened, 1-2 minutes. Remove from heat; stir in sour cream.

4. Arrange half of the potatoes in a greased 1½-qt. or 8-in. square baking dish; top with spinach. Spread half of the hot mushroom sauce over top; sprinkle with 1 cup cheese. Layer with remaining potatoes, sauce and cheese.

5. Bake, uncovered, until heated through and cheese is melted, 12-15 minutes. Let stand 10 minutes before serving.

1 CUP: 269 cal., 14g fat (9g sat. fat), 49mg chol., 471mg sod., 23g carb. (4g sugars, 2g fiber), 11g pro.

VERMICELLI PASTA SALAD

I started making this salad because it's loaded with peppers, my husband's favorite vegetable. Don't be surprised when there are no leftovers to take home after the family reunion, picnic or church potluck.
—*Janie Colle, Hutchinson, KS*

PREP: 20 MIN. + CHILLING • MAKES: 10 SERVINGS

12 oz. uncooked vermicelli
1 bottle (16 oz.) creamy Italian salad dressing
1 small green pepper, chopped
1 small sweet red pepper, chopped
6 green onions, chopped
1 tsp. dill seed
1 tsp. caraway seeds
1 tsp. poppy seeds

Cook vermicelli according to package directions. Drain; transfer to a large bowl. Add remaining ingredients; toss to coat. Refrigerate until cold.

¾ CUP: 309 cal., 18g fat (3g sat. fat), 0 chol., 404mg sod., 30g carb. (5g sugars, 2g fiber), 5g pro.

SPAGHETTI SQUASH WITH APPLES, BACON, & WALNUTS

I've always loved spaghetti squash as an alternative to pasta and enjoy it in the classic marinara style, but I wanted a new recipe so my family and I could enjoy it more often. The savory, salty and sour flavors combine perfectly with a hint of sweet spice. While the squash is baking, prep the rest—it will take only minutes to finish after you shred the squash.
—*Jeff Tori, Johnstown, CO*

PREP: 1 HOUR • COOK: 20 MIN. • MAKES: 6 SERVINGS

1 **medium spaghetti squash**
1 **tsp. ground cumin**
8 **bacon strips, chopped**
8 **green onions, sliced**
2 **Tbsp. butter**
2 **garlic cloves, minced**
¼ **tsp. crushed red pepper flakes**
2 **medium apple, peeled and chopped**
1 **cup apple cider or juice**
2 **Tbsp. maple syrup**
½ **tsp. salt**
1 **dash pepper**
½ **cup chopped walnuts, toasted**
2 **Tbsp. minced fresh parsley**

1. Preheat oven to 400°. Cut squash lengthwise in half; remove and discard seeds. Sprinkle with ½ tsp. cumin. Place squash in a 15x10x1-in. baking pan, cut sides down. Bake until easily pierced with a fork, 35-45 minutes.

2. In a large skillet, cook bacon over medium heat until crisp, stirring occasionally. Remove with a slotted spoon; drain on paper towels. Discard drippings.

3. Add green onions, 2 Tbsp. butter, garlic and pepper flakes; cook and stir over medium heat until tender, 2-3 minutes. Stir in apples, cider, syrup, salt, pepper and remaining cumin. Bring to a boil; cook until slightly thickened, 4-6 minutes.

4. When squash is cool enough to handle, use a fork to separate strands. Add squash to skillet; cook until the liquid is absorbed, 2-3 minutes. Stir in bacon, walnuts and parsley.

NOTE: To toast the nuts, bake in a shallow pan in a 350° oven for 5-10 minutes or cook in a skillet over low heat until lightly browned, stirring occasionally.

¾ CUP: 314 cal., 16g fat (5g sat. fat), 21mg chol., 482mg sod., 39g carb. (14g sugars, 7g fiber), 8g pro.

ORANGE-GLAZED CARROTS, ONIONS & RADISHES

Carrots and radishes give color and crunch to this sweet, spicy side. We never
have leftovers. If you make it ahead, reheat it and add the walnuts just before serving.

—Thomas Faglon, Somerset, NJ

PREP: 15 MIN. • COOK: 20 MIN. • MAKES: 8 SERVINGS

1 **lb. fresh pearl onions**
¼ **cup butter, cubed**
2 **lbs. medium carrots,
  thinly sliced**
12 **radishes, thinly sliced**
½ **cup dark brown sugar**
4 **tsp. grated orange zest**
½ **cup orange juice**
1 **cup chopped walnuts,
  toasted**

1. In a large saucepan, bring 4 cups water to a boil. Add pearl onions; boil 3 minutes. Drain and rinse with cold water. Peel.

2. In a large skillet, heat butter over medium heat. Add carrots, pearl onions, radishes, brown sugar, orange zest and juice; cook, covered, until vegetables are tender, stirring occasionally, 10-15 minutes. Cook, uncovered, until slightly thickened, 5-7 minutes longer. Sprinkle with walnuts.

NOTE: To toast the nuts, bake in a shallow pan in a 350° oven for 5-10 minutes or cook in a skillet over low heat until lightly browned, stirring occasionally.

¾ CUP: 277 cal., 16g fat (5g sat. fat), 15mg chol., 141mg sod., 34g carb. (23g sugars, 5g fiber), 4g pro.

GRANDMA'S EGG NOODLES

You just can't beat the down-home goodness of from-scratch noodles.
Add these to your favorite casserole, stroganoff or chicken soup recipe.

—Mary Stout, Topeka, IN

PREP: 45 MIN. • COOK: 5 MIN. • MAKES: 5 SERVINGS

2 **cups all-purpose flour**
½ **tsp. salt**
2 **large egg yolks**
1 **large egg**
⅓ **cup water**
1 **Tbsp. olive oil**
6 **cups chicken broth**

1. In a small bowl, combine the flour and salt. Make a well in the center. In another bowl, beat the egg yolks, egg, water and oil; pour into well. Stir to form a stiff dough.

2. Turn dough onto a well-floured surface; knead 8-10 times. Divide into thirds. Roll each portion to ⅛-in. thickness. Cut noodles into ¼-in. strips; cut the strips into 2-in. lengths. Cook immediately in boiling broth for 5-7 minutes or until tender; drain.

¾ CUP: 245 cal., 6g fat (1g sat. fat), 128mg chol., 287mg sod., 38g carb. (1g sugars, 1g fiber), 8g pro.

ORANGE-GLAZED
CARROTS, ONIONS
& RADISHES

NUTTY BARLEY BAKE

When I started bringing this distinctive dish to holiday dinners, a lot of people had never seen barley in anything but soup. They have since dubbed me the barley lady, and now I wouldn't dare bring anything but this dish. Even if I double the recipe, I come home with an empty pan.

—Renate Crump, Los Angeles, CA

PREP: 15 MIN. • BAKE: 1¼ HOURS • MAKES: 6 SERVINGS

- 1 medium onion, chopped
- 1 cup medium pearl barley
- ½ cup slivered almonds or pine nuts
- ¼ cup butter, cubed
- ½ cup minced fresh parsley
- ¼ cup thinly sliced green onions
- ¼ tsp. salt
- ⅛ tsp. pepper
- 2 cans (14½ oz. each) beef broth
  Additional parsley and green onions, optional

1. In a large skillet, saute the onion, barley and nuts in butter until barley is lightly browned. Stir in the parsley, green onions, salt and pepper.

2. Transfer to a greased 2-qt. baking dish. Stir in broth. Bake, uncovered, at 350° for 1¼ hours or until the barley is tender and the liquid is absorbed. If desired, sprinkle with additional parsley and green onions.

¾ CUP: 257 cal., 13g fat (5g sat. fat), 20mg chol., 704mg sod., 30g carb. (2g sugars, 7g fiber), 7g pro.

GRANDMA'S SECRET

Most grains become sticky if stirred too much, so leave them alone while they cook. The end result will be fluffier and tastier.

SPICY POTATOES WITH GARLIC AIOLI

This is my take on Spanish patatas bravas. The potatoes are tossed in a flavorful spice mix and then finished to a crispy golden brown. The garlic aioli takes it over the top for an unconventional potato salad that will be a hit at any party.

—*John Stiver, Bowen Island, BC*

PREP: 35 MIN. • **BAKE:** 25 MIN. • **MAKES:** 10 SERVINGS (1¾ CUPS AIOLI)

- 3 lbs. medium Yukon Gold potatoes, cut into 1½-in. cubes (about 8 potatoes)
- 2 Tbsp. olive oil
- 2 garlic cloves, minced
- 2 Tbsp. smoked paprika
- 2 tsp. garlic powder
- 1½ tsp. chili powder
- 1½ tsp. ground cumin
- ¼ tsp. salt
- ¼ tsp. crushed red pepper flakes
- ⅛ tsp. pepper

AIOLI

- 1½ cups mayonnaise
- 3 Tbsp. lemon juice
- 3 garlic cloves, minced
- 1 Tbsp. minced fresh chives plus additional for topping
- 1 tsp. red wine vinegar
- ¼ tsp. salt
- ¼ tsp. pepper

1. Preheat oven to 375°. Place potatoes in a Dutch oven; add water to cover. Bring to a boil. Reduce heat; cook, uncovered, 8-10 minutes or until just tender. Drain; pat dry with paper towels. Transfer potatoes to a mixing bowl. Toss potatoes in oil and minced garlic to coat evenly.

2. Combine the paprika, garlic powder, chili powder, cumin, salt, pepper flakes and pepper; sprinkle over potatoes. Gently toss to coat. Transfer potatoes to 2 greased 15x10x1-in. baking pans, spreading into a single layer. Bake until crispy, about 25 minutes, stirring potatoes and rotating pans halfway through cooking.

3. For aioli, combine ingredients until blended. Transfer potatoes to a serving platter; sprinkle with chives. Serve warm with aioli.

¾ CUP POTATOES WITH ABOUT 3 TBSP. AIOLI: 469 cal., 34g fat (5g sat. fat), 3mg chol., 396mg sod., 37g carb. (3g sugars, 4g fiber), 5g pro.

"The potatoes were crispy and flavorful. The kick from the chili pepper and red pepper were a bonus, and the aioli neutralized the heat a bit. I halved the recipe because there are only four of us, but we ate it all."

—AUG-95, TASTEOFHOME.COM

ROASTED BEETS WITH
ORANGE GREMOLATA
& GOAT CHEESE

ROASTED BEETS WITH ORANGE GREMOLATA & GOAT CHEESE

My grandma always grew beets, then pickled or canned them. I roast them in this special side.
—*Courtney Archibeque, Greeley, CO*

PREP: 25 MIN. • BAKE: 55 MIN. + COOLING • MAKES: 12 SERVINGS

3 medium fresh golden beets (about 1 lb.)
3 medium fresh beets (about 1 lb.)
2 Tbsp. lime juice
2 Tbsp. orange juice
½ tsp. fine sea salt
1 Tbsp. minced fresh parsley
1 Tbsp. minced fresh sage
1 garlic clove, minced
1 tsp. grated orange zest
3 Tbsp. crumbled goat cheese
2 Tbsp. sunflower kernels

1. Preheat oven to 400°. Scrub beets and trim tops by 1 in. Place beets on a double thickness of heavy-duty foil (about 24x12 in.). Fold foil around beets, sealing tightly. Place on a baking sheet. Roast until tender, 55-65 minutes. Open foil carefully to allow steam to escape.

2. When cool enough to handle, peel, halve and slice beets; place in a serving bowl. Add lime juice, orange juice and salt; toss to coat. Combine parsley, sage, garlic and orange zest; sprinkle over beets. Top with goat cheese and sunflower kernels. Serve warm or chilled.

¾ **CUP:** 49 cal., 1g fat (0 sat. fat), 2mg chol., 157mg sod., 9g carb. (6g sugars, 2g fiber), 2g pro. **DIABETIC EXCHANGES:** 1 vegetable.

GREEN BEAN-CHERRY TOMATO SALAD

My grandmother made a cold green bean salad with potatoes for every family barbecue. Now I bring my own version of the recipe to parties. With added color and taste from the cherry tomatoes, this classic favorite is even better.
—*Angela Lemoine, Howell, NJ*

PREP: 25 MIN. • COOK: 10 MIN. • MAKES: 12 SERVINGS

1½ lbs. fresh green beans, trimmed
1 pint cherry tomatoes, halved
1 small red onion, halved and thinly sliced
3 Tbsp. red wine vinegar
1½ tsp. sugar
¾ tsp. dried oregano
¾ tsp. salt
¼ tsp. garlic powder
¼ tsp. pepper
¼ cup olive oil

1. In a 6-qt. stockpot, bring 6 cups water to a boil. Add green beans in batches; cook, uncovered, 2-3 minutes or just until crisp-tender. Remove the beans and immediately drop into ice water. Drain and pat dry.

2. Transfer beans to a large bowl. Add tomatoes and onion; toss to combine. In a small bowl, whisk vinegar, sugar, oregano, salt, garlic powder and pepper. Gradually whisk in oil until blended. Pour over bean mixture; toss to coat.

1 **SERVING:** 65 cal., 5g fat (1g sat. fat), 0 chol., 153mg sod., 6g carb. (2g sugars, 2g fiber), 1g pro. **DIABETIC EXCHANGES:** 1 vegetable, 1 fat.

WILD RICE-STUFFED ACORN SQUASH

I tried many variations of ingredients for the stuffing in my acorn squash. Here's the version I liked best.
—*Michelle Springer, Spring, TX*

PREP: 1 HOUR • **BAKE:** 35 MIN. • **MAKES:** 8 SERVINGS

4 **small acorn squash**
3 **Tbsp. olive oil, divided**
¾ **tsp. salt, divided**
2 **tsp. ground coriander, divided**
½ **tsp. ground nutmeg, divided**
1 **lb. fresh carrots, peeled and cut into ½-in. cubes**
¾ **cup pecan halves, coarsely chopped**
¾ **cup dried cherries, coarsely chopped**
10 **fresh sage leaves, chopped**
2 **garlic cloves, minced**
2 **Tbsp. maple syrup**

FILLING
1 **cup uncooked wild rice**
1 **Tbsp. olive oil**
¾ **cup finely chopped sweet onion**
¼ **tsp. ground cinnamon**
2 **cups vegetable broth**

1. Preheat oven to 375°. Cut squash lengthwise in half; remove and discard seeds. Brush with 2 Tbsp. oil; sprinkle with ¼ tsp. salt, ½ tsp. coriander and ¼ tsp. nutmeg. Place the squash in a 15x10x1-in. baking pan, cut sides up. Bake 35-45 minutes or until easily pierced with a fork.

2. In an 8-in. square dish, combine carrots and remaining 1 Tbsp. oil, ½ tsp. salt, 1 ½ tsp. coriander and ¼ tsp. nutmeg. Bake for 15-20 minutes or just until tender, stirring occasionally. Stir in pecans, cherries, sage, garlic and syrup. Bake 10 minutes longer.

3. Rinse wild rice thoroughly; drain. In a small saucepan, heat oil over medium heat. Add onion; cook and stir 2-3 minutes or until softened. Stir in rice and cinnamon, then add broth. Bring to a boil. Reduce heat; cover and simmer for 40-50 minutes or until rice is fluffy and tender. Drain if necessary.

4. Combine rice and carrot mixtures. Arrange the squash on a serving platter, cut sides up. Fill with rice mixture. Serve warm.

1 STUFFED SQUASH HALF: 409 cal., 14g fat (2g sat. fat), 0 chol., 441mg sod., 70g carb. (24g sugars, 9g fiber), 7g pro.

GRANDMA'S SECRET
Acorn squash is small, round and has a dull, dark-green rind with orange markings. Generally, avoid choosing acorn squash that have too much orange—they tend to be tougher and more fibrous.

SPICED CRAN-APPLE & GRAPE CONSERVE

Faced with an abundance of grapes from my garden,
I wound up using them in various ways. This conserve was an
afterthought, but I received so many compliments from
family and friends that I made sure to write down the recipe.
I served it with crackers and Brie cheese, but it would be
great with pork, chicken, ham and cheesecake, too.
—*Kallee Krong-McCreery, Escondido, CA*

PREP: 2 HOURS • PROCESS: 5 MIN./BATCH • MAKES: 10 HALF-PINTS

6 whole cloves
6 whole allspice berries
8 cups seedless red grapes
6 cups sugar
4 medium tart apples,
  peeled and chopped
  (about 4 cups)

4 cups coarsely chopped
  fresh cranberries
3 Tbsp. lemon juice
  plus enough water
  to equal 1 cup
1½ tsp. ground cinnamon
1 medium tart apple,
  peeled and shredded
  (about 1 cup)

1. Make a spice bag by placing cloves and allspice berries on
a double thickness of cheesecloth. Gather corners of cloth to
enclose seasonings; tie securely with string.

2. In a stockpot, combine next 6 ingredients. Add spice bag. Bring
to a boil. Reduce heat; simmer, uncovered, until mixture begins
to thicken, about 45 minutes. Add shredded apple; simmer until
thickened, 35-45 minutes longer (mixture will thicken more after
cooling). Discard spice bag.

3. Carefully ladle hot mixture into 10 hot sterilized half-pint jars,
leaving ¼-in. headspace. Remove any air bubbles and adjust
headspace, if necessary, by adding additional hot mixture. Wipe
rims. Center lids on jars; screw on bands until fingertip tight.

4. In batches, place jars into canner with simmering water,
ensuring that they are completely covered with water. Bring
to a boil; process for 5 minutes. Remove jars and cool.

NOTE: The processing time listed is for altitudes of 1,000 feet
or less. For altitudes up to 3,000 feet, add 5 minutes; 6,000 feet,
add 10 minutes; 8,000 feet, add 15 minutes; 10,000 feet, add
20 minutes.

2 TBSP.: 77 cal., 0 fat (0 sat. fat), 0 chol., 2mg sod., 20g carb. (19g
sugars, 0 fiber), 0 pro.

TEXAS PECAN RICE

For a special side dish, I dressed up an old recipe to give it a little more
Texas character. Everyone loved the savory flavor and crunchy pecans.
—*Joan Hallford, North Richland Hills, TX*

PREP: 30 MIN. • BAKE: 1 HOUR • MAKES: 10 SERVINGS

½ cup unsalted butter, cubed
1½ cups sliced fresh mushrooms
3 green onions, sliced
2 cups uncooked long grain brown rice
1 garlic clove, minced
1½ cups chopped pecans, toasted
½ tsp. salt
½ tsp. dried thyme
½ tsp. pepper
¼ tsp. ground cumin
3 cans (10½ oz. each) condensed beef consomme, undiluted
2¼ cups water
5 bacon strips, cooked and crumbled
Toasted pecan halves, optional

1. Preheat oven to 400°. In a Dutch oven, heat the butter over medium-high heat. Add mushrooms and green onions; cook and stir until tender, 3-5 minutes. Add rice and garlic; cook and stir 3 minutes. Stir in pecans, salt, thyme, pepper and cumin. Add consomme and water; bring to a boil.

2. Bake, covered, until liquid is absorbed and rice is tender, 1 to 1¼ hours. Transfer to a serving bowl. Top with bacon and, if desired, pecan halves.

¾ CUP: 372 cal., 24g fat (8g sat. fat), 29mg chol., 783mg sod., 32g carb. (2g sugars, 4g fiber), 10g pro.

FROM GRANDMA'S KITCHEN: Don't skip toasting the pecans when making this recipe. Toasting isn't just a way to add color. It also gives the nuts added crunch and brings out tons of nutty flavor that is vital to making a good recipe great.

SHAVED FENNEL SALAD

This salad tastes even more impressive than it looks. It's got an incredible
crunch thanks to the cucumbers, radishes and apples, and the finish
of fennel fronds adds just the faintest hint of licorice flavor.
—*William Milton III, Clemson, SC*

TAKES: 15 MIN. • MAKES: 8 SERVINGS

1 large fennel bulb, fronds reserved
1 English cucumber
1 medium Honeycrisp apple
2 Tbsp. extra virgin olive oil
½ tsp. kosher salt
¼ tsp. coarsely ground pepper
2 radishes, thinly sliced

With a mandoline or vegetable peeler, cut the fennel, cucumber and apple into very thin slices. Transfer to a large bowl; toss with olive oil, salt and pepper. Top with radishes and reserved fennel fronds to serve.

¾ CUP: 55 cal., 4g fat (1g sat. fat), 0 chol., 138mg sod., 6g carb. (4g sugars, 2g fiber), 1g pro. DIABETIC EXCHANGES: 1 vegetable, 1 fat.

TEXAS PECAN RICE

SUPER SIMPLE SCALLOPED POTATOES

I've made many types of scalloped potatoes but I always come back to this rich, creamy, foolproof recipe. The dish gets scraped clean every time I make it.

—*Kallee Krong-McCreery, Escondido, CA*

PREP: 20 MIN. • **BAKE:** 45 MIN. + STANDING • **MAKES:** 10 SERVINGS

- 3 cups heavy whipping cream
- 1½ tsp. salt
- ½ tsp. pepper
- 1 tsp. minced fresh thyme, optional
- 3 lbs. russet potatoes, thinly sliced (about 10 cups)
- Minced fresh parsley, optional

1. Preheat oven to 350°. In a large bowl, combine cream, salt, pepper and, if desired, thyme. Arrange potatoes in a greased 13x9-in. baking dish. Pour cream mixture over top.

2. Bake, uncovered, until potatoes are tender and top is lightly browned, 45-55 minutes. Let stand 10 minutes before serving. If desired, sprinkle with parsley.

¾ **CUP:** 353 cal., 27g fat (17g sat. fat), 99mg chol., 390mg sod., 26g carb. (3g sugars, 3g fiber), 4g pro.

ROASTED ITALIAN GREEN BEANS & TOMATOES

Roasting green beans and tomatoes lets their flavors shine through, and the vibrant colors light up a table. It's the perfect side dish for holidays and special occasions.

—*Brittany Allyn, Mesa, AZ*

TAKES: 25 MIN. • **MAKES:** 8 SERVINGS

- 1½ lbs. fresh green beans, trimmed and halved
- 1 Tbsp. olive oil
- 1 tsp. Italian seasoning
- ½ tsp. salt
- 2 cups grape tomatoes, halved
- ½ cup grated Parmesan cheese

1. Preheat oven to 425°. Place green beans in a 15x10x1-in. baking pan coated with cooking spray. Mix oil, Italian seasoning and salt; drizzle over beans. Toss to coat. Roast 10 minutes, stirring once.

2. Add tomatoes to pan. Roast until beans are crisp-tender and tomatoes are softened, 4-6 minutes longer. Sprinkle with cheese.

¾ **CUP:** 70 cal., 3g fat (1g sat. fat), 4mg chol., 231mg sod., 8g carb. (3g sugars, 3g fiber), 4g pro. **DIABETIC EXCHANGES:** 1 vegetable, ½ fat.

GRANDMA'S SPINACH SALAD

With all its fresh ingredients, this pretty salad was my grandma's favorite.
Even my little ones like it (but don't tell them spinach is good for them)!
—*Shelley Riebel, Armada, MI*

TAKES: 20 MIN. • MAKES: 8 SERVINGS

½ cup sugar
½ cup canola oil
¼ cup white vinegar
½ tsp. celery seed
10 oz. fresh baby spinach
(about 13 cups)
1 small red onion, thinly
sliced
½ lb. sliced fresh
mushrooms
5 hard-boiled large eggs,
sliced
8 bacon strips, cooked and
crumbled

1. Whisk first 4 ingredients until sugar is dissolved.

2. In a 13x9-in. dish, layer half of each of the following: spinach, onion, mushrooms and eggs. Repeat layers. Drizzle salad with dressing; top with bacon.

1¼ CUPS: 280 cal., 21g fat (3g sat. fat), 125mg chol., 214mg sod., 16g carb. (14g sugars, 1g fiber), 9g pro.

HOLIDAY SALSA

When we offer this cream-cheesy salsa of fresh cranberries, cilantro and a little
jalapeno kick, everyone hovers around the serving dish until it's scraped clean.
—*Shelly Pattison, Lubbock, TX*

PREP: 20 MIN. + CHILLING • MAKES: 12 SERVINGS

1 pkg. (12 oz.) fresh or
frozen cranberries
1 cup sugar
6 green onions, chopped
½ cup fresh cilantro leaves,
chopped
1 jalapeno pepper, seeded
and finely chopped
1 pkg. (8 oz.) cream cheese,
softened
Assorted crackers or
tortilla chips

1. Pulse cranberries and sugar in a food processor until coarsely chopped. Stir together with onions, cilantro and jalapeno. Cover and refrigerate several hours or overnight.

2. To serve, place cream cheese on a serving plate. Drain salsa; spoon over cream cheese. Serve with crackers or chips.

1 SERVING: 146 cal., 7g fat (4g sat. fat), 21mg chol., 71mg sod., 22g carb. (19g sugars, 2g fiber), 1g pro.

CHIPOTLE SWEET
POTATO SALAD

CHIPOTLE SWEET POTATO SALAD

I love the velvety taste and texture of sweet potatoes. A friend served
sweet potatoes cooked with peppers and they tasted delicious together.
I took those flavors and developed them into this creamy, smoky potato salad.
—*Carolyn Eskew, Dayton, OH*

PREP: 20 MIN. • BAKE: 25 MIN. + COOLING • MAKES: 9 SERVINGS

3 lbs. sweet potatoes, peeled and cut into ¾-in. pieces (about 7 cups)
¼ cup finely chopped sweet onion
¼ cup finely chopped celery
¼ cup finely chopped seeded fresh poblano pepper
1 jalapeno pepper, seeded and finely chopped
1 cup mayonnaise
2 Tbsp. lime juice
½ to 1 tsp. ground chipotle pepper
½ tsp. salt
¼ tsp. pepper
   Minced fresh cilantro

1. Preheat oven to 425°. Place sweet potatoes in a parchment-lined 15x10x1-in. baking pan; cover tightly with foil. Roast until tender, 25-30 minutes. Cool. Transfer to a large bowl.

2. Add onion, celery, poblano and jalapeno. Combine mayonnaise, lime juice, chipotle pepper, salt and pepper; pour over the potato mixture and toss gently to coat. Refrigerate salad, covered, until serving. Sprinkle with cilantro.

NOTE: Wear disposable gloves when cutting hot peppers; the oils can burn skin. Avoid touching your face.

¾ CUP: 322 cal., 18g fat (3g sat. fat), 2mg chol., 278mg sod., 38g carb. (16g sugars, 5g fiber), 3g pro.

GARLIC ROASTED BRUSSELS SPROUTS

My roommate and I used to make garlicky Brussels sprouts at least twice a week.
Now I make them as a healthy side for all sorts of occasions.
—*Katherine Moore-Colasurd, Cincinnati, OH*

PREP/TOTAL: 30 MIN. • MAKES: 12 SERVINGS

2 lbs. fresh Brussels sprouts, trimmed and halved
2 medium red onions, cut into 1-in. pieces
3 Tbsp. olive oil
7 garlic cloves, finely chopped
1 tsp. salt
½ tsp. pepper

1. Preheat oven to 425°. Divide Brussels sprouts and onions between 2 foil-lined 15x10x1-in. baking pans.

2. In a small bowl, mix oil, garlic, salt and pepper; drizzle half of the mixture over each pan and toss to coat. Roast until tender, 20-25 minutes, stirring occasionally and switching position of pans halfway through.

½ CUP: 69 cal., 4g fat (1g sat. fat), 0 chol., 215mg sod., 8g carb. (2g sugars, 3g fiber), 3g pro. DIABETIC EXCHANGES: 1 vegetable, ½ fat.

GRANDMA'S POULTRY DRESSING

Every family seems to have its own favorite dressing recipe which becomes a tradition, and this is ours. It came from Grandma, who passed it down to my mother. Now our children have carried it into their kitchens. It's truly a good old-fashioned recipe!
—*Norma Howland, Joliet, IL*

PREP: 20 MIN. • **BAKE:** 40 MIN. • **MAKES:** 6 CUPS

1 lb. bulk pork sausage
1 cup 2% milk
7 cups coarse dry bread crumbs
1 cup diced celery
2 large eggs
2 to 3 Tbsp. minced fresh parsley
2 Tbsp. diced onion
½ tsp. salt or salt to taste

1. Preheat oven to 350°. In a large skillet, brown sausage. Drain sausage, discarding drippings. Meanwhile, in a small saucepan, heat milk over medium heat until bubbles form around side of pan. In a large bowl, combine sausage, milk and remaining ingredients.

2. Transfer to a greased 2-qt. baking dish. Cover and bake until lightly browned, about 40 minutes.

½ CUP: 352 cal., 12g fat (4g sat. fat), 52mg chol., 826mg sod., 48g carb. (3g sugars, 2g fiber), 12g pro.

HERBED HARVEST VEGETABLE CASSEROLE

I belong to a cooking club, so I try a lot of new recipes. This one has become one of my favorites. I hope your hungry crew enjoys it as much as mine does.
—*Netty Dyck, St. Catharines, ON*

PREP: 15 MIN. • **BAKE:** 1 HOUR 40 MIN. + STANDING • **MAKES:** 8 SERVINGS

4 new potatoes, cut in ¼-in. slices
¼ cup butter
1 Tbsp. finely chopped fresh sage or 1 tsp. dried sage
1 Tbsp. finely chopped fresh tarragon or 1 tsp. dried tarragon
3 sweet red bell peppers, seeded and diced
1 onion, thinly sliced
½ cup uncooked long-grain rice
3 medium zucchini, thinly sliced
4 medium tomatoes, sliced
1 cup shredded Swiss cheese

1. Grease a 2½-qt. baking dish and arrange half the potato slices in overlapping rows. Dot with half the butter. Sprinkle with half the sage, tarragon, peppers, onion, rice and zucchini. Dot with the remaining butter and repeat layering.

2. Cover and bake at 350° for 1½ hours or until potatoes are tender. Uncover; top with tomato slices and cheese. Bake 10 minutes longer or until tomatoes are warm and cheese is melted. Remove from oven; cover and let stand for 10 minutes before serving.

1 SERVING: 206 cal., 10g fat (6g sat. fat), 28mg chol., 105mg sod., 24g carb. (6g sugars, 4g fiber), 7g pro.

MUSHROOM SOUR CREAM GRAVY

My grandma used to make this gravy. It's delicious served over a biscuit or a piece of bread, open-face style.
—Josephine Mellwig, Naples, FL

PREP: 15 MIN. • COOK: 25 MIN. • MAKES: ABOUT 4½ CUPS

1 lb. small fresh mushrooms, thinly sliced
6 Tbsp. butter, divided
1 large onion, finely chopped
2 celery ribs, chopped
⅓ cup all-purpose flour
¾ tsp. salt
¾ tsp. pepper
2 cups water
½ cup sour cream

1. In a large cast-iron or other heavy skillet, saute mushrooms in 3 Tbsp. butter in batches; remove and set aside. In the same pan, saute onion and celery in 1 Tbsp. butter. Add the flour, salt, pepper and remaining butter; cook and stir until smooth.

2. Gradually add water. Bring mixture to a boil; cook and stir until thickened, about 2 minutes. Stir in mushrooms and heat through. Remove from heat; stir in sour cream.

¼ CUP: 66 cal., 5g fat (3g sat. fat), 12mg chol., 136mg sod., 4g carb. (1g sugars, 1g fiber), 1g pro.

BEST HUSH PUPPIES

Some years ago, I was a cook on a large cattle ranch. One day, I thought back to the hush puppies I'd had as a child on a southern trip, and I ended up creating my own version of them. They go well as part of an old-fashioned fried chicken dinner with mashed potatoes and gravy, buttermilk biscuits, corn on the cob and watermelon pickles.
—Karyl Goodhart, Geraldine, MT

PREP: 15 MIN. • COOK: 20 MIN. • MAKES: 3 DOZEN

2 cups yellow cornmeal
½ cup all-purpose flour
2 Tbsp. sugar
2 tsp. baking powder
1 tsp. salt
½ tsp. baking soda
1 large egg, room temperature, lightly beaten
¾ cup 2% milk
¾ cup cream-style corn
   Oil for deep-fat frying

1. In a large bowl, whisk cornmeal, flour, sugar, baking powder, salt and baking soda. Add the egg, milk and corn; stir together just until combined.

2. In a deep-fat fryer, heat oil to 375°. Drop batter by the Tbsp., a few at a time, into hot oil. Fry until golden brown on both sides. Drain on paper towels. Serve warm.

1 HUSH PUPPY: 66 cal., 2g fat (0 sat. fat), 6mg chol., 129mg sod., 10g carb. (1g sugars, 0 fiber), 1g pro.

GREEN BEAN, CORN & BUTTERMILK SALAD

I love the crunch of green beans and fresh corn, so I combined them with a buttermilk Caesar dressing. This salad is good served immediately, but it's even better after chilling for a few hours.
—*Arlene Erlbach, Morton Grove, IL*

PREP: 25 MIN. • **COOK:** 15 MIN. + CHILLING • **MAKES:** 6 SERVINGS

SIDE DISHES

- ½ **cup reduced-fat mayonnaise**
- ½ **cup buttermilk**
- ½ **cup shredded Parmesan cheese, plus more for topping**
- 1 **Tbsp. lemon juice**
- 1 **tsp. Worcestershire sauce**
- ½ **tsp. garlic powder**
- ½ **tsp. salt**
- ½ **tsp. pepper**
- 1 **Tbsp. olive oil**
- ¾ **lb. fresh green beans, trimmed and cut into 1-in. pieces**
- 4 **medium ears sweet corn**

1. In a small bowl, whisk the mayonnaise, buttermilk, ½ cup Parmesan, lemon juice, Worcestershire sauce, garlic powder, salt and pepper. Refrigerate, covered, until serving.

2. Meanwhile, in a Dutch, bring 8 cups water to a boil. Add beans; cook, uncovered, just until crisp-tender, 2-3 minutes. Drain and immediately drop into ice water. Drain and pat dry; transfer to a serving bowl.

3. Cut corn from cobs. In a large cast-iron or other heavy skillet, heat 1 Tbsp. oil over medium-high heat. Add corn; cook and stir until tender, 6-8 minutes. Remove from heat and add to beans; refrigerate, covered, until chilled.

4. Stir mayonnaise mixture into the vegetables; toss to coat. If desired, sprinkle with additional Parmesan.

1 CUP: 201 cal., 12g fat (3g sat. fat), 13mg chol., 498mg sod., 20g carb. (8g sugars, 3g fiber), 7g pro.

FROM GRANDMA'S KITCHEN: Shocking the beans in ice water stops the cooking process and helps set the vibrant green color.

PICKLED RAINBOW CHARD

Pickling adds pop to fresh foods, especially
Swiss chard stems. In this easy fridge method,
sweet meets tart and it all balances out overnight.
—Taste of Home *Test Kitchen*

PREP: 10 MIN. • **COOK:** 5 MIN. + CHILLING • **MAKES:** 8 SERVINGS

2 bunches rainbow Swiss chard	½ tsp. celery seed
	½ tsp. mustard seed
1 small onion, halved and sliced	1 cup sugar
	1 cup cider vinegar
2 tsp. mixed pickling spices	⅓ cup water

1. Trim leaves from Swiss chard; save for another use. Cut stems into 2-in. pieces; place in a large heatproof nonreactive bowl. Add onion, pickling spices, celery seed and mustard seed.

2. In a small saucepan, combine sugar, vinegar and water; bring to a boil. Cook 1 minute, stirring to dissolve sugar; pour carefully over chard mixture. Cool completely. Refrigerate, covered, overnight, stirring occasionally.

1 SERVING: 48 cal., 0 fat (0 sat. fat), 0 chol., 211mg sod., 11g carb. (8g sugars, 2g fiber), 2g pro.

BUTTERMILK SMASHED POTATOES

Our family loves this decadent potato dish. Serve with your favorite toppings and indulge!
—Marla Clark, Albuquerque, NM

TAKES: 30 MIN. • **MAKES:** 8 SERVINGS

4 lbs. Yukon Gold potatoes, peeled and cubed (about 8 cups)
½ cup butter, softened
1¼ tsp. salt
¼ tsp. pepper
¾ to 1 cup buttermilk
Optional toppings: crumbled cooked bacon, sour cream and thinly sliced green onions

1. Place potatoes in a 6-qt. stockpot; add water to cover. Bring to a boil. Reduce heat; cook, uncovered, until tender, 10-15 minutes.

2. Drain; return to pan. Mash potatoes, gradually adding butter, salt, pepper and enough buttermilk to reach desired consistency. Serve with toppings as desired.

NOTE: To substitute for each cup of buttermilk, use 1 Tbsp. white vinegar or lemon juice plus enough milk to measure 1 cup. Stir, then let stand 5 min. Or, use 1 cup plain yogurt or 1¾ tsp. cream of tartar plus 1 cup milk.

¾ CUP: 313 cal., 12g fat (7g sat. fat), 31mg chol., 531mg sod., 46g carb. (4g sugars, 4g fiber), 6g pro.

BAKED BEANS MOLE

My son and husband love this hearty side dish that is quick and easy to prepare but yet so flavorful. Chocolate, chili and honey mingle to create a rich, savory flavor that's not too spicy and not too sweet.
—*Roxanne Chan, Albany, CA*

PREP: 25 MIN. • **BAKE:** 40 MINUTES • **MAKES:** 8 SERVINGS

¼ lb. fresh chorizo, crumbled
½ cup chopped onion
½ cup chopped sweet red pepper
1 large garlic clove, minced
1 can (15 oz.) black beans, rinsed and drained
1 can (15 oz.) pinto beans, rinsed and drained
1 can (15 oz.) black-eyed peas, rinsed and drained
1 cup salsa (medium or hot)
1 cup chili sauce
2 Tbsp. honey
1 Tbsp. instant coffee granules
½ tsp. ground cinnamon
2 oz. chopped bittersweet or semisweet chocolate
   Minced fresh cilantro

Preheat oven to 375°. In a large, ovenproof skillet with a lid, cook chorizo, onion, red pepper and garlic over medium heat until sausage is browned, 4-6 minutes. Add next 9 ingredients; mix well. Bake, covered, until mixture is thickened and flavors are blended, about 40 minutes. Sprinkle with cilantro.

⅔ CUP: 284 cal., 7g fat (3g sat. fat), 13mg chol., 989mg sod., 40g carb. (14g sugars, 6g fiber), 11g pro.

FROM GRANDMA'S KITCHEN: Pronounced MOH-lay, the word "mole" is generally used in the U.S. to describe a particular type of sauce, one spiced with earthy, rich flavors. Chocolate, cinnamon and other spices are often key ingredients.

ZUCCHINI IN DILL CREAM SAUCE

My husband and I were dairy farmers until we retired, so I always use fresh, real dairy products in my recipes. This creamy sauce combines all of our favorite foods!
—*Josephine Vanden Heuvel, Hart, MI*

TAKES: 30 MIN. • **MAKES:** 8 SERVINGS

7 cups sliced zucchini (¼-in. slices)
¼ cup finely chopped onion
½ cup water
1 tsp. salt
1 tsp. chicken bouillon granules or 1 chicken bouillon cube
½ tsp. dill weed
2 Tbsp. butter, melted
2 tsp. sugar
1 tsp. lemon juice
2 Tbsp. all-purpose flour
¼ cup sour cream

1. In a Dutch oven, combine zucchini, onion, water, salt, bouillon and dill; bring to a boil. Add the butter, sugar and lemon juice; mix. Remove from heat; do not drain.

2. Combine flour and sour cream; stir half the mixture into hot zucchini. Return to heat; add remaining cream mixture and cook until thickened.

¾ CUP: 71 cal., 5g fat (3g sat. fat), 9mg chol., 434mg sod., 7g carb. (4g sugars, 1g fiber), 2g pro. **DIABETIC EXCHANGES:** 1 vegetable, 1 fat.

TRIPLE CHEESE POTATO CAKE WITH HAM

This decadent souffle-like side dish combines the classic flavors of ham, chives and three different cheeses. The crispy crust and fluffy interior make it over-the-top amazing.

—Rebekah Radewahn, Wauwatosa, WI

PREP: 35 MIN. • BAKE: 35 MIN. • MAKES: 12 SERVINGS

¼ cup plus 1 Tbsp. dry bread crumbs, divided
3 lbs. medium potatoes, peeled and cubed (about 8 cups)
½ cup heavy whipping cream
¼ cup butter, cubed
3 Tbsp. minced fresh chives
1 tsp. salt
¼ tsp. pepper
3 large eggs
4 slices Swiss cheese
4 slices part-skim mozzarella cheese
4 oz. thinly sliced deli ham, cut into ½-in. pieces
⅓ cup grated Parmesan cheese
1 Tbsp. butter, melted

1. Preheat oven to 350°. Grease a 9-in. springform pan; dust with ¼ cup bread crumbs.

2. Place potatoes in a Dutch oven; add water to cover. Bring to a boil. Reduce heat; cook, uncovered, 10-15 minutes or until tender. Drain; return to pan. Mash potatoes, gradually adding cream, cubed butter, chives, salt and pepper. Cool slightly.

3. Add eggs, 1 at a time, stirring to blend after each addition. Spread half of the potato mixture into prepared pan. Layer with cheese slices, ham and remaining potatoes. In a small bowl, mix Parmesan cheese and remaining 1 Tbsp. bread crumbs; stir in melted butter. Sprinkle over potatoes.

4. Bake 35-40 minutes or until golden brown. Cool on a wire rack 10 minutes. Loosen side from pan with a knife. Serve warm.

1 PIECE: 241 cal., 15g fat (8g sat. fat), 88mg chol., 520mg sod., 19g carb. (2g sugars, 1g fiber), 10g pro.

GRANDMA'S SECRET

Use a handheld masher, a potato ricer or a fork to mash potatoes. Resist the temptation to dump the cooked potatoes into a food processor or blender. Overmixing will give the spuds a gooey, gluey texture.

CREAMED PEAS

I can still taste these wonderful peas in Mama's delicious white sauce. Our food was pretty plain during the week, so I thought this white sauce made the peas extra special and fitting for a Sunday meal.
—*Imogene Hutton, Brownwood, TX*

TAKES: 15 MIN. • **MAKES:** 4 SERVINGS

1 pkg. (10 oz.) frozen peas
1 Tbsp. butter
1 Tbsp. all-purpose flour
¼ tsp. salt
⅛ tsp. pepper
½ cup whole milk
1 tsp. sugar

Cook peas according to package directions. Meanwhile, in a small saucepan, melt the butter. Stir in the flour, salt and pepper until blended; gradually add milk and sugar. Bring to a boil; cook and stir for 1-2 minutes or until thickened. Drain peas; stir into the sauce and heat through.

½ CUP: 110 cal., 4g fat (2g sat. fat), 12mg chol., 271mg sod., 14g carb. (6g sugars, 3g fiber), 5g pro.

NUTTY APPLE BUTTER

Being a New England native, I love apple-picking season. Grab some apples and peanut butter to make this creamy PB&J riff. Dunk in sliced fruit or graham crackers, or spread it on a sandwich.
—*Brandie Cranshaw, Rapid City, SD*

PREP: 20 MIN. • **COOK:** 8 HOURS • **MAKES:** 5 CUPS

4 lbs. apples (about 8 large), peeled and chopped
¾ to 1 cup sugar
¼ cup water
3 tsp. ground cinnamon
¼ tsp. ground nutmeg
¼ tsp. ground cloves
¼ tsp. ground allspice
¼ cup creamy peanut butter

1. In a greased 5-qt. slow cooker, combine the first 7 ingredients. Cook, covered, on low 8-10 hours or until apples are tender.

2. Whisk in peanut butter until apple mixture is smooth. Cool to room temperature. Store apple butter in an airtight container in the refrigerator.

2 TBSP.: 43 cal., 1g fat (0 sat. fat), 0 chol., 7mg sod., 9g carb. (8g sugars, 1g fiber), 0 pro. **DIABETIC EXCHANGES:** ½ starch.

FROM GRANDMA'S KITCHEN: Because this apple butter takes a long time to cook in the slow cooker, a softer variety like Fuji or golden delicious are the best types of apples to use in this recipe. You can also use Braeburn, Cortland and Idared.

BUTTERNUT SQUASH OVEN RISOTTO

Squash and beer make my risotto taste different and delicious. Plus, cooking it in the oven cuts down on the hands-on time typically spent preparing risotto.
—*Katie Ferrier, Houston, TX*

PREP: 20 MIN. • BAKE: 30 MIN. • MAKES: 10 SERVINGS

6 cups cubed peeled butternut squash (1 in.)	2 cups uncooked arborio rice
4 Tbsp. olive oil, divided	2 garlic cloves, minced
½ tsp. salt	1 cup beer
¼ tsp. pepper	2 Tbsp. butter
1 carton (32 oz.) chicken broth	½ tsp. chili powder
1 cup water	¼ tsp. ground nutmeg
1 small onion, chopped	1 cup grated Parmesan cheese

1. Preheat oven to 375°. Place squash in a greased 15x10x1-in. baking pan. Drizzle with 2 Tbsp. oil; sprinkle with salt and pepper. Toss to coat. Roast on a lower oven rack 30-35 minutes or until tender, stirring occasionally.

2. Meanwhile, in a large saucepan, bring broth and water to a simmer; keep hot. In an ovenproof Dutch oven, heat remaining oil over medium heat. Add onion; cook and stir 4-6 minutes or until tender. Add rice and garlic; cook and stir 1-2 minutes longer or until rice is coated.

3. Stir in beer. Reduce heat to maintain a simmer; cook and stir until beer is absorbed. Stir in 4 cups hot broth mixture. Place Dutch oven on an oven rack above squash; bake, covered, 20-25 minutes or until the rice is tender but firm to the bite, risotto is creamy and liquid is almost absorbed.

4. Remove Dutch oven from oven. Add butter, chili powder, nutmeg and remaining broth mixture. Stir vigorously until blended and liquid is almost absorbed. Stir in roasted squash and cheese. Serve immediately.

¾ CUP: 311 cal., 11g fat (4g sat. fat), 15mg chol., 662mg sod., 46g carb. (4g sugars, 3g fiber), 7g pro.

BLACK-EYED PEAS WITH COLLARD GREENS

This dish has special meaning on New Year's Day, when Southerners
eat greens for future wealth and black-eyed peas for prosperity.

—*Athena Russell, Greenville, SC*

TAKES: 25 MIN. • **MAKES:** 6 SERVINGS

- 2 Tbsp. olive oil
- 1 garlic clove, minced
- 8 cups chopped collard greens
- ½ tsp. salt
- ¼ tsp. cayenne pepper
- 2 cans (15½ oz. each) black-eyed peas, rinsed and drained
- 4 plum tomatoes, seeded and chopped
- ¼ cup lemon juice
- 2 Tbsp. grated Parmesan cheese

In a Dutch oven, heat oil over medium heat. Add garlic; cook and stir 1 minute. Add collard greens, salt and cayenne; cook and stir 6-8 minutes or until greens are tender. Add peas, tomatoes and lemon juice; heat through. Sprinkle servings with cheese.

¾ CUP: 177 cal., 5g fat (1g sat. fat), 1mg chol., 412mg sod., 24g carb. (3g sugars, 6g fiber), 9g pro.

AUNT MARION'S FRUIT SALAD DESSERT

Aunt Marion, my namesake, is like a grandma to me. She gave me
this luscious salad recipe, which goes to all our family reunions, hunt club
suppers and snowmobile club picnics...and I always go home with no leftovers!

—*Marion LaTourette, Honesdale, PA*

PREP: 20 MIN. + CHILLING • **MAKES:** 10 SERVINGS (2½ QT.)

- 1 can (20 oz.) pineapple chunks, drained
- 1 can (15¼ oz.) sliced peaches, drained and cut into bite-size pieces
- 1 can (11 oz.) mandarin oranges, drained
- 3 bananas, sliced
- 2 unpeeled red apples, cut into bite-sized pieces

FRUIT SAUCE
- 1 cup cold whole milk
- ¾ cup sour cream
- ⅓ cup thawed orange juice concentrate
- 1 pkg. (3.4 oz.) instant vanilla pudding mix

In a large bowl, combine fruits. Whisk sauce ingredients until smooth. Gently fold into fruits. Cover and chill for 3-4 hours before serving.

1 CUP: 218 cal., 5g fat (3g sat. fat), 7mg chol., 86mg sod., 44g carb. (37g sugars, 3g fiber), 2g pro.

"We love this recipe as written. Once in a while we'll throw in a handful of coconut for something a little different. This was the first salad my kids helped me make when they were little. They thought it was great fun to be the banana 'choppers.' Definitely a refreshing salad on a hot day or a good old standby for potlucks and picnics."
—BRENDA D, TASTEOFHOME.COM

PARMESAN ROASTED BROCCOLI

Sure, it's simple and healthy but, oh, this roasted broccoli is also delicious. Cutting the stalks into tall trees turns the ordinary veggie into a standout side dish.
—*Holly Sander, Lake Mary, FL*

TAKES: 30 MIN. • **MAKES:** 4 SERVINGS

2 **small broccoli crowns (about 8 oz. each)**
3 **Tbsp. olive oil**
½ **tsp. salt**
½ **tsp. pepper**
¼ **tsp. crushed red pepper flakes**
4 **garlic cloves, thinly sliced**
2 **Tbsp. grated Parmesan cheese**
1 **tsp. grated lemon zest**

1. Preheat oven to 425°. Cut broccoli crowns into quarters from top to bottom. Drizzle with oil; sprinkle with salt, pepper and pepper flakes. Place in a parchment-lined 15x10x1-in. pan.

2. Roast until crisp-tender, 10-12 minutes. Sprinkle with garlic; roast 5 minutes longer. Sprinkle with cheese; roast until cheese is melted and stalks of broccoli are tender, 2-4 minutes longer. Sprinkle with lemon zest.

2 BROCCOLI PIECES: 144 cal., 11g fat (2g sat. fat), 2mg chol., 378mg sod., 9g carb. (2g sugars, 3g fiber), 4g pro. **DIABETIC EXCHANGES:** 2 fat, 1 vegetable.

BUTTERY WHISKEY-GLAZED PEARL ONIONS

I always have pearl onions on hand to add to stews and vegetable medleys—they're good pickled, too. I make this glazed onion dish every Thanksgiving. It can easily be made ahead and reheated.
—*Ann Sheehy, Lawrence, MA*

TAKES: 30 MIN. • **MAKES:** 10 SERVINGS

2 **pkg. (14.4 oz. each) pearl onions**
⅓ **cup cider vinegar**
¼ **cup butter, cubed**
¼ **cup whiskey or apple cider**
¼ **cup maple syrup**
½ **tsp. dried thyme**
½ **tsp. kosher salt**
¼ **tsp. pepper**
1⅓ **cups water**

1. Place all ingredients in a large nonstick skillet; bring to a boil. Reduce heat to medium-low; cook, covered, until onions are tender, 6-8 minutes.

2. Increase heat to medium-high; cook, uncovered, until liquid is almost evaporated and onions are glazed, 10-12 minutes, stirring occasionally. Remove from heat.

¼ CUP: 100 cal., 5g fat (3g sat. fat), 12mg chol., 147mg sod., 13g carb. (9g sugars, 1g fiber), 1g pro.

BLT MACARONI SALAD

A friend served this salad, and I just had to get the recipe. My husband loves BLT sandwiches, so this quickly became one of his favorite side dishes. It's nice to serve on hot and humid days, which we frequently get during summer here in Virginia.
—*Hamilton Myers Jr., Charlottesville, VA*

TAKES: 30 MIN. • **MAKES:** 6 SERVINGS

- ½ cup mayonnaise
- 3 Tbsp. chili sauce
- 2 Tbsp. lemon juice
- 1 tsp. sugar
- 3 cups cooked elbow macaroni
- ½ cup chopped seeded tomato
- 2 Tbsp. chopped green onions
- 3 cups shredded lettuce
- 4 bacon strips, cooked and crumbled

In a large bowl, combine the first 4 ingredients. Add the macaroni, tomato and onions; toss to coat. Cover and refrigerate. Just before serving, add lettuce and bacon; toss to coat.

¾ CUP: 259 cal., 17g fat (3g sat. fat), 10mg chol., 287mg sod., 21g carb. (4g sugars, 2g fiber), 5g pro.

EMILY'S HONEY LIME COLESLAW

Here's a refreshing take on slaw with a honey-lime vinaigrette rather than the traditional mayo. It's a great take-along for picnics and potlucks.
—*Emily Tyra, Lake Ann, MI*

PREP: 20 MIN. + CHILLING • **MAKES:** 8 SERVINGS

- 1½ tsp. grated lime zest
- ¼ cup lime juice
- 2 Tbsp. honey
- 1 garlic clove, minced
- ½ tsp. salt
- ¼ tsp. pepper
- ¼ tsp. crushed red pepper flakes
- 3 Tbsp. canola oil
- 1 small head red cabbage (about ¾ lb.), shredded
- 1 cup shredded carrots (about 2 medium carrots)
- 2 green onions, thinly sliced
- ½ cup fresh cilantro leaves

Whisk together the first 7 ingredients until smooth. Gradually whisk in oil until blended. Combine cabbage, carrots and green onions; toss with lime mixture to lightly coat. Refrigerate, covered, 2 hours. Sprinkle with cilantro.

½ CUP: 86 cal., 5g fat (0 sat. fat), 0 chol., 170mg sod., 10g carb. (7g sugars, 2g fiber), 1g pro. **DIABETIC EXCHANGES:** 1 vegetable, 1 fat.

LEMONY CHICKEN
NOODLE SOUP,
PAGE 189

GRANDMA'S FAVORITE

SOUPS &
STEWS

Grandma knew nothing nourishes the soul like a
steamy, savory bowl of soup. Grab your biggest ladle
because now you can indulge in all her best creations,
from home-style classics to creamy bisques, chunky
stews and slow-cooked favorites. With one spoonful,
you'll feel like you're back in her kitchen.

BROWN RICE MULLIGATAWNY

Mulligatawny is a curry soup filled with vegetables, chicken, apples and rice.
It freezes well, so make a second batch to enjoy later.
—*Sarah Ott, Blanchardville, WI*

PREP: 20 MIN. • COOK: 1 HOUR • MAKES: 5 SERVINGS

2 Tbsp. butter
2 celery ribs, chopped
1 small onion, chopped
1 medium carrot, finely chopped
½ cup chopped fresh mushrooms
1 garlic clove, minced
2 Tbsp. all-purpose flour
1½ tsp. curry powder
⅛ tsp. cayenne pepper
1 carton (32 oz.) reduced-sodium chicken broth
¼ cup uncooked long grain brown rice
2 cups cubed cooked chicken breast
2 cups chopped fresh spinach
½ cup chopped peeled sweet apple
¼ tsp. salt
¼ tsp. pepper
⅛ tsp. dried thyme
5 Tbsp. reduced-fat sour cream

1. In a large saucepan, heat butter over medium heat. Add celery, onion and carrot; cook and stir 5-7 minutes or until tender. Add mushrooms and garlic; cook 1 minute longer.

2. Stir in flour, curry powder and cayenne until blended; cook and stir 5 minutes. Gradually whisk in broth. Bring to a boil, stirring constantly. Add rice. Reduce heat; simmer, covered, 45-50 minutes or until rice is tender.

3. Add chicken, spinach, apple, salt, pepper and thyme; cook, uncovered, 3-5 minutes or until heated through and spinach is wilted. Top each serving with sour cream.

1 CUP WITH 1 TBSP. SOUR CREAM: 229 cal., 8g fat (4g sat. fat), 60mg chol., 689mg sod., 17g carb. (5g sugars, 2g fiber), 22g pro. DIABETIC EXCHANGES: 2 lean meat, 1½ fat, 1 vegetable, ½ starch.

FROM GRANDMA'S KITCHEN: Curry powder is typically a blend with a base of turmeric (a yellow spice from the ginger family) that includes a mix of spices such as cloves, cardamom, ginger, nutmeg, fennel, caraway, ajowan seeds, dried basil, mustard seeds, mace, poppy seeds, sesame seeds, saffron and cinnamon.

GRANDMA'S
SECRET
Always be sure to let your soup
cool to room temperature before
moving it into a freezer container.
Then, put it in the fridge to cool the
temp down (to somewhere below
40°) before freezing.

GARDEN VEGETABLE BEEF SOUP

This soup is my go-to healthy lunch option. It's a wonderful way to eat my vegetables, and it's so comforting during the cold winter months.
—*Dawn Donald, Herron, MI*

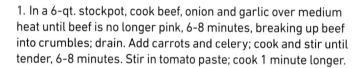

PREP: 20 MIN. • COOK: 50 MIN. • MAKES: 8 SERVINGS (3½ QT.)

- 1½ lbs. lean ground beef (90% lean)
- 1 medium onion, chopped
- 2 garlic cloves, minced
- 1 pkg. (10 oz.) julienned carrots
- 2 celery ribs, chopped
- ¼ cup tomato paste
- 1 can (14½ oz.) diced tomatoes, undrained
- 1½ cups shredded cabbage
- 1 medium zucchini, coarsely chopped
- 1 medium red potato (about 5 oz.), finely chopped
- ½ cup fresh or frozen cut green beans
- 1 tsp. dried basil
- ½ tsp. dried oregano
- ¼ tsp. salt
- ¼ tsp. pepper
- 4 cans (14½ oz. each) reduced-sodium beef broth
  Grated Parmesan cheese, optional

1. In a 6-qt. stockpot, cook beef, onion and garlic over medium heat until beef is no longer pink, 6-8 minutes, breaking up beef into crumbles; drain. Add carrots and celery; cook and stir until tender, 6-8 minutes. Stir in tomato paste; cook 1 minute longer.

2. Add the tomatoes, cabbage, zucchini, potato, green beans, seasonings and broth; bring to a boil. Reduce heat; simmer, covered, 35-45 minutes or until vegetables are tender. If desired, top each serving with cheese.

1¾ CUPS: 207 cal., 7g fat (3g sat. fat), 57mg chol., 621mg sod., 14g carb. (7g sugars, 3g fiber), 21g pro. DIABETIC EXCHANGES: 3 lean meat, 2 vegetable.

THE BEST EVER CHILI

My dad and my father-in-law are the gurus in our chili-loving clan. But after my honeymoon to New Mexico, inspired by the fresh and fragrant chile peppers at the Santa Fe farmers market, I felt it was time to introduce them to my spicy, meaty version with a touch of masa harina.

—Sarah Farmer, Waukesha, WI

PREP: 20 MIN. • **COOK:** 1 HOUR 20 MIN. • **MAKES:** 8 SERVINGS

- 3 dried ancho or guajillo chiles
- 1 to 2 cups boiling water
- 2 Tbsp. tomato paste
- 3 garlic cloves
- ¼ cup chili powder
- 1½ tsp. smoked paprika
- 2 tsp. ground cumin
- 1 lb. ground beef
- 1½ tsp. Montreal steak seasoning
- 2 lbs. beef tri-tip roast, cut into ½-in. cubes
- 2 tsp. salt, divided
- 2 tsp. coarsely ground pepper, divided
- 2 Tbsp. canola oil, divided
- 1 large onion, chopped (about 2 cups)
- 1 poblano pepper, seeded and chopped
- 1 tsp. dried oregano
- 1½ tsp. crushed red pepper flakes
- 3 cups beef stock
- 1 bottle (12 oz.) beer
- 2 cans (14½ oz. each) fire-roasted diced tomatoes, undrained
- 1 can (16 oz.) kidney beans, drained
- 3 Tbsp. masa harina
  Optional: American cheese slices, sour cream, shredded cheddar cheese, diced red onion and corn chips

1. Combine chiles and enough boiling water to cover; let stand until softened, about 15 minutes. Drain, reserving ⅓ cup of the soaking liquid. Discard stems and seeds. Process chiles, tomato paste, garlic and reserved liquid until smooth.

2. In a small skillet, toast chili powder, paprika and cumin over medium heat until aromatic, 3-4 minutes; remove and set aside. In a Dutch oven, cook and stir ground beef and steak seasoning over medium-high heat until the beef is no longer pink, about 5 minutes; remove and drain.

3. Sprinkle steak cubes with 1 tsp. each salt and pepper. In same Dutch oven, brown beef in batches in 1 Tbsp. oil over medium-high heat; remove and set aside. Saute onion and poblano pepper in the remaining 1 Tbsp. oil until tender, about 5 minutes. Stir in toasted spices, oregano and pepper flakes. Add the cooked meats along with stock, beer, tomatoes, beans, remaining 1 tsp. salt and 1 tsp. pepper, and chile paste mixture. Cook over medium heat 20 minutes; reduce heat to low. Stir in masa harina and simmer 30-45 minutes longer. Serve with desired toppings.

FREEZE OPTION: Freeze cooled chili in freezer containers. To use, partially thaw in refrigerator overnight. Heat through in a saucepan, stirring occasionally; add a little broth or water if necessary.

1¾ CUPS: 473 cal., 20g fat (6g sat. fat), 103mg chol., 1554mg sod., 29g carb. (8g sugars, 7g fiber), 41g pro.

FROM GRANDMA'S KITCHEN: The best bowl of chili is even better when you top it with fresh flavors. Sour cream and shredded cheese are classic, but you may also choose to add pungent green or red onions, spicy pickled jalapenos, herbaceous cilantro, acidic lime, creamy avocado or crunchy tortilla chips.

SPECIAL OCCASION BEEF BOURGUIGNON

I've found many rich and satisfying variations for beef Bourguignon, including an intriguing peasant version that used beef cheeks for the meat and a rustic table wine. To make this stew gluten-free, use white rice flour instead of all-purpose.
—*Leo Cotnoir, Johnson City, NY*

PREP: 50 MIN. • BAKE: 2 HOURS • MAKES: 8 SERVINGS

4 bacon strips, chopped
1 beef sirloin tip roast
  (2 lbs.), cut into 1½-in.
  cubes and patted dry
¼ cup all-purpose flour
½ tsp. salt
½ tsp. pepper
1 Tbsp. canola oil
2 medium onions, chopped
2 medium carrots,
  coarsely chopped
½ lb. medium fresh
  mushrooms, quartered
4 garlic cloves, minced
1 Tbsp. tomato paste
2 cups dry red wine
1 cup beef stock
2 bay leaves
½ tsp. dried thyme
8 oz. uncooked egg noodles
  Minced fresh parsley

1. Preheat oven to 325°. In a Dutch oven, cook the bacon over medium-low heat until crisp, stirring occasionally. Remove with a slotted spoon, reserving drippings; drain on paper towels.

2. In batches, brown beef in drippings over medium-high heat; remove from pan. Toss with flour, salt and pepper.

3. In same pan, heat 1 Tbsp. oil over medium heat; saute onions, carrots and mushrooms until onions are tender, 4-5 minutes. Add garlic and tomato paste; cook and stir 1 minute. Add the wine and stock, stirring to loosen browned bits from pan. Add herbs, bacon and beef; bring to a boil.

4. Transfer pot to oven; bake, covered, until the meat is tender, 2 to 2¼ hours. Remove bay leaves.

5. To serve, cook noodles according to package directions; drain. Serve stew with noodles; sprinkle with parsley.

FREEZE OPTION: Freeze cooled stew in freezer containers. To use, partially thaw in the refrigerator overnight. Heat through in a saucepan, stirring occasionally; add a little stock or broth if necessary.

⅔ CUP STEW WITH ⅔ CUP NOODLES: 422 cal., 14g fat (4g sat. fat), 105mg chol., 357mg sod., 31g carb. (4g sugars, 2g fiber), 31g pro. DIABETIC EXCHANGES: 4 lean meat, 2 fat, 1½ starch, 1 vegetable.

CHEESY MEATBALL SOUP

With beef, potatoes and other veggies, this rich-tasting soup is a meal in one. Process cheese sauce makes it taste like a cheeseburger. I serve it with a crusty loaf of French bread.
—Ione Sander, Carlton, MN

PREP: 15 MIN. • COOK: 45 MIN. • MAKES: 6 SERVINGS (2 QT.)

1 large egg
¼ cup dry bread crumbs
½ tsp. salt
1 lb. ground beef
2 cups water
1 cup diced celery
1 cup whole kernel corn, drained
1 cup cubed peeled potatoes
½ cup sliced carrot
½ cup chopped onion
2 beef bouillon cubes
½ tsp. hot pepper sauce
1 jar (16 oz.) cheese dip

1. In a large bowl, combine egg, bread crumbs and salt. Crumble beef over mixture and mix lightly but thoroughly. Shape into 1-in. balls.

2. In a large saucepan, brown meatballs; drain. Add the water, celery, corn, potatoes, carrot, onion, bouillon and hot pepper sauce; bring to a boil. Reduce heat; cover and simmer until the meat is no longer pink and potatoes are tender, about 25 minutes. Stir in the cheese dip; heat through.

1⅓ CUPS: 421 cal., 24g fat (15g sat. fat), 118mg chol., 1959mg sod., 23g carb. (6g sugars, 2g fiber), 26g pro.

BRATWURST SOUP

I came up with this recipe one day when I had some leftover bratwurst. It's been a favorite of my husband's ever since and is requested whenever the guys are hanging out.
—Anna Miller, Churdan, IA

PREP: 10 MIN. • COOK: 25 MIN. • MAKES: 8 SERVINGS (2 QT.)

1 lb. uncooked bratwurst links, casings removed
½ cup chopped onion
1 medium carrot, chopped
2 cans (15½ oz. each) navy beans, rinsed and drained
¼ cup pickled jalapeno slices, chopped
½ tsp. pepper
2 cups reduced-sodium chicken broth
¼ cup all-purpose flour
1½ cups 2% milk, divided
12 slices American cheese

1. In a Dutch oven, cook and crumble bratwurst with onion and carrot over medium heat until the meat is no longer pink, 5-7 minutes; drain.

2. Stir in beans, jalapeno, pepper and broth; bring to a boil. Whisk together flour and ½ cup milk until smooth; stir into soup. Bring to a boil, stirring constantly; cook and stir until thickened, about 5 minutes. Gradually stir in remaining 1 cup milk. Add cheese; cook and stir over low heat until cheese is melted.

1 CUP: 468 cal., 25g fat (11g sat. fat), 53mg chol., 1322mg sod., 33g carb. (5g sugars, 6g fiber), 25g pro.

SOUPS & STEWS

HAM & WHITE BEAN SOUP

I came up with this recipe when I wanted to make dinner in the slow cooker but didn't have time to go to the grocery store. I went through my freezer and cupboards, throwing in what I thought would go well together.
—*Stacey Cornell, Saratoga Springs, NY*

PREP: 20 MIN. • **COOK:** 6 HOURS • **MAKES:** 12 SERVINGS (3 QT.)

- 1 carton (32 oz.) chicken broth
- 1 can (28 oz.) diced tomatoes, undrained
- 1 can (15 to 15½ oz.) cannellini beans, rinsed and drained
- 1 pkg. (10 to 12 oz.) frozen cooked winter squash, thawed
- 1 pkg. (10 oz.) frozen leaf spinach, thawed and squeezed dry
- 1¾ cups cubed fully cooked ham
- 3 medium carrots, peeled, chopped
- 1 large onion, chopped
- 3 garlic cloves, minced
- 1 tsp. reduced-sodium seafood seasoning
- ¼ tsp. pepper
  Grated Parmesan cheese, optional

In a 5- or 6-qt. slow cooker, combine all the ingredients. Cook, covered, on low for 6-8 hours. If desired, sprinkle soup with Parmesan cheese.

1 CUP: 102 cal., 1g fat (0 sat. fat), 14mg chol., 808mg sod., 15g carb. (4g sugars, 4g fiber), 8g pro.

FROM GRANDMA'S KITCHEN: Cannellini beans, like all beans, are members of the legume family and pack a good protein and high-fiber punch. These beans are large, white Italian kidney beans with a nutty, earthy flavor. They retain their shape and texture well, so they're perfect for use in soups and stews.

GRANDMA'S SEAFOOD CHOWDER

My grandmother made this every year on Christmas morning—the only time we ever had it.
Why wait when you can enjoy it any time of year? It's also delicious topped with biscuits.
—*Melissa Obernesser, Oriskany, NY*

PREP: 15 MIN. • **COOK:** 25 MIN. • **MAKES:** 10 SERVINGS (3¼ QT.)

3   Tbsp. plus ¼ cup butter, divided
1   lb. sliced fresh mushrooms
⅓   cup all-purpose flour
1   tsp. salt
⅛   tsp. pepper
4   cups half-and-half cream
1½ cups 2% milk
1   lb. haddock fillets, skin removed, cut into 1-in. pieces
1   lb. uncooked medium shrimp, peeled and deveined
2   cups frozen peas (about 10 oz.)
¾   cup shredded cheddar cheese
1   cup lump crabmeat (about 5 oz.), drained
1   jar (4 oz.) diced pimientos, drained
1   tsp. paprika, optional

1. In a 6-qt. stockpot, heat 3 Tbsp. butter over medium-high heat. Add mushrooms; cook and stir until tender, 8-10 minutes. Remove from pot.

2. In same pot, heat remaining ¼ cup butter over medium heat. Stir in flour, salt and pepper until smooth; gradually whisk in cream and milk. Bring to a boil, stirring constantly; cook and stir until thickened, 2-3 minutes.

3. Stir in haddock, shrimp, peas and sauteed mushrooms; cook until fish just begins to flake easily with a fork and shrimp turn pink, 5-7 minutes. Add cheese, crab and pimientos; stir gently until cheese is melted. If desired, sprinkle servings with paprika.

1¼ CUPS: 390 cal., 23g fat (14g sat. fat), 176mg chol., 596mg sod., 14g carb. (8g sugars, 2g fiber), 28g pro.

"I have made this chowder several times and everyone loved it. Lots of request for the recipe."
—GINNYSWEDER, TASTEOFHOME.COM

SAUSAGE & GREENS SOUP

I always have an abundance of fresh vegetables
on hand, so I wanted to create a delicious soup to enjoy
during the colder months. I found a winner!
—*Angie Pitts, Charleston, SC*

PREP: 20 MIN. • **COOK:** 20 MIN. • **MAKES:** 6 SERVINGS (2¼ QT.)

1 Tbsp. olive oil
2 Italian turkey sausage
   links (4 oz. each), casings
   removed
1 medium onion, chopped
1 celery rib, chopped
1 medium carrot, chopped
1 garlic clove, minced
6 oz. Swiss chard, stems
   removed, chopped (about
   4 cups)

1 can (14½ oz.) no-salt-
   added diced tomatoes,
   undrained
1 bay leaf
1 tsp. rubbed sage
1 tsp. Italian seasoning
½ tsp. pepper
1 carton (32 oz.) reduced-
   sodium chicken broth
1 can (15 oz.) no-salt-added
   cannellini beans, rinsed
   and drained
1 Tbsp. lemon juice

1. In a 6-qt. stockpot, heat oil over medium-high heat. Add
sausage, onion, celery and carrot; cook 6-8 minutes or until
sausage is no longer pink and vegetables are tender, breaking
up sausage into crumbles. Add garlic; cook 1 minute longer.

2. Stir in Swiss chard, tomatoes, bay leaf and seasonings.
Add broth; bring to a boil. Reduce the heat; simmer, covered,
10-12 minutes or until Swiss chard is tender. Stir in beans and
lemon juice; heat through. Remove bay leaf.

1½ CUPS: 155 cal., 5g fat (1g sat. fat), 14mg chol., 658mg sod.,
18g carb. (5g sugars, 5g fiber), 11g pro. **DIABETIC EXCHANGES:**
1 medium-fat meat, 1 vegetable, ½ starch, ½ fat.

GRANDMA'S
SECRET
Vegetables don't always cook at
the same rate. A carrot or potato
will take longer to cook than tender
greens like Swiss chard or spinach.
Know your cook times and add
the hearty vegetables earlier
than the delicate ones.

CREAMY CHICKEN & BROCCOLI STEW

This recipe is so easy to make, but no one would ever guess.
My husband, who doesn't like many chicken dishes, requests it regularly.
—*Mary Watkins, Little Elm, TX*

PREP: 15 MIN. • COOK: 6 HOURS • MAKES: 8 SERVINGS

8 bone-in chicken thighs, skinned (about 3 lbs.)
1 cup Italian salad dressing
½ cup white wine or chicken broth
6 Tbsp. butter, melted, divided
1 Tbsp. dried minced onion
1 Tbsp. garlic powder
1 Tbsp. Italian seasoning
¾ tsp. salt, divided
¾ tsp. pepper, divided
1 can (10¾ oz.) condensed cream of mushroom soup, undiluted
1 pkg. (8 oz.) cream cheese, softened
2 cups frozen broccoli florets, thawed
2 lbs. red potatoes, quartered

1. Place chicken in a 4-qt. slow cooker. Combine the salad dressing, wine, 4 Tbsp. butter, onion, garlic powder, Italian seasoning, ½ tsp. salt and ½ tsp. pepper in a small bowl; pour over chicken.

2. Cover and cook on low for 5 hours. Skim off fat. Remove the chicken from slow cooker with a slotted spoon; shred chicken with 2 forks and return to slow cooker. Combine the soup, cream cheese and 2 cups of liquid from slow cooker in a small bowl until blended; add to slow cooker. Cover and cook 45 minutes longer or until chicken is tender, adding the broccoli during the last 30 minutes of cooking.

3. Meanwhile, place potatoes in a large saucepan and cover with water. Bring to a boil. Reduce heat; cover and simmer until tender, 15-20 minutes. Drain and return to pan. Mash potatoes with the remaining 2 Tbsp. butter and ¼ tsp. each salt and pepper.

4. Serve chicken and broccoli mixture with potatoes.

⅔ CUP CHICKEN MIXTURE WITH ½ CUP POTATOES: 572 cal., 36g fat (14g sat. fat), 142mg chol., 1126mg sod., 28g carb. (5g sugars, 3g fiber), 29g pro.

LOUISIANA
RED BEANS & RICE

LOUISIANA RED BEANS & RICE

Smoked turkey sausage and red pepper flakes add zip to this slow-cooked
version of the New Orleans classic. For extra heat, add red pepper sauce.
—*Julia Bushree, Menifee, CA*

PREP: 20 MIN. • COOK: 3 HOURS • MAKES: 8 SERVINGS

4 cans (16 oz. each)
 kidney beans,
 rinsed and drained
1 can (14½ oz.) diced
 tomatoes, undrained
1 pkg. (14 oz.) smoked
 turkey sausage, sliced
3 celery ribs, chopped
1 large onion, chopped
1 cup chicken broth
1 medium green pepper,
 chopped
1 small sweet red pepper,
 chopped
6 garlic cloves, minced
1 bay leaf
½ tsp. crushed red pepper
 flakes
2 green onions, chopped
 Hot cooked rice

1. In a 4- or 5-qt. slow cooker, combine the first 11 ingredients.
Cook, covered, on low until vegetables are tender, 3-4 hours.

2. Stir before serving. Remove bay leaf. Serve with green onions
and rice.

FREEZE OPTION: Discard bay leaf and freeze cooled bean mixture
in freezer containers. To use, partially thaw in the refrigerator
overnight. Heat through in a saucepan, stirring occasionally and
adding a little broth or water if necessary. Serve as directed.

1 CUP: 291 cal., 3g fat (1g sat. fat), 32mg chol., 1070mg sod., 44g
carb. (8g sugars, 13g fiber), 24g pro.

LEMONY CHICKEN NOODLE SOUP

PICTURED ON PAGE 174

The lemon juice gives this comforting chicken soup enough zip to make it stand out from the rest.
—*Bill Hilbrich, St. Cloud, MN*

TAKES: 30 MIN. • MAKES: 2 SERVINGS

1 small onion, chopped
2 Tbsp. olive oil
1 Tbsp. butter
¼ lb. boneless skinless
 chicken breast, cubed
1 garlic clove, minced
2 cans (14½ oz. each)
 chicken broth
1 medium carrot, cut into
 ¼-in. slices
¼ cup fresh or frozen peas
½ tsp. dried basil
2 cups uncooked medium
 egg noodles
1 to 2 Tbsp. lemon juice

1. In a small saucepan, saute onion in oil and butter until tender.
Add chicken; cook and stir until chicken is lightly browned and
meat is no longer pink. Add garlic; cook 1 minute longer.

2. Stir in the broth, carrot, peas and basil. Bring to a boil. Reduce
heat; cover and simmer for 5 minutes. Add the noodles. Cover and
simmer until noodles are tender, 8-10 minutes. Stir in lemon juice.

1 CUP: 435 cal., 23g fat (6g sat. fat), 83mg chol., 949mg sod., 38g
carb. (7g sugars, 4g fiber), 21g pro.

SWEET POTATO BISQUE

I love to serve this bright orange bisque for special occasions in fall and winter. The recipe includes a minted chili oil to drizzle on top. It's well worth the few extra minutes it takes to make!
—*Lily Julow, Lawrenceville, GA*

PREP: 30 MIN. • COOK: 40 MIN. • MAKES: 8 SERVINGS (2 QT.)

8   bacon strips, finely chopped
6   medium carrots, chopped (2 cups)
1   medium onion, chopped (1 cup)
3   garlic cloves, minced
3   cups water
1¾ lbs. sweet potatoes (about 4 medium), peeled and cubed
3   bay leaves
2½ tsp. curry powder
¾ tsp. salt
½ tsp. ground cinnamon
½ tsp. smoked paprika
½ tsp. pepper
1½ cups heavy whipping cream
1   cup sour cream

MINTED CHILI OIL
18 mint sprigs, chopped
3   Tbsp. olive oil
¼ tsp. sugar
¼ tsp. salt
¼ tsp. crushed red pepper flakes
¼ tsp. pepper

1. In a large saucepan, cook bacon over medium heat until crisp, stirring occasionally. Remove with a slotted spoon; drain on paper towels. Discard drippings, reserving 2 Tbsp. in pan.

2. Add carrots and onion to drippings; cook and stir over medium-high heat until tender. Add garlic; cook 1 minute longer.

3. Stir in water, sweet potatoes, bay leaves, curry, salt, cinnamon, paprika and pepper. Bring to a boil. Reduce the heat; simmer, covered, until vegetables are tender, 10-15 minutes. Discard bay leaves. Stir in cream and sour cream just until blended. Cool.

4. Meanwhile, in a small bowl, combine mint, oil, sugar, salt, pepper flakes and pepper. Let stand 5-10 minutes.

5. Process bisque in batches in a blender until smooth; return all to the pan. Heat through (do not boil). Ladle bisque into bowls; drizzle with minted chili oil.

1 CUP WITH 1½ TSP. MINTED CHILI OIL: 413 cal., 32g fat (16g sat. fat), 90mg chol., 512mg sod., 24g carb. (10g sugars, 4g fiber), 6g pro.

FROM GRANDMA'S KITCHEN: Traditional bisque is a creamy soup made with lobster, shrimp or crab. The classic technique calls for the shells to be ground into a paste and stirred into the broth. Nowadays, bisque recipes have evolved to be pretty much any soup that is creamy in texture and has its ingredients blended, such as this sweet potato bisque.

COMFORTING BEEF STEW

The aroma of slow-simmered stew loaded with root vegetables
is out of this world. This is comfort food personified.
Even my toddlers gobble up this stew!
—*Courtney Percy, Brooksville, FL*

PREP: 20 MIN. • **COOK:** 2½ HOURS • **MAKES:** 6 SERVINGS

2 lbs. beef stew meat
1 tsp. salt
¾ tsp. pepper
3 Tbsp. canola oil
1 Tbsp. butter
1 medium onion, chopped
2 garlic cloves, minced
¼ cup tomato paste
4 cups beef broth

3 Tbsp. all-purpose flour
3 Tbsp. water
5 medium carrots,
   cut into ½-in. pieces
3 medium turnips,
   peeled and cubed
2 Tbsp. minced fresh
   parsley

1. Sprinkle beef with salt and pepper. In a Dutch oven, heat oil
over medium-high heat. Brown beef in batches. Remove with
a slotted spoon.

2. In same pan, heat butter over medium heat. Add onion; cook
and stir 2-3 minutes or until tender. Add garlic; cook 1 minute
longer. Stir in tomato paste. Gradually stir in broth until blended.
Return beef to pan; bring to a boil. Reduce heat; simmer, covered,
1½ hours.

3. In a small bowl, mix flour and water until smooth; gradually stir
into stew. Add carrots and turnips; cook, covered, 30-40 minutes
longer or until stew is thickened and beef and vegetables are
tender. Stir in parsley.

FREEZE OPTION: Freeze cooled stew in freezer containers.
To use, partially thaw in refrigerator overnight. Heat through in
a saucepan, stirring occasionally and adding a little broth to the
stew if necessary.

1½ **CUPS:** 375 cal., 20g fat (6g sat. fat), 99mg chol., 1142mg sod.,
15g carb. (6g sugars, 3g fiber), 33g pro.

THE BEST EVER TOMATO SOUP

Creamy, rich and bursting with brightness, this tomato soup is the ultimate sidekick to a grilled cheese sandwich. Enjoy it as a simple lunch or an easy family dinner.
—*Josh Rink, Milwaukee, WI*

PREP: 20 MINUTES, • COOK: 30 MINUTES • MAKES: 16 SERVINGS (4 QT.)

3 Tbsp. olive oil
3 Tbsp. butter
¼ to ½ tsp. crushed red pepper flakes
3 large carrots, peeled and chopped
1 large onion, chopped
2 garlic cloves, minced
2 tsp. dried basil
3 cans (28 oz. each) whole peeled tomatoes, undrained
1 container (32 oz.) chicken stock
2 Tbsp. tomato paste
3 tsp. sugar
1 tsp. salt
½ tsp. pepper
1 cup heavy whipping cream, optional
   Fresh basil leaves, thinly sliced, optional

1. In a 6-qt. stockpot or Dutch oven, heat oil, butter and pepper flakes over medium heat until butter is melted. Add carrots and onion; cook, uncovered, over medium heat, stirring frequently, until vegetables are softened, 8-10 minutes. Add garlic and dried basil; cook and stir 1 minute longer. Stir in the tomatoes, chicken stock, tomato paste, sugar, salt and pepper; mix well. Bring to a boil. Reduce the heat; simmer, uncovered, to let flavors blend, 20-25 minutes.

2. Remove pan from heat. Using a blender, puree soup in batches until smooth. If desired, slowly stir in the heavy cream, stirring continuously to incorporate; return to stove to heat through. Top servings with fresh basil if desired.

1 CUP: 104 cal., 5g fat (2g sat. fat), 6mg chol., 572mg sod., 15g carb. (10g sugars, 2g fiber), 3g pro. DIABETIC EXCHANGES: 1 starch, 1 fat.

FROM GRANDMA'S KITCHEN: Use canned Roma tomatoes for this tomato soup recipe. They're bright, flavorful and bring the perfect balance of acidity.

HAM, POTATO & PEPPER CHOWDER

I have been serving this chowder for years. When I'm feeding family members who don't eat dairy products, I substitute oil for the butter and use coconut milk or soy creamer instead of heavy cream. It still turns out wonderful!

—*Eileen Stefanski, Wales, WI*

PREP: 20 MIN. • **COOK:** 30 MIN. • **MAKES:** 6 SERVINGS (2 QT.)

- 1½ lbs. potatoes (about 2 large), peeled and cut into 1-in. cubes
- 1 carton (32 oz.) chicken broth, divided
- 2 Tbsp. butter
- 1 large sweet red pepper, coarsely chopped
- 1 large green pepper, coarsely chopped
- 1 large onion, finely chopped
- 1 large carrot, chopped
- 1½ cups cubed fully cooked ham (about 8 oz.)
- 2 Tbsp. chopped seeded jalapeno pepper
- ¼ tsp. white pepper
- ¼ tsp. cayenne pepper
- 1 large egg yolk
- ¼ cup heavy whipping cream
- Optional toppings: Shredded cheddar cheese, cooked and crumbled bacon, minced fresh chives and sour cream

1. Place potatoes and 2 cups broth in a Dutch oven; bring to a boil. Reduce heat; simmer, covered, until the potatoes are tender, 10-15 minutes. Cool slightly. Transfer to a food processor; cover and process until smooth.

2. In same pot, heat butter over medium heat; saute the red and green peppers, onion and carrot until carrot is tender, 8-10 minutes. Add ham, jalapeno and seasonings; cook and stir 1 minute.

3. Stir in pureed potatoes and remaining 2 cups broth; bring just to a boil. In a small bowl, whisk a small amount of hot soup into egg yolk and cream; return all to the pot, whisking constantly. Bring to a gentle boil; cook and stir until thickened, 1-2 minutes. Serve with toppings as desired.

1⅓ **CUPS:** 226 cal., 10g fat (6g sat. fat), 76mg chol., 1124mg sod., 23g carb. (6g sugars, 3g fiber), 11g pro.

BEEF & BEET STEW

When I was child, every Saturday night was Red Flannel Night. Grandpa and I wore our red flannel long underwear to supper and Grandma, the cook, dressed in a long calico dress and sunbonnet. We'd eat Red Flannel Stew spooned over fluffy Southern style biscuits. Grandma learned to make the stew from earlier generations.

—*Kathy Padgett, Diamond City, AR*

PREP: 30 MIN. • **COOK:** 1½ HOURS • **MAKES:** 10 SERVINGS (3½ QT.)

4   whole fresh beets, washed, trimmed and halved
12 cups water, divided
2   lbs. corned beef brisket, trimmed and cut into 1-in. pieces
8   small carrots, sliced
4   medium parsnips, sliced
3   small turnips, peeled and cubed
2   small onions, chopped
2   tsp. each dried parsley flakes, basil and thyme
½   tsp. salt
¼   tsp. pepper

1. In a Dutch oven, bring beets and 8 cups water to a boil. Reduce heat; simmer, uncovered, for 20-25 minutes or until tender. Drain, reserving 4 cups cooking liquid. Peel and dice beets; set aside.

2. In the same pan, combine the corned beef, carrots, parsnips, turnips, onions, seasonings, remaining 4 cups water and the reserved cooking liquid. Bring to a boil. Reduce heat; cover and simmer for 1¼ to 1½ hours or until meat and vegetables are tender. Stir in diced beets; heat through.

SHAKER BEAN SOUP

I like cooking a new recipe every week, and my family loves soup, especially this hearty one. We often enjoyed it while living in Michigan.

—*Deborah Amrine, Fort Myers, FL*

PREP: 15 MIN. + SOAKING • **COOK:** 2¼ HOURS • **MAKES:** 5 QT.

1   lb. dried great northern beans
1   meaty ham bone or 2 smoked ham hocks
8   cups water
1   large onion, chopped
3   celery ribs, diced
2   medium carrots, shredded
    Salt to taste
½   tsp. pepper
½   tsp. dried thyme
1   can (28 oz.) crushed tomatoes in puree
2   Tbsp. brown sugar
1½ cups finely shredded fresh spinach

1. Soak beans according to package directions. In a Dutch oven, bring the beans, ham bone and water to a boil. Reduce heat; cover and simmer for 1½ hours or until meat easily falls off the bone.

2. Remove bone from broth; cool. Trim meat from the bone. Discard bone. Add the meat, onion, celery, carrots, salt, pepper and thyme to broth. Cover and cook for 30-60 minutes or until beans and vegetables are tender.

3. Add tomatoes and brown sugar. Cook 10 minutes longer. Just before serving, add spinach.

1 CUP: 119 cal., 2g fat (1g sat. fat), 6mg chol., 70mg sod., 20g carb. (4g sugars, 6g fiber), 7g pro.

DILL
CHICKEN
SOUP

GRANDMA'S SECRET

It's amazing what a pinch of herbs can do to add an extra layer of "oomph" to soup. A bouquet of wispy, fragrant fronds, dill is a tangy herb that boasts a strong clean, fresh, earthy flavor.

DILL CHICKEN SOUP

I could eat soup for every meal of the day, all year long. I particularly like
dill and spinach—they add a brightness to this light and healthy soup.
—*Robin Haas, Hyde Park, MA*

TAKES: 30 MIN. • MAKES: 6 SERVINGS (2 QT.)

1 Tbsp. canola oil
2 medium carrots, chopped
1 small onion, coarsely
   chopped
2 garlic cloves, minced
½ cup uncooked whole
   wheat orzo pasta
1½ cups coarsely shredded
   rotisserie chicken
6 cups reduced-sodium
   chicken broth
1½ cups frozen peas
   (about 6 oz.)
8 oz. fresh baby spinach
   (about 10 cups)
2 Tbsp. chopped fresh dill
   or 1 Tbsp. dill weed
2 Tbsp. lemon juice
   Coarsely ground pepper,
   optional

1. In a 6-qt. stockpot, heat oil over medium heat. Add carrots, onion and garlic; saute until carrots are tender, 4-5 minutes.

2. Stir in orzo, chicken and broth; bring to a boil. Reduce heat; simmer, uncovered, 5 minutes. Stir in peas, spinach and dill; return to a boil. Reduce heat; simmer, uncovered, until orzo is tender, 3-4 minutes. Stir in lemon juice. If desired, top each serving with coarsely ground pepper.

1⅓ CUPS: 198 cal., 6g fat (1g sat. fat), 31mg chol., 681mg sod., 20g carb. (4g sugars, 5g fiber), 18g pro. **DIABETIC EXCHANGES:** 2 lean meat, 1 starch, 1 vegetable, ½ fat.

HEARTY MINESTRONE SOUP

Packed with sausage and veggies, this soup is not only nutritious,
it's also a great way to use up your garden bounty.
—*Donna Smith, Fairport, NY*

PREP: 25 MIN. • COOK: 30 MIN. • MAKES: 9 SERVINGS

1 lb. bulk Italian sausage
2 cups sliced celery
1 cup chopped onion
6 cups chopped zucchini
1 can (28 oz.) diced
   tomatoes, undrained
1½ cups chopped green
   pepper
1½ tsp. Italian seasoning
1½ tsp. salt
1 tsp. dried oregano
1 tsp. sugar
½ tsp. dried basil
¼ tsp. garlic powder

In a large saucepan, cook the sausage until no longer pink. Remove with a slotted spoon to paper towel to drain, reserving 1 Tbsp. of drippings. Saute the celery and onion in drippings for 5 minutes. Add sausage and remaining ingredients; bring to a boil. Reduce heat; cover and simmer for 20-30 minutes or until the vegetables are tender.

1 CUP: 224 cal., 16g fat (6g sat. fat), 38mg chol., 901mg sod., 12g carb. (7g sugars, 4g fiber), 10g pro.

LAMB STEW

My grandmother used to make this stew as a special Sunday meal. It's also a memorable dish from Ireland. If you like your stew thick and rich, you won't be disappointed.
—*Vickie Desourdy, Washington, NC*

PREP: 40 MIN. • BAKE: 1½ HOURS • MAKES: 8 SERVINGS (250 QT.)

2 lbs. lamb stew meat, cut into 1-in. cubes
1 Tbsp. butter
1 Tbsp. olive oil
1 lb. carrots, sliced
2 medium onions, thinly sliced
2 garlic cloves, minced
1½ cups reduced-sodium chicken broth
1 bottle (12 oz.) Guinness stout or additional reduced-sodium chicken broth
6 medium red potatoes, peeled and cut into 1-in. cubes
4 bay leaves
2 fresh thyme sprigs
2 fresh rosemary sprigs
2 tsp. salt
1½ tsp. pepper
¼ cup heavy whipping cream

1. Preheat oven to 325°. In an ovenproof Dutch oven, brown lamb in butter and oil in batches. Remove and keep warm. In the same pan, saute carrots and onions in drippings until crisp-tender. Add garlic; cook 1 minute. Gradually add broth and beer. Stir in lamb, potatoes, bay leaves, thyme, rosemary, salt and pepper.

2. Cover and bake 1½ to 2 hours or until meat and vegetables are tender, stirring every 30 minutes. Discard bay leaves, thyme and rosemary. Stir in cream; heat through.

FREEZE OPTION: Place individual portions of stew in freezer containers and freeze up to 3 months. To use, partially thaw in refrigerator overnight. Heat through in a saucepan, stirring occasionally; add a little water if necessary.

1¼ CUPS: 311 cal., 12g fat (5g sat. fat), 88mg chol., 829mg sod., 23g carb. (6g sugars, 4g fiber), 26g pro. DIABETIC EXCHANGES: 3 lean meat, 2 vegetable, 1 starch, 1 fat.

FROM GRANDMA'S KITCHEN: If you prefer lamb meat with a mild flavor, purchase grain-fed instead of grass-fed. Domestic lamb is usually grain-fed. Also look for lamb rather than mutton, as mutton has a more robust flavor.

CURRY CHICKEN STEW

My Grandma Inky grew up in India and passed down this recipe to my mother, who then passed it down to me. I tweaked the ingredients a bit to fit my toddler's taste buds, but it's just as scrumptious as the original. This recipe brings back fond memories of my family gathered around the table.

—*Teresa Flowers, Sacramento, CA*

PREP: 15 MIN. • COOK: 4 HOURS • MAKES: 6 SERVINGS

2 cans (14½ oz. each) chicken broth
1 can (10¾ oz.) condensed cream of chicken soup, undiluted
1 tub Knorr concentrated chicken stock (4.66 oz.)
4 garlic cloves, minced
1 Tbsp. curry powder
¼ tsp. salt
¼ tsp. cayenne pepper
¼ tsp. pepper
6 boneless skinless chicken breasts (6 oz. each)
1 medium green pepper, cut into thin strips
1 medium onion, thinly sliced
Hot cooked rice
Chopped fresh cilantro and chutney, optional

1. In a large bowl, combine the first 8 ingredients. Place chicken, green pepper and onion in a 5- or 6-qt. slow cooker; pour broth mixture over top. Cook, covered, on low until the chicken and vegetables are tender, 4-5 hours.

2. Remove chicken and cool slightly. Cut or shred the meat into bite-size pieces and return to slow cooker; heat through. Serve with rice. If desired, top with cilantro and chutney.

1¾ CUPS: 266 cal., 8g fat (2g sat. fat), 101mg chol., 1604mg sod., 9g carb. (2g sugars, 2g fiber), 36g pro.

"Wonderful! I added celery and more green bell pepper. Other than that, I prepared the recipe as written. We have had this meal several times since I first discovered the recipe in November 2019. My whole family loves it."
—SUSAN JOHNSON, TASTEOFHOME.COM

HEARTY NAVY BEAN SOUP

Dried beans and a ham hock create this easy comfort-food classic.
Bean soup is a family favorite in our house, and it's budget-friendly, too.
—*Mildred Lewis, Temple, TX*

PREP: 30 MIN. + SOAKING • COOK: 1¾ HOURS • MAKES: 10 SERVINGS (2½ QT.)

3 cups (1½ lbs.) dried
  navy beans
1 can (14½ oz.) diced
  tomatoes, undrained
1 large onion, chopped
1 meaty ham hock or 1 cup
  diced cooked ham
2 cups chicken broth
2½ cups water
  Salt and pepper to taste
  Minced fresh parsley,
  optional

1. Rinse and sort beans; soak according to package directions.

2. Drain and rinse beans, discarding liquid. Place in a Dutch oven. Add the tomatoes with juice, onion, ham hock, broth, water, salt and pepper. Bring to a boil. Reduce heat; cover and simmer until beans are tender, about 1½ hours.

3. Add more water if necessary. Remove ham hock and let it stand until cool enough to handle. Remove the meat from bone; discard bone. Cut the meat into bite-sized pieces; set aside. (For a thicker soup, cool slightly, then puree the beans in a food processor or blender and return to pan.) Return ham to soup and heat through. Garnish with parsley if desired.

1 CUP: 245 cal., 2g fat (0 sat. fat), 8mg chol., 352mg sod., 42g carb. (5g sugars, 16g fiber), 18g pro. DIABETIC EXCHANGES: 3 starch, 2 lean meat.

DEB'S MUSHROOM & BARLEY SOUP

Nothing is more gratifying that coming home to this rich, comforting soup. I prep the ingredients the evening before and start the slow cooker on my way out the door in the morning.
—*Debra Kamerman, New York, NY*

PREP: 25 MIN. • COOK: 6 HOURS • MAKES: 10 SERVINGS (3½ QT.)

1 lb. sliced baby portobello
  mushrooms
3 medium carrots,
  finely chopped
3 celery ribs,
  finely chopped
1 medium onion,
  finely chopped
1 cup medium pearl barley
1 tsp. dried thyme
1 tsp. pepper
5 cups water
4 cups beef stock
3 tsp. salt, divided
1 large egg, lightly beaten
1 lb. ground turkey

1. Place the first 9 ingredients and 2½ tsp. salt in a 6- or 7-qt. slow cooker.

2. In a large bowl, mix egg and remaining ½ tsp. salt. Add turkey; mix lightly but thoroughly. Shape into 1¼-in. balls; drop gently into slow cooker. Cook, covered, on low until vegetables and barley are tender, 6-8 hours.

1⅓ CUPS: 180 cal., 4g fat (1g sat. fat), 49mg chol., 967mg sod., 22g carb. (4g sugars, 5g fiber), 15g pro.

HEARTY NAVY
BEAN SOUP

CASHEW BUTTER
COOKIES, PAGE 226

GRANDMA'S FAVORITE

COOKIES, BROWNIE'S & BARS

Whether she was loading up the cookie jar or pulling a pan of warm fudgy brownies out of the oven, Grandma always had a sweet surprise at the ready. Stir up a bit of nostalgia with these recipes she knew by heart.

MAPLE WHOOPIE PIES

We have a huge maple syrup industry in New York. I took a basic whoopie pie
recipe and gave it a twist using our beloved maple flavor.

—*Holly Balzer-Harz, Malone, NY*

PREP: 40 MIN. • **BAKE:** 10 MIN./BATCH + COOLING • **MAKES:** ABOUT 2 DOZEN

- ⅓ cup butter, softened
- ¾ cup sugar
- 1 large egg, room temperature
- 1 tsp. vanilla extract
- 1 tsp. maple flavoring
- 2¼ cups all-purpose flour
- 1¼ tsp. baking powder
- 1 tsp. salt
- ½ cup heavy whipping cream
- ½ cup maple syrup
- ½ cup finely chopped pecans, divided

FILLING

- ½ cup butter, softened
- ½ cup shortening
- 1 tsp. maple flavoring
- 4 cups confectioners' sugar
- ¼ cup heavy whipping cream
- 2 Tbsp. maple syrup

1. Preheat oven to 375°. In a large bowl, cream butter and sugar until light and fluffy, 5-7 minutes. Beat in the egg, vanilla and flavoring. In another bowl, whisk flour, baking powder and salt; add to the creamed mixture alternately with cream and syrup, beating well after each addition. Stir in ¼ cup pecans.

2. Drop dough by rounded tablespoonfuls 2 in. apart onto greased baking sheets; sprinkle with remaining ¼ cup pecans. Bake until edges are light brown and tops spring back when lightly touched, 8-10 minutes. Remove from pans to wire racks to cool completely.

3. For filling, in a large bowl, beat butter, shortening and flavoring until creamy. Beat in confectioners' sugar alternately with cream and syrup until smooth. Spread filling on bottoms of half of the cookies; cover with remaining cookies. Store whoopie pies in airtight containers in the refrigerator.

1 WHOOPIE PIE: 306 cal., 15g fat (7g sat. fat), 35mg chol., 183mg sod., 41g carb. (32g sugars, 1g fiber), 2g pro.

GRANDMA'S SECRET

Extra whoopie pies can be stored in the refrigerator and are best enjoyed within about 5 days. You can also freeze whoopie pies in an airtight container for up to 3 months.

JAM-FILLED WREATHS & HEARTS

I make these beautiful wreath-shaped cookies with jewel-red centers every Christmas. The dusting of powdered sugar gives them a snowy look. My mother cut the recipe out of a newspaper some 30 years ago.
—*Monica Wilson, Pomona, NY*

PREP: 25 MIN. + CHILLING • **BAKE:** 10 MIN./BATCH + COOLING
MAKES: ABOUT 3 DOZEN WREATHS OR 4 DOZEN HEARTS

¾ cup butter, softened
1 cup sugar
2 large eggs, room temperature
1½ cups all-purpose flour
1 tsp. baking powder
1 tsp. ground cinnamon
½ tsp. ground allspice
1 cup quick-cooking oats
¾ cup finely chopped nuts
1 jar (18 oz.) seedless raspberry jam
Confectioners' sugar

1. In a bowl, cream butter and sugar. Add eggs, 1 at a time, beating well after each addition. Combine flour, baking powder, cinnamon and allspice; add to the creamed mixture. Stir in oats and nuts; mix well. Refrigerate for 3 hours or until dough is easy to handle.

2. On a floured surface, roll out dough to ⅛-in. thickness. Cut with a 2½-in. round- or 2-in. heart-shaped cookie cutter. Using a 1-in. round- or heart-shaped cookie cutter, cut out the center of half of the cookies. Place solid and window cookies on lightly greased baking sheets.

3. Bake at 400° for 6-8 minutes or until lightly browned. Cool on wire racks.

4. Spread 1 tsp. jam over bottoms of solid cookies; top with window cookies. Dust with confectioners' sugar. Fill centers with additional jam if desired.

1 COOKIE: 166 cal., 7g fat (3g sat. fat), 25mg chol., 58mg sod., 25g carb. (17g sugars, 1g fiber), 2g pro.

"Amazing recipe. Added some Chambord liqueur to this. Light and fluffy."
—BRANDONBRIGGS, TASTEOFHOME.COM

NANNY'S FRUITCAKE COOKIES

My grandmother made a holiday fruitcake every Christmas. I took her recipe
and made it a cookie that's perfect any time with a cup of tea.
—*Amanda Digges, South Windsor, CT*

PREP: 35 MIN. + CHILLING • BAKE: 15 MIN./BATCH • MAKES: ABOUT 4 DOZEN

1⅔ cups chopped pecans
    or walnuts
1⅓ cups golden raisins
1 cup pitted dried plums
    (prunes), chopped
⅔ cup dried apricots,
    finely chopped
½ cup dried cranberries
¼ cup Triple Sec
1 cup butter, softened
½ cup sugar
⅓ cup packed light brown
    sugar
½ tsp. ground nutmeg
1 large egg, room
    temperature
2⅔ cups all-purpose flour

1. Place the first 5 ingredients in a large bowl. Drizzle with Triple Sec and toss to combine. Let stand, covered, overnight. In a large bowl, cream butter, sugars and nutmeg for 5-7 minutes or until light and fluffy. Beat in egg. Gradually beat in flour. Stir in fruit mixture. Divide the dough in half; shape each into a 12x3x1-in. rectangular log. Cover; refrigerate overnight or until firm.

2. Preheat oven to 350°. Uncover and cut dough crosswise into ½-in. slices. Place 2 in. apart on ungreased baking sheets. Bake until edges are light brown, 13-16 minutes. Remove from pans to wire racks to cool.

1 COOKIE: 131 cal., 7g fat (3g sat. fat), 14mg chol., 37mg sod., 17g carb. (9g sugars, 1g fiber), 2g pro.

OLD-FASHIONED PEANUT BUTTER COOKIES

My mother insisted my grandmother write down one recipe for her when Mom got married in 1942.
That was a real effort because Grandma was a traditional pioneer-type cook who added a little of
this and a little of that until it felt right. This treasured recipe is the only one she ever wrote down!
—*Janet Hall, Clinton, WI*

PREP: 15 MIN. • BAKE: 10 MIN./BATCH • MAKES: 3 DOZEN

1 cup shortening
1 cup peanut butter
1 cup sugar
1 cup packed brown sugar
3 large eggs,
    room temperature
3 cups all-purpose flour
2 tsp. baking soda
¼ tsp. salt

1. Preheat oven to 375°. In a large bowl, cream shortening, peanut butter and sugars until light and fluffy, 5-7 minutes. Add the eggs, 1 at a time, beating well after each addition. Combine flour, baking soda and salt; add to creamed mixture and mix well.

2. Roll into 1½-in. balls. Place 3 in. apart on ungreased baking sheets. Flatten with a fork or meat mallet if desired. Bake for 10-15 minutes. Remove to wire racks to cool.

1 COOKIE: 180 cal., 9g fat (2g sat. fat), 18mg chol., 128mg sod., 21g carb. (12g sugars, 1g fiber), 3g pro.

GRANDMA'S PECAN
RUM BARS

GRANDMA'S PECAN RUM BARS

My grandmother handed down the recipe for these gooey bars,
which we all love. The candied cherries are a must!
—*Deborah Pennington, Falkville, AL*

PREP: 20 MIN. • BAKE: 1 HOUR + COOLING • MAKES: 2 DOZEN

4 cups chopped pecans, divided
1 cup butter, softened
2¼ cups packed brown sugar
4 large eggs, room temperature
2 Tbsp. vanilla extract
1 cup all-purpose flour
2¼ cups red candied cherries
1½ cups chopped candied pineapple
½ cup chopped candied citron
⅓ cup rum

1. Sprinkle 3 cups pecans over a greased 15x10x1-in. baking pan.

2. Preheat oven to 350°. In a large bowl, cream butter and brown sugar until light and fluffy, 5-7 minutes. Add eggs, 1 at a time, beating well after each addition. Beat in vanilla. Gradually add flour to creamed mixture, beating well.

3. Spread batter into prepared pan. Combine candied fruit and remaining pecans. Spread fruit and pecans evenly over creamed mixture; press gently to help mixtures adhere. Bake until a toothpick inserted in center comes out clean, about 1 hour. Sprinkle rum over the top; cool completely in pan on a wire rack. Cut into bars. Store in an airtight container.

1 BAR: 401 cal., 22g fat (6g sat. fat), 51mg chol., 123mg sod., 49g carb. (40g sugars, 2g fiber), 4g pro.

BUTTERSCOTCH TOFFEE COOKIES

With its big butterscotch and chocolate flavor, my cookie stands out. I enjoy it with a glass of milk
or a cup of coffee. It's my fallback recipe when I'm short on time and need something delicious fast.
—*Allie Blinder, Norcross, GA*

PREP: 10 MIN. • BAKE: 10 MIN./BATCH • MAKES: 5 DOZEN

2 large eggs, room temperature
½ cup canola oil
1 pkg. butter pecan cake mix (regular size)
1 pkg. (10 to 11 oz.) butterscotch chips
1 pkg. (8 oz.) milk chocolate English toffee bits

1. Preheat oven to 350°. In a large bowl, beat eggs and oil until blended; gradually add cake mix and mix well. Fold in chips and toffee bits.

2. Drop by tablespoonfuls 2 in. apart onto greased baking sheets. Bake until golden brown, 10-12 minutes. Cool 1 minute before removing to wire racks.

1 COOKIE: 95 cal., 5g fat (3g sat. fat), 10mg chol., 70mg sod., 11g carb. (3g sugars, 0 fiber), 1g pro.

FUDGE NUT BROWNIES

There's no brownie recipe or mix I've ever tried that's better than this!
It's so easy—you can mix it in one bowl in just a few minutes. My husband's grandmother
passed the recipe on; now our son makes these brownies for after-school snacks.
—*Becky Albright, Norwalk, OH*

PREP: 15 MIN. • BAKE: 20 MIN. • MAKES: 24 BROWNIES

1⅓ cups all-purpose flour
2 cups sugar
¾ cup baking cocoa
1 tsp. baking powder
½ tsp. salt
½ cup chopped nuts
⅔ cup vegetable oil
4 large eggs, room temperature, lightly beaten
2 tsp. vanilla extract
1 cup chopped nuts, optional

1. Preheat oven to 350°. In a bowl, combine the first 6 ingredients. In another bowl, combine the oil, eggs and vanilla; add to the dry ingredients. Do not overmix.

2. Spread in a 13x9-in. baking pan. Sprinkle with nuts if desired. Bake 20-25 minutes or until a toothpick inserted in center comes out clean. Cool in pan on a wire rack.

1 SERVING: 180 cal., 9g fat (1g sat. fat), 35mg chol., 77mg sod., 24g carb. (16g sugars, 1g fiber), 3g pro.

SILVER BELLS

My mom and grandma are known for their signature Christmas cookies. I decided to create
my own, inspired by one of my favorite Christmas songs. Edible shimmer dust gives them their
iconic shine. Look for the dust in the cake decorating section of craft or grocery stores.
—*Crystal Schlueter, Northglenn, CO*

PREP: 20 MIN. + CHILLING • BAKE: 15 MIN./BATCH + COOLING • MAKES: ABOUT 4 DOZEN

1½ cups butter, softened
3 cups sugar
4 large eggs, room temperature
1 tsp. peppermint extract
1 tsp. vanilla extract
5 cups all-purpose flour
2 tsp. baking powder
1 tsp. salt
1 pkg. (10 to 12 oz.) white baking chips
1 Tbsp. shortening
Black paste food coloring, optional
Silver edible shimmer dust or sugar

1. Cream butter and sugar until light and fluffy, 5-7 minutes. Beat in eggs and extracts. In another bowl, whisk flour, baking powder and salt; gradually beat into creamed mixture. Divide dough into quarters. Shape each into a disk; cover. Refrigerate until firm enough to roll, about 2 hours.

2. Preheat oven to 350°. On a lightly floured surface, roll each portion of dough to ⅛-in. thickness. Cut with a floured 2½-in. bell-shaped cookie cutter. Place 1 in. apart on greased baking sheets. Bake until edges begin to brown, 12-15 minutes. Remove from pans to wire racks to cool completely.

3. In a microwave, melt chips and shortening; stir until smooth. If desired, tint with food coloring. Spread over cookies. Let stand until set; brush with shimmer dust.

1 COOKIE: 188 cal., 8g fat (5g sat. fat), 32mg chol., 126mg sod., 26g carb. (16g sugars, 0 fiber), 2g pro.

GLAZED STRAWBERRY COOKIES

I learned to bake with my grandmother and
mother. I started a new family tradition
when I shared this special recipe with them.
—*Andrea Zulauf, Livonia, NY*

PREP: 45 MIN. + CHILLING • BAKE: 10 MIN./BATCH + COOLING
MAKES: 3½ DOZEN

1 **cup butter, softened**	**FILLING**
1½ **cups confectioners' sugar**	¼ **cup plus 2 Tbsp.**
1 **large egg, room**	**strawberry jelly**
temperature	¾ **cup confectioners' sugar**
1½ **tsp. vanilla extract**	
2½ **cups all-purpose flour**	**ICING**
1½ **oz. strawberry gelatin**	1½ **cups confectioners' sugar**
1 **tsp. baking soda**	3 **Tbsp. 2% milk**
1 **tsp. cream of tartar**	

1. Preheat oven to 375°. In a large bowl, cream butter and
confectioners' sugar until blended. Beat in egg and vanilla.
In another bowl, whisk flour, gelatin, baking soda and cream
of tartar; gradually beat into creamed mixture.

2. Divide dough into 4 portions. Shape each into a disk; cover.
Refrigerate 30 minutes or until firm enough to roll.

3. Preheat oven to 375°. For filling, in a small bowl, beat jelly and
confectioners' sugar. On a lightly floured surface, roll 1 portion
of dough to ⅛-in. thickness. Cut with a floured 2-in. round cookie
cutter. Place about ½ tsp. filling in center of half of the cookies.
Cover with remaining cookies. Press edges with a fork to seal.
Place 2 in. apart on ungreased baking sheets. Repeat with
remaining dough and filling.

4. Bake 10-12 minutes or until edges are light brown. Cool on pans
2 minutes. Remove to wire racks to cool completely.

5. In a small bowl, mix confectioners' sugar and milk until smooth.
Drizzle over cookies; let stand until set. Store in an airtight
container in the refrigerator.

FREEZE OPTION: Transfer wrapped disks to a freezer container;
freeze. To use, thaw dough in refrigerator until soft enough to roll.
Prepare filling and cookies. Bake and decorate as directed.

1 COOKIE: 121 cal., 5g fat (3g sat. fat), 16mg chol., 70mg sod., 19g
carb. (13g sugars, 0 fiber), 1g pro.

MOLASSES COOKIES WITH A KICK

This is a combination of spices that I have used for a long time. It's also one of
my mother's favorite cookies. I get requests from her to make them year-round!

—Tamara Rau, Medina, ND

PREP: 40 MIN. + CHILLING • **BAKE:** 10 MIN./BATCH • **MAKES:** 5 DOZEN

¾ cup butter, softened
½ cup sugar
½ cup packed brown sugar
¼ cup molasses
1 large egg, room
   temperature
1½ tsp. minced fresh
   gingerroot
2¼ cups all-purpose flour
1 tsp. ground cinnamon
¾ tsp. baking soda
½ tsp. ground cloves
¼ to ½ tsp. cayenne pepper
¼ tsp. salt
¼ tsp. ground nutmeg
⅛ tsp. each ground white
   pepper, cardamom and
   coriander
¾ cup turbinado
   (washed raw) sugar

1. In a large bowl, cream butter and sugars until light and fluffy, 5-7 minutes. Beat in the molasses, egg and ginger. Combine the flour, cinnamon, baking soda, cloves, cayenne, salt, nutmeg, white pepper, cardamom and coriander; gradually add to the creamed mixture and mix well. Cover and refrigerate for 1½ hours or until easy to handle.

2. Roll into 1-in. balls; roll in turbinado sugar. Place 3 in. apart on lightly greased baking sheets.

3. Bake at 350° for 8-10 minutes or until set. Cool for 2 minutes before removing from pans to wire racks. Store in an airtight container.

1 COOKIE: 66 cal., 2g fat (2g sat. fat), 9mg chol., 46mg sod., 11g carb. (7g sugars, 0 fiber), 1g pro.

CARROT SPICE THUMBPRINT COOKIES

Carrot cake is a family favorite, and these delicious cookies taste just like it with shredded carrots, dried cranberries, toasted walnuts, cinnamon and cloves. And they're topped with a rich cream cheese frosting. Who could resist? Each cookie is like eating a piece of carrot cake, but with no fork needed!
—*Susan Bickta, Kutztown, PA*

PREP: 30 MIN. • **BAKE:** 10 MIN./BATCH + COOLING • **MAKES:** 5 DOZEN

1   **cup margarine, softened**
1   **cup sugar**
½   **cup packed brown sugar**
2   **large eggs, room temperature**
2   **tsp. vanilla extract**
3   **cups all-purpose flour**
1½ **tsp. ground cinnamon**
1   **tsp. baking powder**
¾   **tsp. salt**
½   **tsp. baking soda**
⅛   **tsp. ground cloves**
1½ **cups shredded carrots**

⅔   **cup chopped walnuts, toasted**
½   **cup dried cranberries**

FROSTING
½   **cup butter, softened**
4   **oz. cream cheese, softened**
2   **cups confectioners' sugar**
1   **tsp. vanilla extract**
    Additional confectioners' sugar

1. Preheat oven to 375°. In a large bowl, cream together the margarine and sugars until light and fluffy, 5-7 minutes. Beat in eggs and vanilla. In another bowl, whisk flour, cinnamon, baking powder, salt, baking soda and cloves; gradually beat into creamed mixture. Stir in carrots, walnuts and cranberries.

2. Drop the dough by rounded tablespoonfuls 2 in. apart onto parchment-lined baking sheets. Press a deep indentation in center of each with the back of a ½-tsp. measure.

3. Bake until edges begin to brown, 10-12 minutes. Reshape the indentations as needed. Cool on pans 5 minutes. Remove to wire racks to cool completely.

4. For frosting, beat butter, cream cheese, confectioners' sugar and vanilla until blended. To serve, fill each cookie with about 1½ tsp. frosting; sprinkle with additional confectioners' sugar. Refrigerate leftover filled cookies.

1 COOKIE: 167 cal., 9g fat (3g sat. fat), 17mg chol., 146mg sod., 21g carb. (14g sugars, 1g fiber), 2g pro.

FIG & ALMOND COOKIES

In our family, holiday cookies—like these nutty fig treats—are a big deal.
I'm so proud to be passing on this Italian tradition to my two boys.
—*Angela Lemoine, Howell, NJ*

PREP: 50 MIN. + CHILLING • **BAKE:** 10 MIN./BATCH + COOLING • **MAKES:** ABOUT 6½ DOZEN

2 large eggs, room
   temperature
1 Tbsp. cold water
2 tsp. vanilla extract
2¾ cups all-purpose flour
1½ cups confectioners' sugar
3 tsp. baking powder
¼ tsp. salt
6 Tbsp. cold butter, cubed

FILLING
8 oz. dried figs (about
   1⅓ cups)
3 Tbsp. unblanched
   almonds
2 Tbsp. apricot preserves
4 tsp. orange juice

GLAZE
1 cup confectioners' sugar
2 Tbsp. 2% milk
½ tsp. vanilla extract

1. In a small bowl, whisk the eggs, cold water and vanilla until blended. Place flour, confectioners' sugar, baking powder and salt in a food processor; pulse until blended. Add butter; pulse until crumbly. While pulsing, add egg mixture just until combined.

2. Divide dough in half. Shape each into a disk; cover. Refrigerate 1 hour or until firm enough to roll.

3. Wipe food processor clean. Add figs and almonds; pulse until chopped. Add preserves and juice; pulse until combined.

4. Preheat oven to 350°. On a lightly floured surface, roll each portion of dough into a 10x8-in. rectangle; cut each lengthwise into four 2-in.-wide strips.

5. Spread about 2 Tbsp. filling down center of each strip. Fold dough over filling; pinch edges to seal. Roll each gently to shape into a log; cut crosswise into 1-in. pieces.

6. Place 1 in. apart on parchment-lined baking sheets. Bake until light brown, 10-12 minutes. Remove from pans to wire racks to cool completely.

7. In a small bowl, mix glaze ingredients until smooth. Drizzle over cookies. Let stand until set.

1 COOKIE: 51 cal., 1g fat (1g sat. fat), 7mg chol., 33mg sod., 9g carb. (5g sugars, 0 fiber), 1g pro.``

"Made these over the holidays—wonderful, super easy and fast, and so close to the old world recipe of real cucidati! Well worth it if you like fig cookies. Makes plenty and they went fast!"
—RUTH, TASTEOFHOME.COM

GRANDMA KRAUSE'S
COCONUT COOKIES

GRANDMA KRAUSE'S COCONUT COOKIES

When my two daughters were young, their great-grandma made them
cookies with oats and coconut. We're so grateful she shared the recipe.
—*Debra Dorn, Dunnellon, FL*

PREP: 40 MIN. + FREEZING • BAKE: 10 MIN./BATCH • MAKES: ABOUT 4 DOZEN

1 cup shortening
1 cup sugar
1 cup packed brown sugar
2 large eggs, room temperature
1 tsp. vanilla extract
2 cups all-purpose flour
1 tsp. baking powder
1 tsp. baking soda
¼ tsp. salt
1 cup old-fashioned oats
1 cup sweetened shredded coconut

1. In a large bowl, beat shortening and sugars until blended. Beat in eggs and vanilla. In another bowl, whisk flour, baking powder, baking soda and salt; gradually beat into sugar mixture. Stir in oats and coconut.

2. Divide dough into 4 portions. On a lightly floured surface, shape each into a 6-in.-long log. Wrap in waxed paper; freeze 2 hours or until firm.

3. Preheat oven to 350°. Unwrap and cut dough crosswise into ½-in. slices, reshaping as needed. Place 2 in. apart on ungreased baking sheets. Bake 10-12 minutes or until golden brown. Cool on pans 5 minutes. Remove to wire racks to cool.

FREEZE OPTION: Place wrapped logs in a freezer container; return to freezer. To use, unwrap the frozen logs and cut into slices. If necessary, let dough stand a few minutes at room temperature before cutting. Prepare and bake as directed.

1 COOKIE: 109 cal., 5g fat (2g sat. fat), 8mg chol., 56mg sod., 15g carb. (10g sugars, 0 fiber), 1g pro.

WYOMING WHOPPER COOKIES

These big country cookies are made to travel—in fact, I came up with this recipe while
trying to match a commercial cookie that was delicious, but too crumbly to carry.
—*Jamie Hirsch, Powell, WY*

TAKES: 30 MIN. • MAKES: 2 DOZEN

⅔ cup butter, cubed
1¼ cups packed brown sugar
¾ cup sugar
3 large eggs, beaten
1½ cups chunky peanut butter
6 cups old-fashioned oats
2 tsp. baking soda
1½ cups raisins
2 cups semisweet chocolate chips

1. In a large saucepan, melt butter over low heat. Stir in the brown sugar, sugar, eggs and peanut butter until smooth. Add oats, baking soda, raisins and chocolate chips (dough will be sticky).

2. Drop on a greased baking sheet with an ice cream scoop or large spoon. Flatten slightly. Bake at 350° for 15 minutes. Remove cookies to a wire rack to cool.

NOTE: Reduced-fat peanut butter is not recommended for this recipe.

2 COOKIES: 768 cal., 39g fat (15g sat. fat), 80mg chol., 499mg sod., 101g carb. (65g sugars, 8g fiber), 17g pro.

WINNING APRICOT BARS

This recipe is down-home baking at its best, and it represents all regions of the country. It's won blue ribbons at county fairs and cookie contests in several states. Easy to make, it's perfect for potluck suppers, bake sales, lunchboxes or snacking.
—*Jill Moritz, Irvine, CA*

PREP: 15 MIN. • **BAKE:** 30 MIN. + COOLING • **MAKES:** 2 DOZEN

¾ cup butter, softened
1 cup sugar
1 large egg, room temperature
½ tsp. vanilla extract
2 cups all-purpose flour
¼ tsp. baking powder
1⅓ cups sweetened shredded coconut
½ cup chopped walnuts
1 jar (10 to 12 oz.) apricot preserves

1. Preheat oven to 350°. In a large bowl, cream butter and sugar until light and fluffy, 5-7 minutes. Beat in egg and vanilla. In a small bowl, whisk flour and baking powder; gradually add to creamed mixture, mixing well. Fold in coconut and walnuts.

2. Press two-thirds of the dough onto the bottom of a greased 13x9-in. baking pan. Spread with preserves; crumble remaining dough over preserves. Bake 30-35 minutes or until golden brown. Cool completely in pan on a wire rack. Cut into bars.

1 BAR: 195 cal., 10g fat (6g sat. fat), 23mg chol., 72mg sod., 27g carb. (16g sugars, 1g fiber), 2g pro.

MONKEY BARS

Mmm! Two of my favorite foods together in one dessert! Smooth peanut butter and sweet banana combine to make these thick muffinlike bars.
—*Tina Haupert, Weymouth, MA*

PREP: 15 MIN. • **BAKE:** 25 MIN. • **MAKES:** 16 SERVINGS

½ cup butter, softened
1 cup packed brown sugar
½ cup creamy peanut butter
1 large egg, room temperature
1 medium ripe banana, mashed
1 tsp. vanilla extract
1 cup whole wheat flour
1 tsp. baking powder
⅛ tsp. salt
Confectioners' sugar, optional

1. Preheat oven to 350°. In a large bowl, beat butter, brown sugar and peanut butter until blended. Gradually beat in egg, banana and vanilla. In another bowl, whisk flour, baking powder and salt; gradually add to butter mixture, mixing well.

2. Spread into an 8-in. square baking dish coated with cooking spray. Bake until a toothpick inserted in center comes out clean, 25-30 minutes. Cool on a wire rack. Cut into bars. If desired, dust with confectioners' sugar.

1 BAR: 188 cal., 10g fat (5g sat. fat), 27mg chol., 139mg sod., 22g carb. (15g sugars, 1g fiber), 4g pro.

SWEDISH GINGERBREAD COOKIES

Making Swedish *pepparkakor*—or gingerbread cookies—
is a holiday tradition for our family. I entered these at
the Iowa State Fair and took home a blue ribbon.
—*Kathleen Olesen, Des Moines, IA*

PREP: 15 MIN. + CHILLING • **BAKE:** 10 MIN./BATCH + COOLING
MAKES: 3 DOZEN

1 cup butter, softened
1 cup sugar
½ cup molasses
1 large egg, room temperature
3¼ cups all-purpose flour
1 Tbsp. ground ginger
1 Tbsp. ground cinnamon
2 tsp. ground cloves
1 tsp. baking soda

FROSTING
3 cups confectioners' sugar
¾ cup shortening
1 Tbsp. vanilla extract
3 to 5 Tbsp. water
Red Hots, optional

1. In a large bowl, cream butter and sugar until light and fluffy, 5-7 minutes. Beat in molasses and egg. In another bowl, whisk flour, ginger, cinnamon, cloves and baking soda; gradually beat into creamed mixture. Divide dough in half. Shape each into a disk; wrap. Refrigerate 1 hour or until firm enough to roll.

2. Preheat oven to 350°. On a lightly floured surface, roll each portion of dough to ¼-in. thickness. Cut with a floured 3½-in. gingerbread man cookie cutter. Place 1 in. apart on greased baking sheets. Bake until edges are firm, 8-10 minutes. Cool on pans 2 minutes. Remove to wire racks to cool completely.

3. For frosting, in a bowl, beat confectioners' sugar, shortening, vanilla and enough water to reach spreading consistency. Decorate cookies with frosting and, if desired, Red Hots.

FREEZE OPTION: Transfer wrapped disks to a resealable freezer container; freeze. To use, thaw dough in refrigerator overnight or until soft enough to roll. Prepare, bake and decorate cookies as directed.

1 COOKIE: 201 cal., 9g fat (4g sat. fat), 19mg chol., 80mg sod., 28g carb. (19g sugars, 0 fiber), 1g pro.

RAISIN PUMPKIN BARS

These moist bars will keep well—if your family doesn't eat them all right away!
They're nice to take to a potluck supper, or as a snack or dessert anytime.

—J.B. Hendrix, Ganado, TX

PREP: 20 MIN. • **BAKE:** 25 MIN. + COOLING • **MAKES:** 2 DOZEN

2 cups sugar
1 can (15 oz.) pumpkin
1 cup canola oil
4 large eggs, room temperature
2 cups all-purpose flour
2 tsp. baking powder
1 tsp. baking soda
1 tsp. ground cinnamon
1 tsp. ground nutmeg
½ tsp. salt
⅛ tsp. ground cloves
½ cup raisins
⅓ cup chopped pecans or walnuts

FROSTING
⅓ cup butter, softened
3 oz. cream cheese, softened
1 Tbsp. 2% milk
1 tsp. vanilla extract
2 cups confectioners' sugar

1. In a large bowl, beat the sugar, pumpkin, oil and eggs. Combine the flour, baking powder, baking soda, cinnamon, nutmeg, salt and cloves; gradually add to pumpkin mixture and mix well. Stir in the raisins and nuts.

2. Pour into a greased 15x10x1-in. baking pan. Bake at 350° for 25-30 minutes or until a toothpick is inserted in the center comes out clean. Cool on a wire rack.

3. For frosting, combine the butter, cream cheese, milk and vanilla in a bowl; beat until smooth. Gradually beat in the confectioners' sugar. Spread over top; cut into bars. Store in the refrigerator.

1 SERVING: 297 cal., 15g fat (4g sat. fat), 46mg chol., 184mg sod., 39g carb. (28g sugars, 1g fiber), 3g pro.

GRANDMA'S SECRET
If you don't have a nut chopper gadget, try using a serrated knife to chop nuts instead of a chef's knife. It will help to keep the nuts from flying off your cutting board.

LEMON SNOWDROPS

I save my snowdrop cookies for special occasions. The crunchy,
buttery sandwich cookie has a puckery lemon filling.
—*Bernice Martinoni, Petaluma, CA*

PREP: 40 MIN. + CHILLING • **BAKE:** 10 MIN./BATCH + COOLING
MAKES: 2 DOZEN

1   **cup butter, softened**
½   **cup confectioners' sugar**
¼   **tsp. salt**
1   **tsp. lemon extract**
2   **cups all-purpose flour**
     Sugar

FILLING
1   **large egg, room**
     temperature, lightly
     beaten
⅔   **cup sugar**
2   **tsp. grated lemon zest**
3   **Tbsp. lemon juice**
4   **tsp. butter**
     Additional confectioners'
     sugar, optional

1. Preheat oven to 350°. Cream butter, confectioners' sugar and
salt until light and fluffy, 5-7 minutes. Beat in extract. Gradually
beat in flour. Shape teaspoons of dough into balls (if necessary,
refrigerate dough, covered, until firm enough to shape). Place 1 in.
apart on ungreased baking sheets; flatten slightly with bottom of
a glass dipped in sugar. Bake until light brown, 10-12 minutes.
Remove cookies from pans to wire racks to cool completely.

2. For filling, whisk together egg, sugar, lemon zest and lemon
juice in a small heavy saucepan over medium-low heat until
blended. Add butter; cook over medium heat, whisking constantly,
until thickened and a thermometer reads at least 170°, about
20 minutes. Remove from heat immediately (do not allow to boil).
Transfer to a small bowl; cool. Press plastic wrap onto surface of
filling. Refrigerate until cold, about 1 hour.

3. To serve, spread lemon filling on half of cookies; cover with
remaining cookies. If desired, dust with confectioners' sugar.
Store leftovers in refrigerator.

FREEZE OPTION: Freeze unfilled, undecorated cookies in freezer
containers. To use, thaw cookies in covered containers. Fill and
decorate as directed.

1 SANDWICH COOKIE: 147 cal., 9g fat (5g sat. fat), 30mg chol., 94mg
sod., 16g carb. (8g sugars, 0 fiber), 1g pro.

RHUBARB CUSTARD BARS

Once I tried these rich, gooey bars, I just had to have the recipe so I could make them for my family and friends. The shortbreadlike crust and the rhubarb and custard layers inspire people to find rhubarb that they can use to fix a batch for themselves.
—*Shari Roach, South Milwaukee, WI*

PREP: 25 MIN. • BAKE: 50 MIN. + CHILLING • MAKES: 3 DOZEN

2 cups all-purpose flour
¼ cup sugar
1 cup cold butter

FILLING
2 cups sugar
7 Tbsp. all-purpose flour
1 cup heavy whipping cream
3 large eggs, room temperature, beaten
5 cups finely chopped fresh or frozen rhubarb, thawed and drained

TOPPING
6 oz. cream cheese, softened
½ cup sugar
½ tsp. vanilla extract
1 cup heavy whipping cream, whipped

1. In a bowl, combine the flour and sugar; cut in butter until the mixture resembles coarse crumbs. Press mixture into a greased 13x9-in. baking pan. Bake at 350° for 10 minutes.

2. Meanwhile, for filling, combine sugar and flour in a bowl. Whisk in the cream and eggs. Stir in the rhubarb. Pour over crust. Bake at 350° until custard is set, 40-45 minutes. Cool.

3. For topping, beat cream cheese, sugar and vanilla until smooth; fold in whipped cream. Spread over top. Cover and chill. Cut into bars. Store in the refrigerator.

1 BAR: 198 cal., 11g fat (7g sat. fat), 52mg chol., 70mg sod., 23g carb. (16g sugars, 1g fiber), 2g pro.

FROM GRANDMA'S KITCHEN: Heavy whipping cream gives custard fillings a luscious, decadent texture, but half-and-half cream or whole milk can be substituted with nice results.

VERMONT MAPLE
COOKIES

VERMONT MAPLE COOKIES

I created this recipe after tasting maple cookies with a maple glaze at a bakery in Stowe, Vermont, some years ago. I get many requests to bring them to bake sales, parties and ski trips.
—*Delores Day, Wolcott, VT*

PREP: 20 MIN. • BAKE: 10 MIN./BATCH + COOLING • MAKES: 5 DOZEN

1 cup butter, softened
¾ cup sugar
¾ cup packed brown sugar
2 large eggs, room temperature
1 tsp. maple flavoring
2½ cups all-purpose flour
1 tsp. baking soda
1 tsp. salt
2 cups white baking chips
1 cup chopped pecans

MAPLE GLAZE
⅓ cup butter, cubed
1¾ cups confectioners' sugar
⅓ cup maple syrup
¼ tsp. maple flavoring

1. Preheat oven to 350°. In a large bowl, cream the butter and sugars until light and fluffy, 5-7 minutes. Beat in eggs and maple flavoring. In another bowl, whisk the flour, baking soda and salt; gradually beat into creamed mixture. Stir in the baking chips and pecans.

2. Drop the dough by rounded tablespoonfuls 2 in. apart onto ungreased baking sheets. Bake 10-12 minutes or until golden brown. Cool on pans 2 minutes. Remove to wire racks to cool completely.

3. For glaze, in a saucepan, melt the butter over medium heat. Remove from heat. Gradually beat in confectioners' sugar, syrup and maple flavoring until smooth.

4. Drizzle over cookies; let dry completely. Store between pieces of waxed paper in airtight containers.

1 COOKIE: 139 cal., 7g fat (4g sat. fat), 18mg chol., 101mg sod., 18g carb. (13g sugars, 0 fiber), 1g pro.

SNICKERDOODLE BLONDIE BARS

When asked to bring a dessert for my boys' football team to share, I whipped up these unique blondies and was instantly named the greatest mom by all.
—*Valonda Seward, Coarsegold, CA*

PREP: 15 MIN. • BAKE: 35 MIN. + COOLING • MAKES: 20 BARS

1 cup butter, softened
2 cups packed brown sugar
3 tsp. vanilla extract
2 large eggs, room temperature
2⅔ cups all-purpose flour
2 tsp. baking powder
1 tsp. ground cinnamon
¼ tsp. ground nutmeg
½ tsp. salt

TOPPING
1½ tsp. sugar
½ tsp. ground cinnamon

1. Preheat oven to 350°. Cream butter and brown sugar until light and fluffy, 5-7 minutes. Beat in the vanilla. Beat in the eggs, 1 at a time, beating well after each addition. In another bowl, whisk together the flour, baking powder, spices and salt; gradually beat into the creamed mixture. Spread into a greased 9-in. square baking pan.

2. Mix topping ingredients; sprinkle over top. Bake until set and golden brown, 35-40 minutes. Cool completely in pan on a wire rack. Cut into bars.

1 BAR: 235 cal., 10g fat (6g sat. fat), 45mg chol., 180mg sod., 35g carb. (22g sugars, 1g fiber), 2g pro.

GINGER-CREAM BARS

I rediscovered this nearly forgotten old-time recipe recently and it became everyone's favorite. Even small children have asked for these frosted bars as nursery treats.
—*Carol Nagelkirk, Holland, MI*

PREP: 20 MIN. • **BAKE:** 20 MIN. • **MAKES:** 5 DOZEN

1 cup butter, softened
1 cup sugar
2 cups all-purpose flour
1 tsp. salt
2 tsp. baking soda
1 Tbsp. ground cinnamon
1 Tbsp. ground cloves
1 Tbsp. ground ginger
2 large eggs, room temperature
½ cup molasses
1 cup hot brewed coffee

FROSTING
½ cup butter, softened
3 oz. cream cheese, softened
2 cups confectioners' sugar
2 tsp. vanilla extract
Chopped nuts, optional

1. Preheat oven to 350°. Cream butter and sugar. Sift together the flour, salt, baking soda and spices; add to creamed mixture. Add eggs, 1 at a time, beating well after each addition, and molasses. Blend in coffee. Spread the batter in a 15x10x1-in. baking pan.

2. Bake 20-25 minutes. Cool. For frosting, cream the butter and cream cheese; add confectioners' sugar and vanilla. Spread over bars. If desired, top with nuts.

1 BAR: 101 cal., 5g fat (3g sat. fat), 20mg chol., 126mg sod., 13g carb. (9g sugars, 0 fiber), 1g pro.

CASHEW BUTTER COOKIES

PICTURED ON PAGE 202

These cashew butter cookies are on a more sophisticated level than peanut butter. They are vegan and gluten-free, so you'll be able to share with all your friends.
—Taste of Home *Test Kitchen*

PREP: 15 MIN. • **BAKE:** 20 MIN./BATCH • **MAKES:** 20 COOKIES

1 cup creamy cashew butter
¼ cup maple syrup
¼ cup ground flaxseed
¼ tsp. salt

1. In a large bowl, mix all ingredients. Roll level tablespoons into balls. Place on an ungreased baking sheet; flatten with a fork.

2. Bake at 350° for 18 minutes. Remove to a wire rack to cool.

1 COOKIE: 90 cal., 7g fat (1g sat. fat), 0 chol., 61mg sod., 8g carb. (5g sugars, 1g fiber), 2g pro.

S'MORES BROWNIES

Our family adores our daughter's fudgy s'mores brownies.
The cinnamon graham cracker crust and dark chocolate brownies
bring our passion for the classic treat to a whole new level!
—*Jennifer Gilbert, Brighton, MI*

PREP: 20 MIN. • BAKE: 30 MIN. • MAKES: 2 DOZEN

1½ cups graham cracker crumbs (about 10 whole crackers)
¼ cup sugar
1 tsp. ground cinnamon
½ cup butter, melted

BROWNIES
1 oz. unsweetened baking chocolate
½ cup butter, softened
1¼ cups sugar
3 large eggs, room temperature

1 tsp. vanilla extract
1¼ cups all-purpose flour
⅓ cup dark baking cocoa
½ tsp. baking powder
¼ tsp. salt
1 cup miniature marshmallows

TOPPING
1 cup miniature marshmallows
5 whole graham crackers, broken into bite-sized pieces

1. Preheat oven to 350°. Combine cracker crumbs, sugar and cinnamon. Stir in melted butter. Press onto the bottom of an ungreased 13x9-in. baking pan. Bake until lightly browned, 7-9 minutes. Cool on a wire rack.

2. For brownies, melt the unsweetened chocolate on high in a microwave, stirring every 30 seconds. Cool slightly. Cream the butter and sugar on medium speed for 5-7 minutes or until light and fluffy. Add eggs, 1 at a time, beating well after each addition; beat in the melted chocolate and vanilla. In another bowl, whisk together flour, cocoa, baking powder and salt; stir into creamed mixture. Fold in 1 cup miniature marshmallows.

3. Spread the batter over graham cracker crust. Top with 1 cup marshmallows and broken graham crackers. Bake until center is set, 18-22 minutes (do not overbake).

1 BROWNIE: 215 cal., 10g fat (6g sat. fat), 44mg chol., 157mg sod., 30g carb. (17g sugars, 1g fiber), 3g pro.

FROSTED OATMEAL COOKIES

A woman in my small Iowa hometown sold these cookies. When my grandmother asked her for the recipe, the woman agreed to give it to her if she promised not to make them until the woman was too old to sell them. Grandmother kept her promise, and this special recipe has been a family favorite for years.
—*Bonnie Capper-Eckstein, Maple Grove, MN*

PREP: 45 MIN. + CHILLING • **BAKE:** 10 MIN./BATCH + COOLING • **MAKES:** ABOUT 4 DOZEN

1   **cup butter, softened**
2   **cups packed brown sugar**
2   **large eggs, room temperature**
2   **cups all-purpose flour**
2   **cups quick-cooking oats**
1   **tsp. baking soda**
1   **tsp. salt**
1   **tsp. ground allspice**
1   **tsp. ground cinnamon**
¼   **tsp. ground cloves**
1   **cup raisins**
1   **cup chopped pecans, optional**

FROSTING
5   **cups confectioners' sugar**
¼   **cup butter, melted**
⅓   **to ½ cup 2% milk**
    White sprinkles, optional

1. Cream butter and brown sugar for 5-7 minutes or until light and fluffy. Beat in eggs. In another bowl, whisk the next 7 ingredients; gradually beat into creamed mixture. Stir in the raisins and, if desired, pecans. Divide dough in half. Shape each into a disk; cover. Refrigerate until firm enough to roll, about 1 hour.

2. Preheat oven to 350°. On a lightly floured surface, roll each portion of dough to ¼-in. thickness. Cut with a floured 2¾-in. round cookie cutter. Place 2 in. apart on greased baking sheets. Bake until light brown, 7-9 minutes. Cool 2 minutes before removing from pans to wire racks to cool completely.

3. For frosting, beat confectioners' sugar, butter and enough milk to reach spreading consistency. Spread over cookies. If desired, top with white sprinkles.

1 COOKIE: 164 cal., 5g fat (3g sat. fat), 20mg chol., 116mg sod., 29g carb. (22g sugars, 1g fiber), 1g pro.

FROM GRANDMA'S KITCHEN: Are your oatmeal cookies too crunchy and hard after baking? Overmixing is usually the culprit when you end up with dry, tough cookies. Mix the ingredients at a slow speed, or better yet, mix by hand with a rubber spatula or wooden spoon just until the ingredients are combined. Also, when a cookie recipe calls for butter, don't substitute shortening, which can produce a drier cookie.

FAMILY TREE FUDGY BROWNIES

Personalized with names, these rich brownies with a
gooey marshmallow layer will surely be a hit with the families
you know. Mine, for one, absolutely loves chocolate!

—*Latressa Allen, Fort Worth, TX*

PREP: 20 MIN. + CHILLING • BAKE: 30 MIN. + COOLING • MAKES: 2 DOZEN

4 oz. unsweetened
  chocolate, chopped
1 cup butter, cubed
2 cups sugar
1 cup all-purpose flour
⅛ tsp. salt
4 large eggs, room
  temperature, beaten
1 cup chopped pecans
3 cups miniature
  marshmallows

FROSTING

2 oz. unsweetened
  chocolate
½ cup butter, cubed
½ cup evaporated milk
5 cups confectioners' sugar
½ tsp. vanilla extract
1 can (16 oz.) vanilla
  frosting or 2 cups vanilla
  frosting of your choice
  Liquid or paste food
  coloring, optional

1. In a large saucepan, heat chocolate and butter until melted;
remove from the heat. Combine sugar, flour and salt; stir into
chocolate mixture. Add eggs and pecans. Pour into a greased
13x9-in. baking pan.

2. Bake at 350° for 25-30 minutes or until brownies begin to pull
away from sides of pan. Sprinkle with marshmallows; return to
oven for 2-3 minutes or until marshmallows are melted. Spread
with a knife; cool.

3. In saucepan, heat chocolate, butter and milk, until chocolate
and butter are melted. Remove from heat; stir in confectioners'
sugar and vanilla until smooth.

4. Frost brownies. Refrigerate overnight. Cut into bars. Cut a
small hole in the corner of a pastry or plastic bag. Tint vanilla
frosting with food coloring if desired; place frosting in the bag.
Pipe names on brownies.

1 SERVING: 450 cal., 21g fat (10g sat. fat), 68mg chol., 186mg sod.,
65g carb. (55g sugars, 1g fiber), 3g pro.

FROM GRANDMA'S KITCHEN: Do your brownies crumble when cut?
Next time be sure to allow the brownies to cool completely before
cutting them. Use a sawing motion when cutting and warm the
blade of the knife in hot water, dry, then cut. Clean and rewarm the
knife after each cut.

GRANDMA'S RASPBERRY RUGELACH

I remember sitting on the couch in my great-grandmother's house with a pad and pen as she told me each ingredient and measurement for her special rugelach. Some of the ingredients are different from the typical version. My whole family cherishes this heirloom recipe.

—Dalya Rubin, Boca Raton, FL

PREP: 45 MIN. + CHILLING • BAKE: 25 MIN./BATCH + COOLING • MAKES: ABOUT 5 DOZEN

1½ cups margarine, softened
⅓ cup sugar
3 tsp. vanilla extract
 Pinch salt
1 cup heavy whipping cream
4 to 4½ cups all-purpose flour
1 cup seedless raspberry jam

OPTIONAL GLAZE
1 cup confectioners' sugar
4 tsp. 2% milk

1. In a large bowl, beat margarine, sugar, vanilla and salt on medium-low until combined. Slowly beat in whipping cream. Gradually beat in enough flour until dough is no longer sticky. Divide dough into 4 portions, then flatten into disks. Wrap; refrigerate at least 2 hours or overnight.

2. Preheat oven to 350°. On a lightly floured surface, roll each portion of dough into a 12-in. circle; spread each with ¼ cup raspberry jam. Cut each circle into 16 wedges.

3. Gently roll up wedges from the wide ends. Place 2 in. apart on parchment-lined baking sheets, point side down. Bake for 25-30 minutes or until light golden. Remove to wire racks to cool.

4. If desired, combine confectioners' sugar and milk until smooth. Drizzle over cooled rugelach.

1 COOKIE: 96 cal., 6g fat (2g sat. fat), 4mg chol., 53mg sod., 10g carb. (4g sugars, 0 fiber), 1g pro.

JELLY BEAN COOKIES

It's a family tradition for my grandmother and me to make these colorful cookies every year for the holidays.

—Cheyenne Fink, Pleasantville, PA

PREP: 15 MIN. • BAKE: 10 MIN./BATCH • MAKES: ABOUT 2½ DOZEN

½ cup shortening
¾ cup sugar
1 large egg, room temperature
2 Tbsp. 2% milk
1 tsp. vanilla extract
1½ cups all-purpose flour
1¼ tsp. baking powder
½ tsp. salt
¾ cup small jelly beans

1. Preheat oven to 350°. In a large bowl, cream shortening and sugar until blended. Beat in egg, milk and vanilla. In another bowl, whisk flour, baking powder and salt; gradually beat into creamed mixture. Stir in jelly beans.

2. Drop dough by tablespoonfuls 1½ in. apart onto greased or parchment-lined baking sheets. Bake 8-10 minutes or until edges are light golden brown. Cool on pans 2 minutes. Remove to wire racks to cool.

1 COOKIE: 91 cal., 3g fat (1g sat. fat), 6mg chol., 61mg sod., 15g carb. (9g sugars, 0 fiber), 1g pro.

CARAMEL PEANUT BARS

CARAMEL PEANUT BARS

Rich chocolate, crunchy peanuts and gooey caramel peek out
from between golden oat and crumb layers. Delicious!
—*Ardyce Piehl, Wisconsin Dells, WI*

PREP: 25 MIN. • **BAKE:** 15 MIN. + COOLING • **MAKES:** 3 DOZEN

1½ cups quick-cooking oats
1½ cups all-purpose flour
1¼ cups packed brown sugar
¾ tsp. baking soda
¼ tsp. salt
¾ cup butter, melted
1 pkg. (14 oz.) caramels
½ cup heavy whipping
   cream
1½ cups semisweet
   chocolate chips
¾ cup chopped peanuts

1. In a bowl, combine the first 5 ingredients; stir in butter. Set aside 1 cup for topping. Press remaining mixture into a greased 13x9-in. baking pan. Bake at 350° for 10 minutes or until lightly browned.

2. In a heavy saucepan or microwave, melt caramels with cream, stirring often. Sprinkle the chocolate chips and peanuts over the crust; top with caramel mixture. Sprinkle with the reserved oat mixture. Bake for 15-20 minutes or until topping is golden brown. Cool completely on a wire rack. Cut into bars.

1 BAR: 197 cal., 10g fat (5g sat. fat), 16mg chol., 113mg sod., 27g carb. (19g sugars, 1g fiber), 3g pro.

SOFT CORNMEAL COOKIES

If you haven't tried cornmeal cookies before, here's your chance. Use this versatile
cookie as the base for an ice cream sandwich or crumble over strawberry shortcake.
—*Gina Martin, Spooner, WI*

TAKES: 30 MIN. • **MAKES:** ABOUT 2 DOZEN

1½ cups yellow cornmeal
1½ cups all-purpose flour
½ cup plus ⅓ cup sugar
½ cup nonfat dry milk
   powder
3 tsp. baking powder
½ tsp. salt
½ cup cold butter
¼ cup cream cheese
¾ cup 2% milk
½ cup chopped walnuts,
   optional

1. Preheat oven to 375°. In a large bowl, combine cornmeal, flour, ½ cup sugar, powdered milk, baking powder and salt. Cut in the butter and cream cheese until crumbly. Add milk and, if desired, walnuts; stir until blended. Shape into 1½-in. balls. Place the remaining ⅓ cup sugar in a shallow bowl; roll cookies in sugar.

2. Place cookies 2 in. apart on greased baking sheets. Flatten slightly with bottom of a drinking glass dipped in sugar. Bake 13-15 minutes or until edges are light brown. Remove to wire racks to cool.

1 COOKIE: 143 cal., 5g fat (3g sat. fat), 14mg chol., 151mg sod., 22g carb. (8g sugars, 1g fiber), 2g pro.

ROASTED STRAWBERRY
SHEET CAKE, PAGE 239

GRANDMA'S FAVORITE

CAKES & PIES

Forget boxed caked mixes or store-bought pies.
When you want to create oven-fresh, made-at-home
bakery pleasures just like Grandma's, turn to these
old-fashioned standbys. From flaky slices of bubbly,
fruit-filled pies to buttery cakes swirled with dreamy
frosting, there's something here for every sweet tooth.

CONTEST-WINNING CHOCOLATE POTATO CAKE

I won grand champion honors in a potato festival baking contest with this moist chocolate cake. The icing recipe can be doubled for real sweet tooths. A great-grandma, I've spent over 85 years on the farm.
—*Catherine Hahn, Winamac, IN*

PREP: 40 MIN. • **BAKE:** 25 MIN. + COOLING • **MAKES:** 12 SERVINGS

1 cup butter, softened
2 cups sugar
2 large eggs, room temperature
1 cup cold mashed potatoes (without added milk and butter)
1 tsp. vanilla extract
2 cups all-purpose flour
½ cup baking cocoa
1 tsp. baking soda
1 cup whole milk
1 cup chopped walnuts or pecans

CARAMEL ICING

½ cup butter, cubed
1 cup packed brown sugar
¼ cup evaporated milk
2 cups confectioners' sugar
½ tsp. vanilla extract

1. In a large bowl, cream butter and sugar for 5-7 minutes or until light and fluffy. Add 1 egg at a time, beating well after each addition. Add potatoes and vanilla. Combine the flour, cocoa and baking soda; gradually add to creamed mixture alternately with milk, beating well after each addition. Stir in nuts.

2. Pour into 2 greased and floured 9-in. round baking pans. Bake at 350° until a toothpick inserted in the center comes out clean, 25-30 minutes. Cool for 10 minutes before removing from pans to wire racks to cool completely.

3. For icing, in a saucepan over low heat, cook butter and brown sugar until the butter is melted and mixture is smooth. Stir in evaporated milk; bring to a boil, stirring constantly. Remove from the heat; cool to room temperature. Stir in confectioners' sugar and vanilla until smooth. Spread between layers and over top of the cake.

1 PIECE: 671 cal., 31g fat (15g sat. fat), 101mg chol., 374mg sod., 94g carb. (71g sugars, 2g fiber), 8g pro.

AUNT LOU'S FRESH APPLE CAKE

My Great-Aunt Lou made a luscious apple cake that became a family tradition. My mom makes it for our annual beach trip to the Outer Banks in North Carolina.
—*Cristy King, Scott Depot, WV*

PREP: 15 MIN. • **BAKE:** 50 MIN. + COOLING • **MAKES:** 12 SERVINGS

2 cups sugar
1 cup canola oil
3 large eggs, room temperature
2 tsp. vanilla extract
3 cups all-purpose flour
1 tsp. salt
1 tsp. baking powder
3 cups chopped peeled apples (about 3 medium)
Confectioners' sugar

1. Preheat oven to 350°. Grease and flour a 10-in. fluted tube pan.

2. In a large bowl, beat the sugar, oil, eggs and vanilla until well blended. In another bowl, whisk flour, salt and baking powder; gradually beat into oil mixture. Stir in apples. Transfer batter to prepared pan.

3. Bake until a toothpick inserted in the center comes out clean, 50-60 minutes. Cool in pan 10 minutes. Run a knife around sides and center of tube pan. Remove the cake to a wire rack to cool completely. Dust with confectioners' sugar.

1 PIECE: 445 cal., 20g fat (2g sat. fat), 47mg chol., 249mg sod., 62g carb. (37g sugars, 2g fiber), 5g pro.

BUTTERMILK CAKE WITH CARAMEL ICING

Moist and tender, this cake melts in your mouth. It's been a favorite cake recipe of my family since the 1970s and it goes over really well at church potlucks and bake sales.

—Anna Jean Allen, West Liberty, KY

PREP: 35 MIN. • **BAKE:** 45 MIN. + COOLING • **MAKES:** 16 SERVINGS

1 **cup butter, softened**	**ICING**
2⅓ **cups sugar**	¼ **cup butter, cubed**
1½ **tsp. vanilla extract**	½ **cup packed brown sugar**
3 **large eggs, room temperature**	⅓ **cup heavy whipping cream**
3 **cups all-purpose flour**	1 **cup confectioners' sugar**
1 **tsp. baking powder**	
½ **tsp. baking soda**	
1 **cup buttermilk**	

1. Preheat oven to 350°. Grease and flour a 10-in. fluted tube pan.

2. Cream butter and sugar until light and fluffy, 5-7 minutes. Beat in vanilla; add eggs, 1 at a time, beating well after each addition. In another bowl, whisk together the flour, baking powder and baking soda; add to creamed mixture alternately with buttermilk (batter will be thick). Transfer to prepared pan.

3. Bake until a toothpick inserted in the center comes out clean, 45-50 minutes. Cool in pan 10 minutes before removing to a wire rack to cool completely.

4. For icing, in a small saucepan, combine butter, brown sugar and cream; bring to a boil over medium heat, stirring constantly. Remove from heat; cool 5-10 minutes. Gradually beat in the confectioners' sugar; spoon over cake.

1 PIECE: 419 cal., 17g fat (11g sat. fat), 79mg chol., 230mg sod., 63g carb. (44g sugars, 1g fiber), 4g pro.

GRANDMA'S SECRET

Ensure your cake comes out of the pan cleanly by greasing the pan well. Always use shortening to grease fluted tube pans, even ones with nonstick coating. Then dust with flour and tap away the excess.

ROASTED STRAWBERRY SHEET CAKE

PICTURED ON PAGE 234

My Grandma Gigi loved summer berry cakes. Almost any time I'd call her during the warmer months, she'd invite me over to taste her latest masterpiece. This cake is an ode to her.

—*Kristin Bowers, Rancho Palos Verdes, CA*

PREP: 1 HOUR • BAKE: 30 MIN. + COOLING • MAKES: 24 SERVINGS

4 lbs. halved fresh
   strawberries
½ cup sugar

CAKE
1 cup butter, softened
1½ cups sugar
2 large eggs, room
   temperature
2 tsp. almond extract
3 cups all-purpose flour
3 tsp. baking powder
2 tsp. salt
1 cup 2% milk
¼ cup turbinado (washed
   raw) sugar

1. Preheat oven to 350°. Place strawberries on a parchment-lined rimmed baking sheet. Sprinkle with sugar and toss to coat. Bake until just tender, 35-40 minutes. Cool slightly.

2. Meanwhile, grease a 15x10x1-in. baking pan. In a large bowl, cream butter and sugar until light and fluffy, 5-7 minutes. Add eggs, 1 at a time, beating well after each addition. Beat in extract. In another bowl, whisk the flour, baking powder and salt; add to creamed mixture alternately with milk, beating well after each addition (batter may appear curdled).

3. Transfer the batter to prepared pan. Top with 3 cups roasted strawberries; sprinkle with turbinado sugar. Reserve remaining strawberries for serving. Bake until a toothpick inserted in center comes out clean, 30-35 minutes. Cool completely in pan on a wire rack. Serve with reserved roasted strawberries.

1 PIECE: 235 cal., 9g fat (5g sat. fat), 37mg chol., 329mg sod., 37g carb. (23g sugars, 2g fiber), 3g pro.

GRANDMA'S LEMON POPPY SEED CAKE

This is from a collection of family recipes. My granddaughter, Riley, likes that it tastes like lemons and is refreshingly sweet. It's always wonderful.

—*Phyllis Harmon, Nelson, WI*

PREP: 20 MIN. • BAKE: 30 MIN. + COOLING • MAKES: 15 SERVINGS

1 pkg. lemon cake mix
   (regular size)
1 pkg. (3.4 oz.) instant
   vanilla pudding mix
4 large eggs, room
   temperature
1 cup water
½ cup canola oil
¼ cup poppy seeds

DRIZZLE
2 cups confectioners' sugar
2 Tbsp. water
2 Tbsp. lemon juice

1. In a large bowl, combine the cake mix, pudding mix, eggs, water and oil; beat on low speed for 30 seconds. Beat on medium for 2 minutes. Fold in poppy seeds. Transfer to a greased and floured 13x9-in. baking pan. Bake at 350° for 30-35 minutes or until a toothpick inserted in the center comes out clean. Cool on a wire rack.

2. For drizzle, in a small bowl, combine the confectioners' sugar, water and lemon juice; drizzle over cake.

1 PIECE: 320 cal., 12g fat (2g sat. fat), 56mg chol., 335mg sod., 51g carb. (36g sugars, 0 fiber), 3g pro.

GRAN'S
APPLE CAKE

GRAN'S APPLE CAKE

My grandmother occasionally brought over this wonderful cake warm from the oven.
This recipe is such a treasure. Even though I've lightened it up, it's still a family favorite.
—Lauris Conrad, Turlock, CA

PREP: 20 MIN. • BAKE: 35 MIN. + COOLING • MAKES: 24 SERVINGS

1⅔ cups sugar
2 large eggs, room
   temperature
½ cup unsweetened
   applesauce
2 Tbsp. canola oil
2 tsp. vanilla extract
2 cups all-purpose flour
2 tsp. baking soda
2 tsp. ground cinnamon
¾ tsp. salt
6 cups chopped peeled
   tart apples
½ cup chopped pecans

FROSTING
4 oz. reduced-fat cream
   cheese
2 Tbsp. butter, softened
1 tsp. vanilla extract
1 cup confectioners' sugar

1. Preheat oven to 350°. Coat a 13x9-in. baking pan with cooking spray.

2. In a large bowl, beat sugar, eggs, applesauce, oil and vanilla until well blended. In another bowl, whisk flour, baking soda, cinnamon and salt; gradually beat into sugar mixture. Fold in apples and pecans.

3. Transfer to prepared pan. Bake 35-40 minutes or until top is golden brown and a toothpick inserted in center comes out clean. Cool completely in pan on a wire rack.

4. In a small bowl, beat cream cheese, butter and vanilla until smooth. Gradually beat in confectioners' sugar (mixture will be soft). Spread over cake. Refrigerate leftovers.

1 PIECE: 181 cal., 5g fat (2g sat. fat), 21mg chol., 213mg sod., 32g carb. (22g sugars, 1g fiber), 2g pro. DIABETIC EXCHANGES: 2 starch, 1 fat.

PENNSYLVANIA DUTCH FUNNY CAKE

I can still remember my grandma serving this delicious cake on the big wooden table in her farm
kitchen. Every time I bake this unique dessert, it takes me back to those special days at Grandma's.
—Diane Ganssle, Bethlehem, PA

PREP: 20 MIN. • BAKE: 40 MIN. • MAKES: 2 CAKES (8 SERVINGS EACH)

2 cups sugar, divided
½ cup baking cocoa
1½ cups whole milk, divided
2 sheets refrigerated
   pie crust
2 cups all-purpose flour
2 tsp. baking powder
¼ tsp. salt
1 large egg, room
   temperature
2 Tbsp. shortening
1 tsp. vanilla extract
   Whipped cream, optional

In a small saucepan, combine 1 cup of sugar and cocoa. Blend in ½ cup milk. Cook and stir over medium heat until mixture comes to a boil. Cook and stir until thickened, about 2 minutes. Unroll crusts into 9-in. pie plates; flute edges. Pour mixture into crusts, tipping to coat crusts halfway up the sides; set aside. In a bowl, combine flour, baking powder, salt and remaining sugar. Add the egg, shortening, vanilla and remaining milk; beat until smooth. Starting at the edges, spoon the batter into crusts, completely covering the chocolate. Bake at 350° for 40 minutes or until a toothpick inserted in the center comes out clean. Serve warm or chilled, with whipped cream if desired.

1 PIECE: 314 cal., 10g fat (4g sat. fat), 21mg chol., 203mg sod., 53g carb. (27g sugars, 1g fiber), 4g pro.

GRANDMA'S CARROT CAKE

My grandma was very special to me. She had a big country kitchen that was full of wonderful aromas any time we visited. This was one of her prized cake recipes, and it continues to be a favorite from generation to generation.

—Denise Strasz, Detroit, MI

PREP: 30 MIN. • **BAKE:** 50 MIN. + COOLING • **MAKES:** 16 SERVINGS

2 cups sugar
1½ cups canola oil
4 large eggs, room temperature
2 tsp. vanilla extract
2½ cups all-purpose flour
1½ tsp. baking soda
½ tsp. salt
1 tsp. ground cinnamon
3 cups shredded carrots (about 6 medium)
1 cup chopped walnuts

FROSTING
1 pkg. (8 oz.) cream cheese, softened
¼ cup butter, softened
3 cups confectioners' sugar

1. Preheat oven to 350°. Grease and flour a 10-in. fluted tube pan.

2. Beat first 4 ingredients until well blended. Whisk together the flour, baking soda, salt and cinnamon; gradually beat into sugar mixture. Stir in carrots and walnuts.

3. Transfer to prepared pan. Bake until a toothpick inserted in center comes out clean, 50-60 minutes. Cool in pan 10 minutes before removing to a wire rack; cool completely.

4. For frosting, beat cream cheese and butter until smooth. Gradually beat in confectioners' sugar. Spread over cake.

1 PIECE: 593 cal., 35g fat (7g sat. fat), 68mg chol., 292mg sod., 67g carb. (49g sugars, 2g fiber), 6g pro.

FROM GRANDMA'S KITCHEN: Cakes made with oil tend to retain more moisture than cakes made with butter or shortening. Canola oil is best for this cake because it has a nice neutral flavor that doesn't interfere or clash with any of the other flavors in the cake.

GINGERBREAD PUDDING CAKE

Sweet spices and a half cup of molasses give my dessert a delightful old-fashioned flavor. It's pretty topped with a dollop of whipped cream.
—*Barbara Cook, Yuma, AZ*

PREP: 20 MIN. • **COOK:** 2 HOURS + STANDING • **MAKES:** 8 SERVINGS

½ cup molasses	½ tsp. ground cinnamon
1 cup water	½ tsp. ground ginger
¼ cup butter, softened	¼ tsp. ground allspice
¼ cup sugar	⅛ tsp. ground nutmeg
1 large egg white, room temperature	½ cup chopped pecans
1 tsp. vanilla extract	6 Tbsp. brown sugar
1¼ cups all-purpose flour	¾ cup hot water
¾ tsp. baking soda	⅔ cup butter, melted
¼ tsp. salt	Sweetened whipped cream, optional

1. Mix molasses and 1 cup water. Cream softened butter and sugar until light and fluffy, 5-7 minutes; beat in egg white and vanilla. In another bowl, whisk together flour, baking soda, salt and spices; add to creamed mixture alternately with molasses mixture, beating well after each addition. Fold in pecans.

2. Pour into a greased 3-qt. slow cooker. Sprinkle with brown sugar. Mix hot water and melted butter; pour over the batter (do not stir).

3. Cook, covered, on high until a toothpick inserted in center comes out clean, 2-2½ hours. Turn off slow cooker; let stand 15 minutes. If desired, serve with whipped cream.

1 SERVING: 431 cal., 26g fat (14g sat. fat), 56mg chol., 377mg sod., 48g carb. (32g sugars, 1g fiber), 3g pro.

FRESH CHERRY PIE

Want to learn how to make cherry pie from scratch? Here's the place to start. This ruby-red pie is just sweet enough, with a hint of almond flavor and a good level of cinnamon. The cherries peeking out of the lattice crust makes it so pretty, too.

—*Josie Bochek, Sturgeon Bay, WI*

PREP: 25 MIN. • BAKE: 55 MIN. + COOLING • MAKES: 8 SERVINGS

1¼ cups sugar
⅓ cup cornstarch
1 cup cherry juice blend
4 cups fresh tart cherries, pitted or frozen pitted tart cherries, thawed
½ tsp. ground cinnamon
¼ tsp. ground nutmeg
¼ tsp. almond extract

DOUGH
2 cups all-purpose flour
½ tsp. salt
⅔ cup shortening
5 to 7 Tbsp. cold water
1 large egg, beaten, optional

1. Preheat oven to 425°. In a large saucepan, combine sugar and cornstarch; gradually stir in cherry juice until smooth. Bring to a boil; cook and stir until thickened, about 2 minutes. Remove from the heat. Add cherries, cinnamon, nutmeg and extract; set aside.

2. In a large bowl, combine flour and salt; cut in shortening until crumbly. Gradually add cold water, tossing with a fork until a ball forms. Divide the dough in half so that 1 ball is slightly larger than the other.

3. On a lightly floured surface, roll out larger ball to fit a 9-in. pie plate. Transfer dough to pie plate; trim even with edge of plate. Add filling. Roll out remaining dough; make a lattice crust. Trim, seal and flute edge. If desired, brush with egg wash.

4. Bake for 10 minutes. Reduce heat to 375°; bake until crust is golden brown, 45-50 minutes. Cool on a wire rack.

1 PIECE: 466 cal., 17g fat (4g sat. fat), 23mg chol., 161mg sod., 73g carb. (41g sugars, 2g fiber), 5g pro.

"Awesome! An old-fashioned cherry pie from scratch. I always loved the combo of cherry and almond together. Simply the best."
—SUEFALK, TASTEOFHOME.COM

MOM'S CUSTARD PIE

Just a single bite of this traditional custard pie takes me back to the days when Mom would fix this pie for Dad, Grandfather and me. Mom also regularly prepared pies for large gatherings. This dessert was often requested.
—*Barbara Hyatt, Folsom, CA*

PREP: 25 MIN. + CHILLING • **BAKE:** 40 MIN. + COOLING • **MAKES:** 8 SERVINGS

Dough for single-crust pie
4 **large eggs, room temperature**
½ **cup sugar**
¼ **tsp. salt**
1 **tsp. vanilla extract**
2½ **cups 2% milk**
¼ **tsp. ground nutmeg**

1. On a lightly floured surface, roll dough to a ⅛-in.-thick circle; transfer to a 9-in. pie plate. Trim crust to ½ in. beyond rim of plate; flute edge. Refrigerate 30 minutes. Preheat oven to 425°. Line the unpricked crust with a double thickness of foil. Fill crust with pie weights, dried beans or uncooked rice. Bake on a lower oven rack until edge is light golden brown, 15-20 minutes. Remove foil and weights; bake until bottom is golden brown, 3-6 minutes longer. Cool on a wire rack. Reduce oven setting to 350°.

2. Separate 1 egg; set the white aside in a large bowl and let stand 15 minutes. In a small bowl, beat yolk and remaining eggs just until combined. Blend in the sugar, salt and vanilla. Stir in milk. Beat reserved egg white until stiff peaks form; fold into egg mixture.

3. Carefully pour into crust. Cover edge of pie with foil. Bake for 25 minutes. Remove foil; bake until a knife inserted in the center comes out clean, 15-20 minutes longer. Cool on a wire rack. Sprinkle with nutmeg. Store in the refrigerator.

DOUGH FOR SINGLE-CRUST PIE (9 IN.): Combine 1¼ cups all-purpose flour and ¼ tsp. salt; cut in ½ cup cold butter until crumbly. Gradually add 3-5 Tbsp. ice water, tossing with a fork until the dough holds together when pressed. Shape into a disk; wrap and refrigerate for 1 hour.

1 PIECE: 254 cal., 12g fat (5g sat. fat), 122mg chol., 243mg sod., 29g carb. (17g sugars, 0 fiber), 7g pro.

GERMAN CHOCOLATE CAKE

This cake is my husband's favorite! Every bite has a light crunch from the pecans, a sweet taste of coconut and a drizzle of chocolate.
—*Joyce Platfoot, Wapakoneta, OH*

PREP: 30 MIN. • BAKE: 30 MIN. + COOLING • MAKES: 12 SERVINGS

4 oz. German sweet chocolate, chopped
½ cup water
1 cup butter, softened
2 cups sugar
4 large eggs, separated, room temperature
1 tsp. vanilla extract
2½ cups cake flour
1 tsp. baking soda
½ tsp. salt
1 cup buttermilk

FROSTING

1½ cups sugar
1½ cups evaporated milk
¾ cup butter
5 large egg yolks, room temperature, beaten
2 cups sweetened shredded coconut
1½ cups chopped pecans
1½ tsp. vanilla extract

ICING

1 tsp. shortening
2 oz. semisweet chocolate

1. Line 3 greased 9-in. round baking pans with waxed paper. Grease waxed paper and set aside. In small saucepan, melt chocolate with water over low heat; cool.

2. Preheat oven to 350°. In a large bowl, cream butter and sugar until light and fluffy, 5-7 minutes. Beat in 4 egg yolks, 1 at a time, beating well after each addition. Blend in melted chocolate and vanilla. Combine flour, baking soda and salt; add to the creamed mixture alternately with the buttermilk, beating well after each addition.

3. In a small bowl and with clean beaters, beat the 4 egg whites until stiff peaks form. Fold a fourth of the egg whites into creamed mixture; fold in remaining whites.

4. Pour batter into prepared pans. Bake 24-28 minutes or until a toothpick inserted in center comes out clean. Cool 10 minutes before removing from pans to wire racks to cool completely.

5. For frosting, in a small saucepan, heat sugar, milk, butter and egg yolks over medium-low heat until mixture is thickened and golden brown, stirring constantly. Remove from heat. Stir in coconut, pecans and vanilla. Cool until thick enough to spread. Spread a third of frosting over each cake layer and stack layers.

6. In a microwave, melt chocolate and shortening; stir until smooth. Drizzle over cake.

1 PIECE: 910 cal., 53g fat (28g sat. fat), 237mg chol., 511mg sod., 103g carb. (76g sugars, 4g fiber), 11g pro.

GRANDMA'S SOUR CREAM RAISIN PIE

The aroma of this pie baking in my farm kitchen oven reminds me of my
dear grandma, who made this pretty pie for special occasions.
—*Beverly Medalen, Willow City, ND*

PREP: 30 MIN. • BAKE: 10 MIN. + CHILLING • MAKES: 8 SERVINGS

1 cup raisins
⅔ cup sugar
3 Tbsp. cornstarch
⅛ tsp. salt
⅛ tsp. ground cloves
½ tsp. ground cinnamon
1 cup sour cream
½ cup 2% milk
3 large egg yolks, room
   temperature
½ cup chopped nuts,
   optional
1 pie shell (9 in.), baked

MERINGUE
3 large egg whites, room
   temperature
¼ tsp. salt
6 Tbsp. sugar

1. In a small saucepan, place raisins and enough water to cover; bring to a boil. Remove from the heat; set aside.

2. In a large saucepan, combine the sugar, cornstarch, salt, cloves and cinnamon. Stir in sour cream and milk until smooth. Cook and stir over medium-high heat until thickened and bubbly. Reduce heat to low; cook and stir for 2 minutes longer. Remove from the heat. Stir a small amount of hot filling into egg yolks; return all to the pan, stirring constantly. Bring to a gentle boil; cook and stir for 2 minutes. Remove from the heat.

3. Drain raisins, reserving ½ cup liquid. Gently stir liquid into filling. Add raisins, and nuts if desired. Pour into pie crust.

4. For meringue, in a small bowl, beat egg whites and salt on medium speed until soft peaks form. Gradually beat in sugar, 1 Tbsp. at a time, on high until stiff peaks form. Spread over hot filling, sealing edge to crust.

5. Bake at 350° for 15 minutes or until golden brown. Cool on a wire rack for 1 hour; refrigerate for 1-2 hours before serving. Refrigerate leftovers.

1 PIECE: 381 cal., 15g fat (7g sat. fat), 82mg chol., 253mg sod., 58g carb. (40g sugars, 1g fiber), 5g pro.

FROM GRANDMA'S KITCHEN: For the strongest and most stable meringue, add ⅛ tsp. cream of tartar for every egg white before beating—it's an acid that stabilizes the egg white. If you don't have any on hand, use ½ tsp. lemon juice for every egg white. (Or if you have a copper-lined bowl, using that will produce the same effect.)

THE BEST SWEET POTATO PIE

I love this recipe's rich sweet potato flavor and irresistibly buttery crust.
Sour cream makes the filling super smooth, and the brown sugar and spices
make it extra cozy. There's no doubt that this is the best sweet potato pie!
—*Shannon Norris, Cudahy, WI*

PREP: 1½ HOURS + CHILLING • **BAKE:** 35 MIN. + COOLING • **MAKES:** 8 SERVINGS

CRUST
- 1 **large egg yolk**
- ¼ to ½ **cup ice water, divided**
- 2½ **cups all-purpose flour**
- 3 **Tbsp. sugar**
- ½ **tsp. salt**
- ½ **cup cold shortening, cubed**
- ½ **cup cold butter, cubed**

FILLING
- 2½ **lbs. sweet potatoes**
- ⅔ **cup packed brown sugar**
- ½ **cup sour cream**
- 3 **large eggs, lightly beaten**
- ⅓ **cup butter, melted**
- 1 **Tbsp. bourbon**
- 2 **tsp. vanilla extract**
- 1½ **tsp. ground cinnamon**
- ½ **tsp. ground nutmeg**
- ½ **tsp. salt**
  Optional toppings: Whipped cream and sugared cranberries

1. In a small bowl, mix egg yolk with ¼ cup ice water; set aside. Place the flour, sugar and salt in a food processor; pulse until blended. Add shortening and butter; pulse until shortening and butter are the size of peas. While pulsing, add egg yolk mixture. Add just enough of remaining ice water to form moist crumbs. Divide dough in half. Shape each into a disk; wrap and refrigerate 1 hour or overnight.

2. Preheat oven to 400°. Scrub the sweet potatoes; place in a 13x9-in. baking pan with 1½ cups water. Bake 45-50 minutes or until tender. Meanwhile, on a lightly floured surface, roll 1 disk of dough to a ⅛-in.-thick circle; transfer to a 9-in. deep-dish pie plate. Trim crust to ½ in. beyond rim of plate; flute edge. Roll remaining disk to ⅛-in. thickness; cut into desired shapes with floured 1-in. cookie cutters. Place on a parchment-lined baking sheet. Refrigerate crust and cutouts for at least 30 minutes.

3. Peel potatoes when they are cool enough to handle; place in a food processor. Pulse to coarsely mash. Add brown sugar and the next 8 ingredients; blend until smooth. Pour filling into chilled crust. Bake on lowest oven rack 15 minutes. Reduce oven setting to 350°; bake until center is just set, 20-25 minutes. Bake crust cutouts on an upper oven rack until golden brown, 10-12 minutes. Cool on a wire rack; decorate the pie with cutouts and toppings as desired.

1 PIECE: 726 cal., 37g fat (18g sat. fat), 147mg chol., 500mg sod., 88g carb. (38g sugars, 6g fiber), 10g pro.

APPLE CRANBERRY SLAB PIE

My husband loves pie, so I made one with apples, raspberries and cranberries. It's so good, I bend the rules and let the grandkids have it for breakfast.
—*Brenda Smith, Curran, MI*

PREP: 45 MIN. • BAKE: 40 MIN. + COOLING • MAKES: 15 SERVINGS

Dough for 2 double-crust pies
1½ cups sugar
¼ cup all-purpose flour
4 medium tart apples, peeled and sliced (about 4½ cups)
4 cups frozen or fresh raspberries
2 cups fresh or frozen cranberries
2 tsp. grated orange zest
½ cup orange juice
1 tsp. ground nutmeg
1 tsp. ground cinnamon
Optional: Additional orange juice and sugar

1. Divide dough into 2 portions so that 1 is slightly larger than the other; wrap and refrigerate 1 hour or overnight.

2. In a Dutch oven, mix sugar and flour; stir in fruit, orange zest, orange juice and spices. Bring to a boil over medium-high heat. Reduce heat; simmer, uncovered, 10-12 minutes or until apples are tender and juices are thickened, stirring occasionally. Cool mixture slightly.

3. Preheat oven to 375°. Roll out larger portion of dough between 2 pieces of waxed paper into a 16x12-in. rectangle. Remove top sheet of waxed paper; place a 13x9-in. baking pan upside down over crust. Lifting with waxed paper, carefully invert crust into pan. Remove waxed paper; press crust onto bottom and up sides of pan. Add filling.

4. On a well-floured surface, roll the remaining dough into a 14x10-in. rectangle; cut into ¾-in.-wide strips. Arrange strips over filling, sealing ends to bottom crust. If desired, brush crust with additional orange juice; sprinkle with additional sugar.

5. Bake 40-50 minutes or until crust is golden brown and filling is bubbly. Cool on a wire rack.

DOUGH FOR 2 DOUBLE-CRUST PIES (9 IN.): In a large bowl, combine 4½ cups all-purpose flour, 1 Tbsp. sugar and 2 tsp. salt; cut in 1¾ cups shortening until crumbly. Whisk 1 large egg, 1 Tbsp. white vinegar and ½ cup ice water; gradually add to flour mixture, tossing with a fork until dough holds together when pressed.

1 PIECE: 478 cal., 23g fat (6g sat. fat), 12mg chol., 322mg sod., 62g carb. (28g sugars, 3g fiber), 5g pro.

AUNT MURNA'S JAM CAKE

I remember Aunt Murna telling me that she created her jam cake recipe as a young girl.
She made improvements over the years, such as soaking the raisins in
crushed pineapple. This cake is a favorite at our annual family reunions.
—*Eddie Robinson, Lawrenceburg, KY*

PREP: 20 MIN. + SOAKING • BAKE: 50 MIN. + COOLING • MAKES: 16 SERVINGS

1 cup raisins
1 can (8 oz.) crushed
   pineapple, undrained
1 cup butter, softened
1 cup sugar
4 large eggs, room
   temperature
1 jar (12 oz.) blackberry
   jam or 1 cup homemade
   blackberry jam
⅔ cup buttermilk
2½ cups all-purpose flour
⅓ cup baking cocoa
1 tsp. baking soda
1 tsp. ground cinnamon
1 tsp. ground nutmeg
½ tsp. ground cloves
1 cup chopped pecans

CARAMEL ICING
1 cup butter, cubed
2 cups packed brown sugar
½ cup 2% milk
3½ to 4 cups sifted
   confectioners' sugar

1. Soak raisins in pineapple and juice several hours or overnight.

2. In a large bowl, cream butter and sugar until light and fluffy, 5-7 minutes. Add the eggs, 1 at a time, beating well after each addition. Add jam and buttermilk; beat until well blended. Sift together dry ingredients; add to batter. Beat on low just until combined. Stir in the raisins, pineapple and pecans.

3. Pour into 2 greased and floured 9-in. round baking pans. Bake at 350° until a toothpick inserted in the center comes out clean, about 50 minutes. Cool in pans for 10 minutes before removing to wire racks.

4. For icing, melt butter in a saucepan over medium heat. Stir in brown sugar and milk; bring to a boil. Remove from the heat. Cool just until warm; beat in enough confectioners' sugar for icing to reach spreading consistency. Add more sugar for thicker icing or more milk to thin it. Frost cooled cake.

1 PIECE: 694 cal., 30g fat (15g sat. fat), 116mg chol., 353mg sod., 105g carb. (83g sugars, 2g fiber), 6g pro.

BUTTERMILK PECAN PIE

Here is the treasured "golden oldie" that my grandmother made whenever we'd come to visit. Grandma grew her own pecans—we never tired of cracking and shelling them when we knew we'd be treated to her special pie!

—Mildred Sherrer, Fort Worth, TX

PREP: 15 MIN. • **BAKE:** 55 MIN. + COOLING • **MAKES:** 8 SERVINGS

- ½ cup butter, softened
- 2 cups sugar
- 5 large eggs, room temperature
- 2 Tbsp. all-purpose flour
- 2 Tbsp. lemon juice
- 1 tsp. vanilla extract
- 1 cup buttermilk
- 1 cup chopped pecans
  Dough for single-crust deep-dish pie

1. Preheat oven to 325°. In a bowl, cream butter and sugar until light and fluffy, 5-7 minutes. Add eggs, 1 at a time, beating well after each addition. Blend in flour, lemon juice and vanilla. Stir in buttermilk and pecans.

2. On a lightly floured surface, roll dough to a ⅛-in.-thick circle; transfer to a 9-in. deep-dish pie plate. Trim crust to ½ in. beyond rim of plate; flute edge.

3. Add filling. Bake until set, 55-60 minutes. Cool on a wire rack. Store in the refrigerator.

DOUGH FOR SINGLE-CRUST PIE (9 IN.): Combine 1½ cups of all-purpose flour and ¼ tsp. salt; cut in ⅔ cup cold butter until crumbly. Gradually add 3-6 Tbsp. ice water, tossing with a fork until the dough holds together when pressed. Shape into a disk; wrap and refrigerate 1 hour.

1 PIECE: 691 cal., 41g fat (20g sat. fat), 191mg chol., 401mg sod., 75g carb. (53g sugars, 2g fiber), 9g pro.

GRANDMA'S SECRET

Once cooled, this pecan pie should be kept in the refrigerator. Pecan pie can be left at room temperature for serving for about 2 hours. After that, it's best to store it in the refrigerator. Cover to keep the pie fresh.

BLACKBERRY-ORANGE CAKE

My grandmother made luscious fruit pies and cobblers using blackberries from her garden.
I decided to follow her lead and create a blackberry cake that's always lovely with a summer meal.
—*Lisa Varner, El Paso, TX*

PREP: 20 MIN. • BAKE: 40 MIN. + COOLING • MAKES: 10 SERVINGS

- ½ cup butter, softened
- 1 cup sugar, divided
- 1 large egg, room temperature
- 1 tsp. grated orange zest
- 1½ cups plus 1 Tbsp. all-purpose flour, divided
- ½ tsp. baking soda
- ⅛ tsp. salt
- ½ cup sour cream or plain yogurt
- 2 cups fresh blackberries
  Confectioners' sugar, optional

1. Preheat oven to 350°. Grease and flour a 9-in. springform pan.

2. In a large bowl, cream butter and ¾ cup sugar until light and fluffy, 5-7 minutes. Beat in egg and orange zest. In another bowl, whisk 1½ cups flour, baking soda and salt; add to the creamed mixture alternately with sour cream, beating well after each addition. Transfer to prepared pan.

3. In a bowl, toss blackberries with remaining flour; arrange over batter. Sprinkle with the remaining sugar. Bake 40-45 minutes or until a toothpick inserted in the center of cake portion comes out clean.

4. Loosen sides from pan with a knife; remove rim from pan. Cool on a wire rack; serve warm or at room temperature. If desired, dust with confectioners' sugar before serving.

1 PIECE: 274 cal., 12g fat (7g sat. fat), 51mg chol., 177mg sod., 38g carb. (22g sugars, 2g fiber), 4g pro.

MOLASSES PUMPKIN PIE

When our sons come home at Thanksgiving to hunt with their dad, I make this pie recipe from
Grandma Fetting. We celebrate Thanksgiving in our cabin in the North Woods, a 40-year-old tradition.
—*Lois Fetting, Nelson, WI*

PREP: 10 MIN. + CHILLING • BAKE: 40 MIN. + COOLING • MAKES: 8 SERVINGS

- 1 sheet refrigerated pie crust
- 2 large eggs
- ½ cup sugar
- 1 tsp. ground cinnamon
- ½ tsp. salt
- ½ tsp. ground ginger
- ½ tsp. ground nutmeg
- 1 can (15 oz.) pumpkin
- 3 Tbsp. molasses
- ¾ cup evaporated milk
  Whipped topping

1. Unroll crust into a 9-in. pie plate. Trim to ½ in. beyond edge of plate; flute edge. Set aside.

2. In a large bowl, beat the eggs, sugar, cinnamon, salt, ginger and nutmeg. Beat in pumpkin and molasses; gradually add milk. Pour into crust. Cover edge loosely with foil.

3. Bake at 425° for 10 minutes. Remove foil. Reduce heat 350°; bake 28-32 minutes longer or until a knife inserted in the center comes out clean. Cool on a wire rack for 2 hours. Chill until ready to serve. Serve with whipped topping. Refrigerate leftovers.

1 PIECE: 257 cal., 10g fat (5g sat. fat), 66mg chol., 291mg sod., 37g carb. (22g sugars, 2g fiber), 5g pro.

MOM'S PEACH PIE

This pie is overflowing with fresh peach flavor, and the homey streusel topping makes it extra special. Each sweet slice is packed with old-fashioned appeal.
—*Sally Holbrook, Pasadena, CA*

PREP: 25 MIN. • BAKE: 40 MIN. • MAKES: 8 SERVINGS

Dough for single-crust pie
1 **large egg white, lightly beaten**
6 **cups sliced peeled fresh peaches**
2 **Tbsp. plus ¾ cup all-purpose flour, divided**
½ **cup packed brown sugar**
⅓ **cup sugar**
¼ **cup cold butter, cubed**

1. On a lightly floured surface, roll dough to a ⅛-in.-thick circle; transfer to a 9-in. pie plate. Trim crust to ½ in. beyond rim of plate; flute edge. Brush egg white over crust; refrigerate crust while making filling.

2. In a large bowl, combine peaches and 2 Tbsp. flour; toss to coat. In a small bowl, combine the remaining ¾ cup flour and sugars; cut in the butter until mixture resembles fine crumbs. Sprinkle two-thirds into crust; top with peach mixture. Sprinkle with remaining crumb mixture.

3. Bake at 375° for 40-45 minutes or until filling is bubbly and peaches are tender. Cover with foil during the last 15 minutes if pie begins to brown too quickly.

DOUGH FOR SINGLE-CRUST PIE (9 IN.): Combine 1¼ cups all-purpose flour and ¼ tsp. salt; cut in ½ cup cold butter until crumbly. Gradually add 3-5 Tbsp. ice water, tossing with a fork until the dough holds together when pressed. Shape into a disk; wrap and refrigerate 1 hour.

1 PIECE: 404 cal., 18g fat (11g sat. fat), 45mg chol., 212mg sod., 58g carb. (32g sugars, 3g fiber), 5g pro.

"We loved this pie recipe! The only thing I did differently was to sprinkle in some blueberries with the peaches. I will definitely put this in my summer pie rotation!"
—PUNKYJOE81, TASTEOFHOME.COM

OLD-FASHIONED CARROT CAKE
WITH CREAM CHEESE FROSTING

A pleasingly moist cake, this treat is the one I requested that my mom make each year for my birthday. It's dotted with sweet carrots and a hint of cinnamon. The fluffy buttery frosting is scrumptious with chopped walnuts stirred in. One piece of this cake is never enough!

—*Kim Orr, West Grove, PA*

PREP: 30 MIN. • **BAKE:** 35 MIN. + COOLING • **MAKES:** 16 SERVINGS

4 **large eggs, room**
   temperature
2 **cups sugar**
1 **cup canola oil**
2 **cups all-purpose flour**
2 **to 3 tsp. ground cinnamon**
¾ **tsp. baking soda**
½ **tsp. baking powder**
¼ **tsp. salt**
¼ **tsp. ground nutmeg**
2 **cups grated carrots**

FROSTING

½ **cup butter, softened**
3 **oz. cream cheese,**
   softened
1 **tsp. vanilla extract**
3¾ **cups confectioners' sugar**
2 **to 3 Tbsp. 2% milk**
1 **cup chopped walnuts,**
   optional
   Optional: Orange and
   green food coloring

1. In a large bowl, combine the eggs, sugar and oil. Combine the flour, cinnamon, baking soda, baking powder, salt and nutmeg; beat into egg mixture. Stir in carrots.

2. Pour into 2 greased and floured 9-in. round baking pans. Bake at 350° for 35-40 minutes or until a toothpick inserted in center comes out clean. Cool for 10 minutes before removing from pans to wire racks to cool completely.

3. For frosting, in another large bowl, cream butter and cream cheese until light and fluffy, 3-4 minutes. Beat in vanilla. Gradually beat in confectioners' sugar. Add enough milk to achieve desired spreading consistency. Reserve ½ cup frosting for decorating if desired. If desired, stir walnuts into remaining frosting.

4. Spread frosting between layers and over top and sides of cake. If decorating the cake, tint ¼ cup reserved frosting orange and ¼ cup green. Cut a small hole in the corner of pastry or plastic bag; insert #7 round pastry tip. Fill the bag with orange frosting. Pipe 16 carrots on top of cake, so each piece will have a carrot. Using #67 leaf pastry tip and the green frosting, pipe a leaf at the top of each carrot.

5. Store cake in the refrigerator.

1 PIECE: 531 cal., 28g fat (7g sat. fat), 67mg chol., 203mg sod., 68g carb. (54g sugars, 1g fiber), 5g pro.

CAST-IRON CHERRY-BERRY PEACH PIE

I had an overabundant supply of cherries one year, so I adapted several recipes to use them up. I knew this one was a keeper when I received phone calls from my mother and grandmother complimenting me on this pie.
—*Amy Hartke, Elgin, IL*

PREP: 30 MIN. + CHILLING • BAKE: 50 MIN. + COOLING • MAKES: 8 SERVINGS

2½ cups all-purpose flour
2 Tbsp. sugar
½ tsp. salt
1 cup cold butter, cubed
6 to 8 Tbsp. cold water

FILLING
2 cups fresh or frozen sliced peaches, thawed
1¾ cups pitted fresh dark sweet cherries or 1 can (15 oz.) pitted dark sweet cherries, drained
1 cup fresh or frozen blueberries, thawed
1 tsp. vanilla extract
½ tsp. almond extract
1½ cups sugar
¼ cup all-purpose flour
¼ cup quick-cooking tapioca
½ tsp. salt
½ tsp. ground nutmeg
1 Tbsp. butter

1. In a large bowl, mix the flour, sugar and salt; cut in butter until crumbly. Gradually add water, tossing with a fork until the dough holds together when pressed. Divide dough into 2 portions. Shape each into a disk; cover and refrigerate for 1 hour or overnight.

2. In a large bowl, combine peaches, cherries, blueberries and extracts. Combine sugar, flour, tapioca, salt and nutmeg; sprinkle over fruit and gently toss to coat. Let stand for 15 minutes.

3. Preheat oven to 375°. On a lightly floured surface, roll half of dough to a ⅛-in.-thick circle; transfer to a 9-in. cast-iron skillet or other ovenproof skillet. Trim to ½ in. beyond rim of plate. Add filling; dot with butter.

4. Roll remaining dough to a ⅛-in.-thick circle; cut into ½-in.-wide strips. Arrange over filling in a lattice pattern. Trim and seal strips to edge of bottom crust; flute edge. Bake until the crust is golden brown and filling is bubbly, 50-55 minutes. Cover edge with foil during the last 15 minutes to prevent overbrowning if necessary. Cool on a wire rack.

1 PIECE: 601 cal., 25g fat (16g sat. fat), 65mg chol., 491mg sod., 91g carb. (49g sugars, 2g fiber), 5g pro.

BEE STING CAKE

The bee sting cake, or *bienenstich,* originated in Germany. It gets its playful name from the sweet honey-almond topping. The recipe may look daunting, but it's well worth the effort. Take each step at a time, and you'll be surprised how easy it is to make.
—Taste of Home *Test Kitchen*

PREP: 45 MIN. • BAKE: 30 MIN. + COOLING • MAKES: 8 SERVINGS

¼ **cup sugar**
3 **Tbsp. cornstarch**
¼ **tsp. salt**
1½ **cups whole milk**
3 **large egg yolks**
2 **Tbsp. butter, cubed**
2 **tsp. vanilla extract**
½ **cup heavy whipping cream, whipped**

CAKE
¼ **cup sugar**
1 **envelope (¼ oz.) active dry yeast**
¼ **tsp. salt**
2¾ **cups all-purpose flour, divided**
¾ **cup whole milk**
⅓ **cup butter, cubed**
2 **large eggs, room temperature**

ALMOND TOPPING
¼ **cup butter**
3 **Tbsp. honey**
2 **Tbsp. sugar**
1 **cup sliced almonds**

1. For filling, in a small heavy saucepan, mix sugar, cornstarch and salt. Whisk in the milk. Cook and stir over medium heat until thickened and bubbly. Reduce heat to low; cook and stir 2 minutes longer. Remove from the heat. In a small bowl, whisk egg yolks. Whisk a small amount of hot mixture into egg yolks; return all to pan, whisking constantly. Bring to a gentle boil; cook and stir for 2 minutes. Remove from the heat. Stir in the butter until melted. Immediately transfer to a clean bowl; stir in the vanilla. Cool for 30 minutes. Press plastic wrap onto surface of filling; refrigerate until cold.

2. Whisk custard gently. Fold in half the whipped cream. Fold in remaining whipped cream. Cover and refrigerate.

3. While custard is chilling, make dough. In a large bowl, mix sugar, yeast, salt and 1 cup flour. In a small saucepan, heat milk and butter to 120°-130°. Add to dry ingredients; beat on medium speed 1 minute. Add eggs; beat on high 1 minute. Stir in enough remaining flour to form a soft dough (dough will be sticky).

4. Turn dough onto a well floured surface; knead until smooth and elastic, 6-8 minutes. Place in a greased bowl, turning once to grease the top. Cover and let rise in a warm place until doubled, about 1 hour.

5. While the dough is rising, make almond topping. In a small saucepan over medium heat, melt butter, honey and sugar. Cook and stir until the sugar is dissolved. Remove from heat; stir in almonds. Cool slightly and set aside.

6. Punch down dough. Turn onto a lightly floured surface; roll into a 9-in. circle. Transfer to greased 9-in. springform baking pan, pressing to evenly fill pan with dough. Spoon almond mixture over dough and gently spread to cover entire surface. Cover pan with a kitchen towel; let rise in a warm place 25-30 minutes or until doubled. Preheat oven to 350°. Bake until topping is golden brown, 25-30 minutes. Cool on a wire rack 10 minutes. Loosen sides from pan with a knife. Cool 1 hour longer.

7. Remove cake from base of springform pan. Using a long serrated knife, cut cake horizontally in half; spread filling over cake. Replace top of cake. Serve immediately. Chill leftovers.

1 PIECE: 548 cal., 32g fat (16g sat. fat), 178mg chol., 314mg sod., 56g carb. (18g sugars, 3g fiber), 11g pro.

COCONUT PINEAPPLE UPSIDE-DOWN CAKE

This recipe is one of my favorites. The tropical flavors remind me of being on vacation with my family in the Caribbean. It brings back so many fun memories.
—*Stephanie Pichelli, Toronto, ON*

PREP: 30 MIN. • **BAKE:** 55 MIN. + COOLING • **MAKES:** 12 SERVINGS

- 1 can (20 oz.) unsweetened sliced pineapple, drained
- ¾ cup unsalted butter, softened
- ¼ cup coconut oil
- 1½ cups sugar
- 2 large egg yolks, room temperature
- 1 tsp. coconut extract
- 3 cups cake flour
- 3 tsp. baking powder
- ½ tsp. salt
- 1 can (13.66 oz.) coconut milk
- 6 large egg whites, room temperature
- ⅛ tsp. cream of tartar
  Toasted sweetened shredded coconut, optional

1. Preheat oven to 350°. Arrange pineapple in a single layer in a well seasoned 12-in. cast-iron or other ovenproof skillet.

2. In a large bowl, cream butter, coconut oil and sugar until light and fluffy, 5-7 minutes. Add egg yolks, 1 at a time, beating well after each addition. Beat in coconut extract. In another bowl, whisk flour, baking powder and salt; add to creamed mixture alternately with coconut milk, beating well after each addition.

3. With clean beaters, beat the egg whites and cream of tartar on high speed just until stiff but not dry. Fold a fourth of the egg whites into batter, then fold in remaining egg whites. Spread over the pineapple. Bake until a toothpick inserted in center comes out clean, 55-60 minutes. Cool 10 minutes before inverting onto a serving plate. Serve warm, with toasted coconut if desired.

1 PIECE: 458 cal., 22g fat (17g sat. fat), 61mg chol., 262mg sod., 59g carb. (31g sugars, 1g fiber), 6g pro.

EASY CREAM PIE

Fresh berries and cream pie—it's a simple, classic combination just like Grandma used to make. My version gets you out of the kitchen and into your patio lounge chair quickly. Enjoy!
—*Gina Nistico, Denver, CO*

PREP: 10 MIN. • BAKE: 15 MIN. + CHILLING • MAKES: 8 SERVINGS

2¾ cups graham cracker crumbs
¾ cup sugar, divided
½ cup butter, melted
1 envelope unflavored gelatin
¼ cup cold water
2 pkg. (8 oz. each) cream cheese, softened
2 cups heavy whipping cream
2 tsp. vanilla extract
Mixed fresh berries, optional

1. Preheat oven to 350°. Combine cracker crumbs and ¼ cup sugar with melted butter. Using the bottom of a glass, press cracker mixture onto bottom and up the sides of a greased 9-in. deep-dish pie plate. Bake until set, 12-15 minutes. Cool completely on a wire rack.

2. Meanwhile, sprinkle the gelatin over cold water; let stand for 5 minutes. Beat cream cheese and remaining sugar until smooth. Slowly beat in cream and vanilla. Microwave gelatin on high until melted, about 10 seconds; beat into the cream cheese mixture. Transfer the filling to crust. Refrigerate, covered, until set, about 3 hours.

3. If desired, top with mixed fresh berries.

1 PIECE: 731 cal., 56g fat (33g sat. fat), 156mg chol., 445mg sod., 51g carb. (31g sugars, 1g fiber), 8g pro.

FRUITCAKE PIE

This recipe came from a friend who knows how much we love fruitcake. The pie has similar flavors, but is easier to make than a large batch of fruitcake. I usually serve it with whipped cream. It's excellent with ice cream, too.
—*Doris Heath, Franklin, NC*

PREP: 20 MIN. • BAKE: 35 MIN. + COOLING • MAKES: 8 SERVINGS

1 sheet refrigerated pie crust
1 cup pecan halves, divided
¾ cup red candied cherries, divided
½ cup chopped dates
¼ cup chopped candied pineapple
6 Tbsp. butter, softened
½ cup packed brown sugar
3 large eggs, room temperature, lightly beaten
½ cup light corn syrup
¼ tsp. each ground cloves, ginger and nutmeg

1. Unroll crust into a 9-in. pie plate. Trim crust to ½ in. beyond rim of plate; flute edge. Set aside. Chop ½ cup pecans; set remaining pecan halves aside. Chop ½ cup cherries; halve remaining cherries and set aside. Combine the dates, pineapple and chopped pecans and cherries; sprinkle over crust.

2. In a small bowl, cream butter and brown sugar until light and fluffy, 5-7 minutes. Beat in the eggs, corn syrup, cloves, ginger and nutmeg. Pour over fruit mixture. Top with the reserved pecan and cherry halves.

3. Bake at 350° for 35-40 minutes or until set. Cool on a wire rack. Refrigerate leftovers.

1 PIECE: 519 cal., 27g fat (10g sat. fat), 107mg chol., 219mg sod., 68g carb. (40g sugars, 2g fiber), 5g pro.

CHOCOLATE CAKE WITH CHOCOLATE FROSTING

I once sent this rich chocolate cake to my kids' teacher. It vanished, so I had to make another one!

—*Megan Moelbert, Springville, NY*

PREP: 40 MIN. • BAKE: 30 MIN. + COOLING • MAKES: 16 SERVINGS

2 cups sugar
2 cups water
⅔ cup canola oil
2 Tbsp. white vinegar
2 tsp. vanilla extract
3 cups all-purpose flour
⅓ cup plus 1 Tbsp. baking cocoa, sifted
2 tsp. baking soda
1 tsp. salt

FROSTING
3¾ cups confectioners' sugar
⅓ cup baking cocoa
1 cup butter, softened
1 tsp. vanilla extract
3 to 5 Tbsp. 2% milk

1. Preheat oven to 350°. Line bottoms of 2 greased 9-in. round baking pans with parchment; grease parchment.

2. In a large bowl, beat sugar, water, oil, vinegar and vanilla until well blended. In another large bowl, whisk flour, sifted cocoa, baking soda and salt; gradually add to sugar mixture, beating until smooth.

3. Transfer the batter to prepared pans. Bake until a toothpick inserted in center comes out clean, 30-35 minutes. Cool in pans 10 minutes before removing to wire racks; remove parchment. Cool completely.

4. For frosting, sift confectioners' sugar and cocoa together. In a large bowl, beat butter and vanilla until blended. Beat in the confectioners' sugar mixture alternately with enough milk to reach desired consistency. Spread frosting between layers and over top and sides of cake.

1 PIECE: 491 cal., 22g fat (8g sat. fat), 31mg chol., 399mg sod., 74g carb. (53g sugars, 1g fiber), 3g pro.

PINK LEMONADE STAND CAKE

If you love a moist and creamy cake, this is it. Lemon juice and lemonade give the layers a tangy, citrusy touch, and the cream cheese frosting with sprinkles makes it extra pretty.
—*Lauren McAnelly, Des Moines, IA*

PREP: 50 MIN. • **BAKE:** 20 MIN. + COOLING • **MAKES:** 12 SERVINGS

CAKES & PIES

1 cup buttermilk
2 Tbsp. lemon juice
2 Tbsp. seedless strawberry jam, warmed
2 Tbsp. thawed pink lemonade concentrate
2 Tbsp. grenadine syrup
1 cup unsalted butter, softened
1¼ cups sugar
3 Tbsp. grated lemon zest
4 large eggs, room temperature
½ tsp. vanilla extract
2½ cups all-purpose flour
1 tsp. baking powder
½ tsp. baking soda
½ tsp. salt

FROSTING

1 cup unsalted butter, softened
1 pkg. (8 oz.) cream cheese, softened
1 Tbsp. grated lemon zest
4 cups confectioners' sugar
⅓ cup plus 3 Tbsp. thawed pink lemonade concentrate, divided
Pink sprinkles

1. Preheat oven to 350°. Line bottoms of 3 greased 8-in. round baking pans with parchment; grease parchment.

2. In a small bowl, whisk the first 5 ingredients until blended. In a large bowl, cream butter, sugar and lemon zest until light and fluffy, 5-7 minutes. Add eggs, 1 at a time, beating well after each addition. Beat in vanilla. In another bowl, whisk flour, baking powder, baking soda and salt; add to creamed mixture alternately with buttermilk mixture, beating well after each addition.

3. Transfer the batter to prepared pans. Bake until a toothpick inserted in center comes out clean, 20-24 minutes. Cool in pans 10 minutes before removing to wire racks; remove parchment. Cool completely.

4. For frosting, in a large bowl, beat butter, cream cheese and lemon zest until smooth. Gradually beat in confectioners' sugar and ⅓ cup lemonade concentrate. If necessary, refrigerate until spreadable, up to 1 hour.

5. Place 1 cake layer on a serving plate. Brush 1 Tbsp. lemonade concentrate over cake; spread with ½ cup frosting. Repeat layers. Top with the remaining cake layer; brush the remaining lemonade concentrate over top. Spread remaining frosting over top and sides of cake.

6. Decorate with sprinkles. Refrigerate until serving.

1 PIECE: 732 cal., 39g fat (24g sat. fat), 172mg chol., 291mg sod., 91g carb. (68g sugars, 1g fiber), 7g pro.

PEACH BLUEBERRY PIE

What a flavor! That's what I hear most often when guests taste this dessert. I invented it one day when I was short on peaches.
—*Sue Thumma, Shepherd, MI*

PREP: 15 MIN. • BAKE: 40 MIN. + COOLING • MAKES: 8 SERVINGS

1 cup sugar
⅓ cup all-purpose flour
½ tsp. ground cinnamon
⅛ tsp. ground allspice
3 cups sliced peeled fresh peaches

1 cup fresh or frozen unsweetened blueberries
Dough for double-crust pie
1 Tbsp. butter
1 Tbsp. 2% milk
Cinnamon sugar

1. In a large bowl, combine sugar, flour, cinnamon and allspice. Add peaches and blueberries; toss to coat.

2. Preheat oven to 400°. On a lightly floured surface, roll half of dough to a ⅛-in.-thick circle; transfer to a 9-in. pie plate. Trim even with rim. Add filling; dot with butter.

3. Roll remaining dough to a ⅛-in.-thick circle; cut into ½-in.-wide strips. Arrange over filling in a lattice pattern. Trim and seal strips to edge of bottom crust; flute edge. Brush lattice strips with milk; sprinkle with cinnamon sugar.

4. Bake until the crust is golden brown and the filling is bubbly, 40-45 minutes. Cool on a wire rack.

NOTE: If using frozen blueberries, use without thawing to avoid discoloring the batter.

DOUGH FOR DOUBLE-CRUST PIE (9 IN.): Combine 2½ cups all-purpose flour and ½ tsp. salt; cut in 1 cup cold butter until crumbly. Gradually add ⅓ to ⅔ cup ice water, tossing with a fork until dough holds together when pressed. Divide dough in half. Shape each into a disk; wrap and refrigerate 1 hour.

1 PIECE: 406 cal., 16g fat (7g sat. fat), 14mg chol., 215mg sod., 65g carb. (34g sugars, 2g fiber), 3g pro.

GRANDMA'S OLD-FASHIONED
STRAWBERRY SHORTCAKE,
PAGE 281

GRANDMA'S FAVORITE

DESSERTS

Life is short...eat dessert first! It's easier than
ever to enjoy a sweet indulgence with Grandma's
best-loved recipes. Whether it's a fruity cobbler
or creamy pudding to top off a weeknight dinner
or a luscious cheesecake for a holiday buffet,
re-create that magic—one sweet recipe at a time.

ROASTED BANANA & PECAN CHEESECAKE

We keep bananas on hand, but with just two of us in the house they ripen faster than we can eat them. That makes them perfect for roasting and baking into this cheesecake with a nutty crust.
—*Patricia Harmon, Baden, PA*

PREP: 45 MIN. + COOLING • **BAKE:** 45 MIN. + CHILLING • **MAKES:** 12 SERVINGS

3 medium ripe bananas, unpeeled
1¾ cups crushed pecan shortbread cookies
3 Tbsp. butter, melted

FILLING
2 pkg. (8 oz. each) cream cheese, softened
1 pkg. (8 oz.) reduced-fat cream cheese
½ cup sugar
¼ cup plus 2 Tbsp. packed brown sugar, divided
1 tsp. vanilla extract
2 Tbsp. spiced rum, optional
4 large eggs, room temperature, lightly beaten
½ cup chopped pecans
½ tsp. ground cinnamon
12 pecan halves, toasted
Chocolate syrup

1. Preheat oven to 400°. Place the unpeeled bananas in an 8-in. square baking dish. Bake 10-12 minutes or until banana peels are black. Cool to room temperature. Reduce oven setting to 325°.

2. Place a greased 9-in. springform pan on a double thickness of heavy-duty foil (about 18 in. square). Wrap foil securely around pan. Place on a baking sheet.

3. In a small bowl, mix cookie crumbs and melted butter. Press onto bottom and 1 in. up side of prepared springform pan. Bake until set, 8-10 minutes. Cool on a wire rack.

4. In a large bowl, beat cream cheese, sugar and ¼ cup brown sugar until smooth. Beat in vanilla and, if desired, rum. Add the eggs; beat on low speed just until blended. Remove ½ cup cream cheese mixture to a small bowl. Pour remaining filling into crust.

5. Peel and place roasted bananas in a food processor; process until smooth. Add to reserved cream cheese mixture; stir in the chopped pecans, cinnamon and remaining brown sugar. Pour over plain cream cheese mixture. Cut through cream cheese filling with a knife to swirl.

6. Place springform pan in a larger baking pan; add 1 in. hot water to larger pan. Bake until center is just set and top appears dull, 45-55 minutes. Remove springform pan from water bath. Cool cheesecake on a wire rack 10 minutes, then run a knife around the edge of the cake to loosen it from the pan; remove foil. Cool 1 hour longer. Refrigerate cheesecake overnight, covering when completely cooled.

7. Remove rim from pan. Top with pecan halves; drizzle with chocolate syrup.

NOTE: To toast nuts, bake in a shallow pan in a 350° oven for 5-10 minutes or cook in a skillet over low heat until lightly browned, stirring occasionally.

1 PIECE: 430 cal., 30g fat (14g sat. fat), 126mg chol., 308mg sod., 33g carb. (24g sugars, 2g fiber), 8g pro.

SLOW-COOKER BERRY COMPOTE

This is a decades-old recipe my grandma made
when I was younger, and it reminds me of her. She always
added extra blueberries to help thicken the sauce.

—*Diane Higgins, Tampa, FL*

PREP: 15 MIN. • **COOK:** 3 HOURS • **MAKES:** 16 SERVINGS (4 CUPS)

¼ **cup sugar**

2 **Tbsp. cornstarch**

1 **cup water**

1 **can (15 oz.) pitted dark sweet cherries, undrained**

1 **pint fresh or frozen unsweetened blueberries**

1 **cup packed brown sugar**

½ **cup chopped walnuts**

¼ **cup all-purpose flour**

¼ **cup sliced almonds**

¼ **cup old-fashioned oats**

1 **tsp. ground cinnamon**

¼ **tsp. ground nutmeg**

Dash salt

½ **cup cold butter**

Vanilla ice cream, optional

1. In a small bowl, mix sugar, cornstarch and water until smooth. Transfer to a greased 3-qt. slow cooker. Stir in the cherries and blueberries. In a large bowl, combine brown sugar, walnuts, flour, almonds, oats, cinnamon, nutmeg and salt; cut in butter until crumbly. Sprinkle over fruit mixture.

2. Cook, covered, on high 3 hours or until bubbly and thickened. If desired, serve warm with vanilla ice cream.

¼ **CUP:** 256 cal., 12g fat (5g sat. fat), 20mg chol., 80mg sod., 37g carb. (30g sugars, 2g fiber), 2g pro.

FROM GRANDMA'S KITCHEN: Fruit compote is fruit cooked with sugar, spices and sometimes other ingredients to produce a warm, chunky fruit syrup. It's often served as a dessert with ice cream or yogurt, or use it to top pancakes, waffles, French toast or oatmeal.

LEMON SCHAUM TORTE

Schaum torte is a classic Austrian dessert that consists of meringue layers filled with fruit and topped with whipped cream. This modified version conveniently bakes in a 13x9-inch pan.
—*Cindy Steffen, Cedarburg, WI*

PREP: 50 MIN. • BAKE: 1 HOUR + STANDING • MAKES: 15 SERVINGS

- 6 large egg whites
- 1 tsp. vanilla extract
- ⅛ tsp. cream of tartar
- 2 cups sugar, divided
- 9 large egg yolks
- ½ cup lemon juice
- 1 Tbsp. grated lemon zest
- 4 cups heavy whipping cream
- ⅔ cup confectioners' sugar
  Ground cinnamon

1. Place the egg whites in a large bowl and let stand at room temperature for 30 minutes. Add vanilla and cream of tartar. Beat on medium until soft peaks form. Gradually beat in 1 cup sugar, 2 Tbsp. at a time, on high speed until stiff glossy peaks form and sugar is dissolved.

2. Spread meringue on the bottom and up the sides of a greased 13x9-in. baking dish. Bake at 275° for 1 hour. Turn oven off and let stand in oven for 1 hour. Do not open door. Remove from the oven; cool on wire rack.

3. In a large saucepan, combine the egg yolks, lemon juice, lemon zest and remaining sugar. Cook and stir over medium heat until mixture is thickened and coats the back of a spoon. Transfer to small bowl; cool.

4. In a chilled bowl, beat cream until it begins to thicken. Add the confectioners' sugar; beat until stiff peaks form. Spread half over meringue; cover with lemon mixture. Top with remaining whipped cream. Sprinkle with cinnamon. Refrigerate leftovers.

1 PIECE: 388 cal., 27g fat (16g sat. fat), 215mg chol., 51mg sod., 35g carb. (33g sugars, 0 fiber), 4g pro.

GRANDMA DAVIDSON'S BAKED APPLE PUDDING

My savvy grandmother whipped up this homey cinnamon-scented apple pudding during the Depression. Many of us still make it today.
—*Holly Sharp, Warren, ON*

PREP: 15 MIN. • BAKE: 40 MIN. + STANDING • MAKES: 6 SERVINGS

- 1 cup packed brown sugar
- 1 cup all-purpose flour
- 2 tsp. baking powder
- ½ tsp. salt
- ½ tsp. ground cinnamon
- ½ cup 2% milk
- 3 medium tart apples, peeled and chopped
- 2 Tbsp. butter, cubed
- 2 cups boiling water
  Vanilla ice cream, optional

1. Preheat oven to 400°. In a large bowl, mix first 5 ingredients. Add the milk; stir just until blended. Fold in apples. Transfer to a greased 2½-qt. deep baking dish. Dot with butter.

2. Pour boiling water over top. Bake, uncovered, 40-45 minutes or until golden brown. Let stand 15 minutes before serving. If desired, serve with ice cream.

1 CUP: 291 cal., 5g fat (3g sat. fat), 12mg chol., 381mg sod., 61g carb. (43g sugars, 2g fiber), 3g pro.

BANANA CRUMB PUDDING

Friends and family ask me to make my thick and creamy banana pudding for all occasions. They can't get enough of the wonderful flavor of the fruit and the vanilla wafer crumbs. You can also top the classic southern treat with meringue instead of whipped cream.
—*Yvonnia Butner, Pinnacle, NC*

PREP: 15 MIN. • COOK: 20 MIN. + CHILLING • MAKES: 15 SERVINGS

- 1   cup sugar
- ½   cup cornstarch
- 6   cups 2% milk
- 5   large egg yolks
- ¼   cup butter, cubed
- 2   tsp. vanilla extract
- 1   tsp. kosher salt
- 2   pkg. (11 oz. each) vanilla wafers
- 7   medium bananas, sliced

TOPPING

- 2   cups heavy whipping cream
- 6   Tbsp. sugar

1. In a large heavy saucepan, mix sugar and cornstarch. Whisk in milk. Cook and stir over medium heat until thickened and bubbly. Reduce heat to low; cook and stir 2 minutes longer. Remove from the heat.

2. In a bowl, whisk a small amount of hot mixture into egg yolks; return all to pan, whisking constantly. Bring to a gentle boil; cook and stir 2 minutes. Remove from heat. Stir in butter, vanilla and salt. Cool 15 minutes, stirring occasionally.

3. Reserve 1 banana and 1 cup whole wafers for topping. Crush 2 cups wafers and set aside. In a 13x9-in. baking dish, place a single layer of whole wafers, filling gaps with crushed wafers. Layer with a third of the bananas and pudding. Repeat layers twice. Press plastic onto the surface of pudding. Refrigerate, covered, overnight.

4. In a bowl, beat heavy cream until it begins to thicken. Add sugar; beat until soft peaks form (do not overmix). Just before serving, spread whipped cream over pudding; top with reserved banana and wafers.

¾ CUP: 535 cal., 27g fat (13g sat. fat), 121mg chol., 370mg sod., 70g carb. (46g sugars, 1g fiber), 7g pro.

GRANDMA'S SECRET

If your bananas are ripe but you're not ready to use them, put them in a sealed plastic bag in the fridge. Their peels will brown but the fruit inside won't. You can keep them there for an extra 4-5 days.

RHUBARB TART

The rhubarb flavor in this tart balances nicely with the honey and amaretto. The mascarpone cheese makes it rich and creamy. Sometimes I'll even double the rhubarb for really sumptuous tarts.

—*Ellen Riley, Murfreesboro, TN*

PREP: 35 MIN. • BAKE: 15 MIN. + COOLING • MAKES: 2 TARTS (8 SERVINGS EACH)

1 pkg. frozen puff pastry (17.30 oz.), thawed
1 large egg
1 Tbsp. water

RHUBARB TOPPING
12 rhubarb ribs (½ in. x 7 in.)
1 cup orange juice
½ cup honey
2 Tbsp. amaretto

FILLING
1 pkg. (8 oz.) mascarpone cheese
2 Tbsp. amaretto
1 Tbsp. honey

1. Preheat oven to 400°. Unfold 1 pastry sheet and place on a parchment-lined baking sheet; repeat with remaining pastry sheet. Whisk egg and water; brush over pastries. Using a sharp knife, score a 1-in. border around edges of pastry sheets (do not cut through). With a fork, prick the center of pastries. Bake until golden brown, about 15 minutes. With a spatula, press down center portion of pastries, leaving outer edges intact. Remove to wire racks to cool.

2. Meanwhile, for topping, arrange rhubarb in a single layer in a 13x9-in. baking dish. Combine orange juice, honey and amaretto; pour over rhubarb. Bake at 400° until rhubarb is just tender but still holds its shape, about 10 minutes. Remove with a slotted spoon, reserving cooking liquid; let rhubarb cool. Transfer the reserved cooking liquid to a small saucepan; bring to a boil over medium-high heat. Reduce heat; simmer until reduced to ½ cup, about 20 minutes. Cool.

3. For filling, stir together mascarpone cheese, amaretto and honey until smooth. Spread mascarpone mixture over center of each pastry. Top with rhubarb ribs. Brush rhubarb with cooled cooking liquid. Refrigerate leftovers.

1 PIECE: 259 cal., 15g fat (6g sat. fat), 29mg chol., 115mg sod., 26g carb. (8g sugars, 3g fiber), 4g pro.

FROM GRANDMA'S KITCHEN: For many rhubarb tart recipes, you can use frozen rhubarb instead of fresh with equally good results. But in this case, you definitely want to use the fresh, long stalks to achieve the spectacular look.

APPLE DUMPLINGS WITH SAUCE

These warm and comforting apple dumplings are incredible by themselves or served with ice cream. You can decorate each dumpling by cutting 1-inch leaves and a ½-inch stem from the leftover dough.

—Robin Lendon, Cincinnati, OH

PREP: 1 HOUR + CHILLING • BAKE: 50 MIN. • MAKES: 8 SERVINGS

3 cups all-purpose flour
1 tsp. salt
1 cup shortening
⅓ cup cold water
8 medium tart apples, peeled and cored
8 tsp. butter

9 tsp. cinnamon sugar, divided

SAUCE
1½ cups packed brown sugar
1 cup water
½ cup butter, cubed

1. In a large bowl, combine flour and salt; cut in shortening until crumbly. Gradually add water, tossing with a fork until dough forms a ball. Divide into 8 portions. Cover and refrigerate at least 30 minutes or until easy to handle.

2. Preheat the oven to 350°. Roll each portion of dough between 2 lightly floured sheets of waxed paper into a 7-in. square. Place an apple on each square. Place 1 tsp. butter and 1 tsp. cinnamon sugar in the center of each apple.

3. Gently bring up corners of dough to each center, trimming any excess; pinch edges to seal. If desired, cut out apple leaves and stems from dough scraps; attach to dumplings with water. Place in a greased 13x9-in. baking dish. Sprinkle with the remaining cinnamon sugar.

4. In a large saucepan, combine sauce ingredients. Bring just to a boil, stirring until blended. Pour over the apples; sprinkle with remaining cinnamon sugar.

5. Bake until the apples are tender and pastry is golden brown, 50-55 minutes, basting occasionally with sauce. Serve warm.

1 DUMPLING: 764 cal., 40g fat (16g sat. fat), 41mg chol., 429mg sod., 97g carb. (59g sugars, 3g fiber), 5g pro.

RED, WHITE & BLUE DESSERT

I slightly changed a recipe I found and ended up with this rich, fresh-tasting dessert.
Decorated to resemble a flag, it's perfect for the Fourth of July or any other patriotic occasion.
—*Sue Gronholz, Beaver Dam, WI*

TAKES: 20 MIN. • MAKES: 18 SERVINGS

2 **pkg. (8 oz. each) cream cheese, softened**
½ **cup sugar**
½ **tsp. vanilla extract**
½ **tsp. almond extract**
2 **cups heavy whipping cream, whipped**
2 **qt. strawberries, halved, divided**
2 **qt. blueberries, divided**

1. In a large bowl, beat cream cheese, sugar and extracts until fluffy. Fold in whipped cream. Place a third of the mixture in a 4-qt. bowl. Reserve 20 strawberry halves and ½ cup blueberries for garnish.

2. Layer half of the remaining strawberries and blueberries over cream mixture. Top with another third of the cream mixture and the remaining berries. Spread the remaining cream mixture on top. Use the reserved strawberries and blueberries to make a flag on top.

1 CUP: 168 cal., 10g fat (6g sat. fat), 32mg chol., 44mg sod., 20g carb. (15g sugars, 3g fiber), 2g pro.

HOMEMADE BUTTERSCOTCH PUDDING

Homemade pudding reminds me of my grandma and how she turned milk and eggs into
creamy textures before my eyes. The butterscotch in this recipe adds a sweet caramel touch.
—*Teresa Wilkes, Pembroke, GA*

PREP: 10 MIN. • COOK: 10 MIN. + CHILLING • MAKES: 6 SERVINGS

½ **cup sugar**
½ **cup packed dark brown sugar**
3 **Tbsp. cornstarch**
¼ **tsp. salt**
⅛ **tsp. ground nutmeg**
3 **cups 2% milk**
3 **large egg yolks**
2 **Tbsp. butter, cubed**
2 **tsp. vanilla extract**
   Whipped cream, optional

1. In a large heavy saucepan, combine the first 5 ingredients. Stir in milk until smooth. Cook and stir over medium-high heat until thickened and bubbly. Reduce heat to low; cook and stir 2 minutes longer. Remove from the heat.

2. Stir a small amount of hot mixture into the egg yolks; return all to the pan. Bring to a gentle boil, stirring constantly; cook 2 minutes or until mixture is thickened and coats the back of a spoon. Remove from the heat.

3. Stir in the butter and vanilla. Cool for 15 minutes, stirring occasionally. Transfer pudding to 6 dessert dishes. Cover and refrigerate until chilled. Garnish with whipped cream if desired.

½ CUP: 273 cal., 8g fat (5g sat. fat), 122mg chol., 198mg sod., 45g carb. (40g sugars, 0 fiber), 5g pro.

GRANDMA'S DIVINITY

*Every year, my grandmother and I made divinity,
just the two of us. I still make it to this day.*
—*Anne Clayborne, Walland, TN*

PREP: 5 MIN. • COOK: 40 MIN. + STANDING • MAKES: 60 PIECES (1½ LBS.)

2 **large egg whites**
3 **cups sugar**
⅔ **cup water**
½ **cup light corn syrup**
1 **tsp. vanilla extract**
1 **cup chopped pecans**

1. Place egg whites in the bowl of a stand mixer; let stand at room temperature for 30 minutes. Meanwhile, line three 15x10x1-in. pans with waxed paper.

2. In a large heavy saucepan, combine the sugar, water and corn syrup; bring to a boil, stirring constantly to dissolve sugar. Cook, without stirring, over medium heat until a candy thermometer reads 252° (hard-ball stage). Just before the temperature is reached, beat egg whites on medium speed until stiff peaks form.

3. Slowly add hot sugar mixture in a thin stream over egg whites, beating constantly and scraping sides of bowl occasionally. Add vanilla. Beat until candy holds its shape, 5-6 minutes. (Do not overmix or candy will get stiff and crumbly.) Immediately fold in the pecans.

4. Quickly drop mixture by heaping teaspoonfuls onto prepared pans. Let stand at room temperature until dry to the touch. Store between sheets of waxed paper in an airtight container at room temperature.

NOTE: We recommend that you test your candy thermometer before each use by bringing water to a boil; the thermometer should read 212°. Adjust your recipe temperature up or down based on your test.

1 PIECE: 61 cal., 1g fat (0 sat. fat), 0 chol., 4mg sod., 13g carb. (12g sugars, 0 fiber), 0 pro.

GRANDMA'S OLD-FASHIONED
STRAWBERRY SHORTCAKE
PICTURED ON PAGE 268

Classic strawberry shortcake is often topped with whipped cream but my grandma
added a scoop of her homemade vanilla ice cream. Either way, it's divine.
—*Angela Lively, Conroe, TX*

PREP: 30 MIN. + STANDING • **BAKE:** 20 MIN. + COOLING • **MAKES:** 8 SERVINGS

6 **cups sliced fresh
    strawberries**
½ **cup sugar**
1 **tsp. vanilla extract**

SHORTCAKE
3 **cups all-purpose flour**
5 **Tbsp. sugar, divided**
3 **tsp. baking powder**
1 **tsp. baking soda**
½ **tsp. salt**
¾ **cup cold butter, cubed**
1¼ **cups buttermilk**
2 **Tbsp. heavy whipping
    cream**

TOPPING
1½ **cups heavy whipping
    cream**
2 **Tbsp. sugar**
½ **tsp. vanilla extract**

1. Combine strawberries with sugar and vanilla; mash slightly.
Let stand at least 30 minutes, tossing occasionally.

2. Preheat oven to 400°. For shortcakes, whisk together flour,
4 Tbsp. sugar, baking powder, baking soda and salt. Cut in butter
until crumbly. Add buttermilk; stir just until combined (do not
overmix). Drop batter by ⅓ cupfuls 2 in. apart onto an ungreased
baking sheet. Brush with 2 Tbsp. heavy cream; sprinkle with
remaining 1 Tbsp. sugar. Bake until golden, 18-20 minutes.
Remove to wire racks to cool completely.

3. For topping, beat heavy whipping cream until it begins to
thicken. Add sugar and vanilla; beat until soft peaks form. To
serve, cut the shortcakes in half; top with strawberries and
whipped cream.

**1 SHORTCAKE WITH ½ CUP STRAWBERRIES AND ⅓ CUP WHIPPED
CREAM:** 638 cal., 36g fat (22g sat. fat), 102mg chol., 710mg sod., 72g
carb. (33g sugars, 4g fiber), 9g pro.

FROM GRANDMA'S KITCHEN: Make sure the butter is cold and cut it
in until it's about the size of peas. As it melts during baking, this will
create the small air pockets that give the biscuit its flakiness.

BAKED
SWEET POTATO
PUDDING

BAKED SWEET POTATO PUDDING

I always have lots of leftover sweet potatoes, but when I make this, they're gone faster than you can say Thanksgiving! Any ice cream flavor will do, though vanilla bean seems to be an ideal companion.

—*Joyce Welling, Swanton, OH*

PREP: 25 MIN. • BAKE: 50 MIN. • MAKES: 8 SERVINGS

4 **cups mashed sweet**
  potatoes
½ **cup heavy whipping**
  cream
3 **large eggs, separated**
2 **Tbsp. lemon juice**
1 **tsp. grated lemon zest**
½ **tsp. ground cinnamon**
½ **tsp. ground ginger**
¼ **tsp. ground cloves**
1 **cup sweetened shredded**
  coconut, divided
⅓ **cup packed brown sugar**
⅓ **cup slivered almonds**
  Vanilla ice cream,
  optional

1. In a large bowl, beat the potatoes, cream, egg yolks, lemon juice, lemon zest and spices until smooth. Fold in ⅔ cup coconut.

2. In a large bowl with clean beaters, beat egg whites on medium speed until soft peaks form. Gradually beat in the brown sugar, 1 Tbsp. at a time, on high until stiff glossy peaks form and sugar is dissolved.

3. With a spatula, stir a fourth of the egg whites into sweet potato mixture until no white streaks remain. Fold in remaining egg whites until combined.

4. Transfer to a greased 11x7-in. baking dish. Sprinkle with the almonds and remaining coconut. Bake at 325° for 50-55 minutes or until a knife inserted in center comes out clean. Serve warm, with ice cream if desired.

¾ **CUP:** 324 cal., 14g fat (8g sat. fat), 100mg chol., 111mg sod., 46g carb. (23g sugars, 5g fiber), 6g pro.

NEW ENGLAND INDIAN PUDDING

This recipe was inspired by traditional New England Indian pudding.
My version is made in the slow cooker instead of baking hours in the oven.
Use real molasses—if it's too strong, cut the amount down to ⅓ cup.

—*Susan Bickta, Kutztown, PA*

PREP: 15 MIN. • COOK: 3½ HOURS • MAKES: 8 SERVINGS

1 **pkg. (8½ oz.) cornbread/**
  muffin mix
1 **pkg. (3.4 oz.) instant**
  butterscotch pudding mix
4 **cups whole milk**
3 **large eggs, lightly beaten**
½ **cup molasses**
1 **tsp. ground cinnamon**
¼ **tsp. ground cloves**
¼ **tsp. ground ginger**
  Optional: Vanilla ice
  cream or sweetened
  whipped cream

1. In a large bowl, whisk cornbread mix, pudding mix and milk until blended. Add the eggs, molasses and spices; whisk until combined. Transfer to a greased 4- or 5-qt. slow cooker. Cover and cook on high for 1 hour.

2. Reduce heat to low. Stir pudding, making sure to scrape sides of slow cooker well. Cover and cook until very thick, 2½-3 hours longer, stirring once per hour. Serve pudding warm, with vanilla ice cream or whipped cream if desired.

⅔ **CUP:** 330 cal., 9g fat (4g sat. fat), 83mg chol., 526mg sod., 51g carb. (36g sugars, 2g fiber), 8g pro.

AUNT RUTH'S FAMOUS
BUTTERSCOTCH CHEESECAKE

Aunt Ruth was our nanny when I was little, and she made this cheesecake often.
It was torture when my sister and I had to wait until the next day to have a piece since it
had to chill overnight. When I visited my old neighborhood and stopped by Aunt Ruth's house, she
offered me a piece of her wonderful cheesecake. I made sure to leave with a copy of the recipe!

—Trisha Kruse, Eagle, ID

PREP: 30 MIN. • **BAKE:** 65 MIN. + CHILLING • **MAKES:** 12 SERVINGS

1½ **cups graham cracker crumbs**
⅓ **cup packed brown sugar**
⅓ **cup butter, melted**
1 **can (14 oz.) sweetened condensed milk**
¾ **cup cold 2% milk**
1 **pkg. (3.4 oz.) instant butterscotch pudding mix**
3 **pkg. (8 oz. each) cream cheese, softened**
1 **tsp. vanilla extract**
3 **large eggs, room temperature, lightly beaten**
  Optional: Whipped cream and crushed butterscotch candies

1. Place a greased 9-in. springform pan on a double thickness of heavy-duty foil (about 18 in. square). Securely wrap foil around pan. In a small bowl, combine cracker crumbs and sugar; stir in butter. Press onto the bottom of prepared pan. Place pan on a baking sheet. Bake at 325° for 10 minutes. Cool on a wire rack.

2. In a small bowl, whisk the milks and pudding mix for 2 minutes. Let stand for 2 minutes or until soft-set.

3. Meanwhile, in a large bowl, beat cream cheese until smooth. Beat in pudding and vanilla. Add eggs; beat on low speed just until combined. Pour mixture over crust. Place springform pan in a large baking pan; add 1 in. of hot water to larger pan.

4. Bake at 325° for 65-75 minutes or until center is almost set and top appears dull. Remove springform pan from water bath. Cool on a wire rack for 10 minutes.

5. Carefully run a knife around edge of pan to loosen; cool 1 hour longer. Refrigerate overnight, covering when completely cooled. Garnish with whipped cream and butterscotch candies if desired.

1 PIECE: 473 cal., 30g fat (18g sat. fat), 141mg chol., 460mg sod., 42g carb. (34g sugars, 0 fiber), 10g pro.

"Absolutely delicious! I didn't change a thing—cooked for 65 minutes and voila! Out popped an immaculate butterscotch cheesecake. I decorated it with chocolate chips and butterscotch drizzle. I will make this again."
—CDEVL, TASTEOFHOME.COM

BLUEBERRY CORNMEAL COBBLER

Cornbread, blueberries and maple syrup butter give this special dessert a taste that's different from any cobbler you've had before. I came across the recipe many years ago.
—*Judy Watson, Tipton, IN*

PREP: 20 MIN. + STANDING • **BAKE:** 35 MIN. • **MAKES:** 12 SERVINGS

4 cups fresh blueberries
1 cup plus 2 Tbsp. sugar
1 Tbsp. quick-cooking tapioca
2 tsp. grated lemon zest
1 tsp. ground cinnamon
¼ to ½ tsp. ground nutmeg

TOPPING
½ cup butter, softened, divided

1 cup confectioners' sugar
1 large egg, room temperature
1 cup all-purpose flour
½ cup cornmeal
2 tsp. baking powder
½ tsp. baking soda
½ tsp. salt
¾ cup buttermilk
2 Tbsp. maple syrup

1. In a large bowl, combine the blueberries, sugar, tapioca, lemon zest, cinnamon and nutmeg. Let stand for 15 minutes. Pour into a greased 11x7-in. baking dish.

2. In a small bowl, beat ¼ cup butter and confectioners' sugar. Add egg; beat well. Combine the flour, cornmeal, baking powder, baking soda and salt; add to creamed mixture alternately with buttermilk, beating just until combined. Pour over berry mixture.

3. Bake at 375° until a toothpick inserted in the center comes out clean, 35-40 minutes.

4. In a small saucepan, melt remaining butter over low heat. Remove from heat; stir in the syrup. Brush over cornbread. Broil 4-6 in. from the heat until bubbly, 1-2 minutes. Serve warm.

1 PIECE: 290 cal., 9g fat (5g sat. fat), 39mg chol., 317mg sod., 52g carb. (35g sugars, 2g fiber), 3g pro.

TINY TIM'S PLUM PUDDING

We first read about this English tradition in Charles Dickens' novella *A Christmas Carol*. In the story, everyone clapped for plum pudding. Since then, our family has made this pudding every year for Christmas, and it is truly worthy of applause.
—*Ruthanne Karel, Hudsonville, MI*

PREP: 30 MIN. • **COOK:** 2 HOURS • **MAKES:** 12 SERVINGS (1½ CUPS SAUCE)

DESSERTS

½ cup butter, softened
¾ cup packed brown sugar
3 large eggs, room temperature
¾ cup dry bread crumbs
½ cup all-purpose flour
1 Tbsp. grated orange zest
1 tsp. ground cinnamon
½ tsp. baking soda
½ tsp. ground nutmeg
¼ tsp. salt
¼ tsp. ground cloves
2 cans (15 oz. each) plums, drained, pitted and chopped
1¾ cups chopped dates
1 cup golden raisins
1 cup shredded carrots
½ cup dried currants

HARD SAUCE
½ cup butter, softened
3 cups confectioners' sugar
¼ cup dark rum or orange juice

1. Generously grease an 8-cup pudding mold, metal gelatin mold or ovenproof bowl; set aside.

2. In a large bowl, cream butter and brown sugar until light and fluffy, 5-7 minutes. Add eggs, 1 at a time, beating well after each addition. In another bowl, mix bread crumbs, flour, orange zest, cinnamon, baking soda, nutmeg, salt and cloves; gradually add to creamed mixture. Fold in the plums, dates, raisins, carrots and currants.

3. Transfer to prepared pudding mold. Cover tightly with heavy-duty foil; tie foil with kitchen string to secure.

4. Place on a rack in a stockpot; add 3 in. hot water to pot. Bring water to a gentle boil; steam cake, covered, until a toothpick inserted in center comes out clean, 2-2½ hours, adding more water to pot as needed. Remove pudding from pot; let stand for 5 minutes before unmolding.

5. Meanwhile, in a bowl, beat hard sauce ingredients until smooth and creamy. Unmold pudding onto a serving plate; serve warm with sauce.

1 PIECE WITH 2 TBSP. SAUCE: 550 cal., 17g fat (10g sat. fat), 93mg chol., 292mg sod., 98g carb. (80g sugars, 5g fiber), 5g pro.

CRANBERRY-ORANGE CRUMB TART

After my sister took the family to the local cranberry festival, my mom bet me
that I couldn't make a holiday dessert out of cranberries and oranges.
Considering the tart was gone before the holidays arrived, I think I won!
—*Heather Cunningham, Whitman, MA*

PREP: 35 MIN. + STANDING • BAKE: 10 MIN. + COOLING • MAKES: 12 SERVINGS

2 cups crushed cinnamon
   graham crackers (about
   14 whole crackers),
   divided
½ cup sugar, divided
6 Tbsp. butter, melted
¼ cup all-purpose flour
¼ cup packed brown sugar
¼ cup cold butter, cubed

FILLING
1 large navel orange
1 cup sugar
3 Tbsp. quick-cooking
   tapioca
¼ tsp. baking soda
¼ tsp. ground cinnamon
⅛ tsp. ground allspice
4 cups fresh or frozen
   cranberries, thawed
2 Tbsp. brandy or
   cranberry juice

1. Preheat oven to 375°. In a small bowl, mix 1¾ cups crushed crackers and ¼ cup sugar; stir in melted butter. Press onto bottom and up side of an ungreased 11-in. fluted tart pan with removable bottom. Bake 7-8 minutes or until edge is lightly browned. Cool on a wire rack.

2. For topping, in a small bowl, mix flour, brown sugar, and remaining crushed crackers and sugar; cut in cold butter until crumbly. Refrigerate while preparing filling.

3. Finely grate 1 Tbsp. zest from orange. Cut a thin slice from the top and bottom of the orange; stand orange upright on a cutting board. Cut off peel and outer membrane, starting from the top. Holding orange over a bowl to catch juices, remove orange sections by cutting along the membrane. Squeeze membrane to reserve additional juice.

4. In a large saucepan, mix sugar, tapioca, baking soda, cinnamon and allspice. Add cranberries, brandy, grated zest and reserved juice; toss to coat. Let stand 15 minutes. Preheat oven to 425°.

5. Bring cranberry mixture to a full boil, stirring constantly. Add orange sections; heat through. Pour mixture into crust; sprinkle with topping. Bake 10-15 minutes or until topping is golden brown. Cool on a wire rack.

1 PIECE: 332 cal., 11g fat (6g sat. fat), 25mg chol., 207mg sod., 56g carb. (38g sugars, 3g fiber), 2g pro.

FROM GRANDMA'S KITCHEN: Pies and tarts are similar, but there are a few key differences. Pies are baked in pans with sloped sides and can have a single or double crust. Pies are served right out of the dish. Tarts are baked in a shallow-sided tart pan and removed from the pan before serving. A tart pan with a removable bottom is invaluable for avid tart bakers. The removable bottom makes it simple to get the pastry out in one piece and still look gorgeous.

APPLE HONEY TAPIOCA PUDDING

I'm glad that apple season is long, since my
family requests this pudding quite often!
—*Amy Kraemer, Glencoe, MN*

TAKES: 25 MIN. • MAKES: 6 SERVINGS

4 cups sliced peeled tart
apples, cut in eighths
¾ cup honey
3 Tbsp. butter
1 Tbsp. lemon juice
½ tsp. salt

½ tsp. ground cinnamon
2½ cups water
⅓ cup quick-cooking
tapioca
Cream, ice cream or
whipped cream

1. In a Dutch oven, combine the first 6 ingredients. Cover and
simmer just until apples are tender.

2. Using a slotted spoon, transfer apples to a bowl. Add water and
tapioca to pan. Cook and stir until thickened and clear. Pour over
apples. Serve warm with cream, ice cream or whipped cream.

1 CUP: 257 cal., 6g fat (4g sat. fat), 15mg chol., 256mg sod., 55g
carb. (42g sugars, 2g fiber), 0 pro.

COCONUT CREME CHOCOLATES

My marshmallow-filled chocolate confections are a fun way
to treat my children and grandchildren when they visit.
—*Dolores Wilder, Texas City, TX*

PREP: 15 MIN. + CHILLING • MAKES: 2½ DOZEN

1 jar (7 oz.) marshmallow
creme
2⅔ cups sweetened
shredded coconut,
toasted
1 tsp. vanilla extract
Dash salt
1 milk chocolate candy bar
(5 oz.), chopped
1½ tsp. shortening

1. In a large bowl, mix marshmallow creme, coconut, vanilla and
salt until blended. Refrigerate, covered, at least 1 hour.

2. Shape mixture into 1-in. balls. Place on a waxed paper-lined
baking sheet. Refrigerate, covered, at least 3 hours.

3. In a microwave, melt the chocolate and shortening; stir until
smooth. Dip coconut balls in chocolate; allow excess to drip off.
Place on waxed paper; let stand until set.

NOTE: To toast coconut, bake in a shallow pan in a 350° oven for
5-10 minutes or cook in a skillet over low heat until golden brown,
stirring occasionally.

1 PIECE: 91 cal., 5g fat (3g sat. fat), 1mg chol., 36mg sod., 12g carb.
(10g sugars, 1g fiber), 1g pro.

ICE CREAM CONE
TREATS

ICE CREAM CONE TREATS

I came up with this recipe as a way for my grandkids to enjoy Rice Krispies treats without getting sticky hands. You can also pack the cereal mixture into paper cups and insert a wooden pop stick to create cute pops.

—Mabel Nolan, Vancouver, WA

TAKES: 20 MIN. • MAKES: 1 DOZEN

12 ice cream sugar cones
   Melted semisweet
   chocolate, optional
   Colored sprinkles
4 cups miniature
   marshmallows
3 Tbsp. butter
6 cups Rice Krispies

1. If desired, dip ice cream cones in melted chocolate to coat edges; stand in juice glasses or coffee mugs.

2. Place sprinkles in a shallow bowl. In a microwave or in a large saucepan over low heat, melt marshmallows and butter; stir until smooth. Remove from heat; stir in cereal.

3. Working quickly, use buttered hands to shape mixture into 12 balls; pack firmly into cones. Dip tops in sprinkles.

1 TREAT: 174 cal., 4g fat (2g sat. fat), 8mg chol., 142mg sod., 34g carb. (14g sugars, 0 fiber), 2g pro.

CINNAMON PEANUT BRITTLE

I made this sweet and crunchy candy for Christmas and sent some with my husband to work. His co-workers liked it so much they asked for more. It has a lovely glossy appearance, is packed with peanuts and gets a different flavor from cinnamon.

—Grace Miller, Mansfield, OH

PREP: 5 MIN. • COOK: 10 MIN. + CHILLING • MAKES: 20 SERVINGS (1¼ LBS.)

1 cup sugar
½ cup light corn syrup
2 cups salted peanuts
1 tsp. butter
½ tsp. ground cinnamon
1 tsp. baking soda
1 tsp. vanilla extract

1. In a 2-qt. microwave-safe bowl, combine sugar and corn syrup. Heat, uncovered, on high for 3 minutes; stir. Heat 2¼ minutes longer. Stir in peanuts, butter and cinnamon.

2. Microwave, uncovered, on high until the mixture turns a light amber color (mixture will be very hot), 20-30 seconds. Quickly stir in baking soda and vanilla until light and foamy.

3. Immediately pour onto a greased baking sheet and spread with a metal spatula. Refrigerate until firm, about 20 minutes; break into small pieces. Store in an airtight container.

1 OZ.: 153 cal., 8g fat (1g sat. fat), 1mg chol., 116mg sod., 19g carb. (17g sugars, 1g fiber), 4g pro.

CARAMEL RHUBARB COBBLER

I came up with this recipe after hearing a friend fondly recall his grandmother's rhubarb dumplings. My son especially likes rhubarb, and this old-fashioned dessert lets those special stalks star.

—Beverly Shebs, Pinehurst, NC

PREP: 25 MIN. • BAKE: 35 MIN. • MAKES: 6 SERVINGS

7 Tbsp. butter, divided
¾ cup packed brown sugar
½ cup sugar, divided
3 Tbsp. cornstarch
1¼ cups water
6 cups chopped fresh or frozen rhubarb, thawed
3 to 4 drops red food coloring, optional
1¼ cups all-purpose flour
1½ tsp. baking powder
¼ tsp. salt
⅓ cup 2% milk
   Cinnamon sugar
   Optional: Whipped cream or ice cream

1. In a saucepan over medium heat, melt 3 Tbsp. butter. Add the brown sugar, ¼ cup sugar and cornstarch. Gradually stir in water and rhubarb; cook and stir until thickened, 5-8 minutes. Add red food coloring if desired. Pour into a greased 2-qt. baking dish and set aside.

2. In another bowl, combine the flour, baking powder, salt and remaining sugar. Melt remaining butter; add to dry ingredients with milk. Mix well. Drop by tablespoonfuls onto rhubarb mixture. Bake at 350° for 35-40 minutes or until the fruit is bubbly and the top is golden brown. Sprinkle with cinnamon sugar. Serve warm, with whipped cream or ice cream if desired.

1 SERVING: 429 cal., 14g fat (9g sat. fat), 38mg chol., 357mg sod., 73g carb. (47g sugars, 3g fiber), 4g pro.

MOM'S HAZELNUT & CHOCOLATE BREAD PUDDING

Mom combined her love of hazelnut spread and bread pudding into one delicious recipe. I adapted it for my slow cooker to save time in the kitchen. It's a great make-ahead dessert.

—Jo Hahn, Newport News, VA

PREP: 15 MIN. • COOK: 4 HOURS • MAKES: 12 SERVINGS

¼ cup unsalted butter
2 Tbsp. semisweet chocolate chips
8 cups cubed challah or brioche
½ cup chopped hazelnuts
4 large eggs
1½ cups fat-free milk
½ cup fat-free half-and-half
½ cup Nutella
¼ cup sugar
½ tsp. vanilla extract
¼ tsp. salt
   Sweetened whipped cream, optional

1. Microwave the butter and chocolate chips for 30-45 seconds or until melted; stir until smooth. Cool. In a 3- or 4-qt. slow cooker coated with cooking spray, combine bread cubes and hazelnuts. In a large bowl, combine next 7 ingredients, mixing well. Add the chocolate mixture to bowl; whisk until smooth.

2. Pour egg mixture over bread and hazelnuts, gently pressing bread cubes to help them absorb liquid. Cook, covered, on low 4-5 hours or until a knife inserted in the center comes out clean. Serve warm, dolloped with whipped cream if desired.

½ CUP: 259 cal., 14g fat (4g sat. fat), 85mg chol., 190mg sod., 28g carb. (15g sugars, 1g fiber), 7g pro.

BUTTER PECAN CHEESECAKE

Fall always makes me yearn for this pecan cheesecake,
but it's delicious in any season. You'll want to put
it on your list of favorite holiday desserts.
—*Laura Sylvester, Mechanicsville, VA*

PREP: 30 MIN. • **BAKE:** 70 MIN. + CHILLING • **MAKES:** 16 SERVINGS

1½ cups graham cracker
    crumbs
½ cup finely chopped
    pecans
⅓ cup sugar
⅓ cup butter, melted

FILLING
3 pkg. (8 oz. each) cream
    cheese, softened

1½ cups sugar
2 cups sour cream
1 tsp. vanilla extract
½ tsp. butter flavoring
3 large eggs, room
    temperature, lightly
    beaten
1 cup finely chopped
    pecans

1. Preheat oven to 325°. In a large bowl, combine the graham
cracker crumbs, pecans, sugar and butter; set aside ⅓ cup for
topping. Press remaining crumb mixture onto the bottom and
1 in. up the side of a greased 9-in. springform pan.

2. Place springform pan on a double thickness of heavy-duty foil
(about 18 in. square). Securely wrap foil around pan.

3. In a large bowl, beat cream cheese and sugar until smooth.
Beat in the sour cream, vanilla and butter flavoring. Add eggs;
beat on low speed just until combined. Fold in pecans. Pour into
crust; sprinkle with reserved crumb mixture. Place springform
pan in a large baking pan; add 1 in. of hot water to larger pan.

4. Bake until the center is almost set, 70-80 minutes. Remove
springform pan from the water bath. Cool cheesecake on a wire
rack for 10 minutes. Carefully run a knife around edge of pan to
loosen; cool 1 hour longer. Refrigerate overnight, covering when
completely cooled. Remove rim of pan.

1 PIECE: 456 cal., 33g fat (16g sat. fat), 116mg chol., 224mg sod.,
33g carb. (27g sugars, 1g fiber), 7g pro.

APPLE PANDOWDY

I found the recipe for this apple pandowdy in an old cookbook. The dessert is tangy and delicious.
—*Doreen Lindquist, Thompson, MB*

PREP: 25 MIN. • BAKE: 55 MIN. • MAKES: 9 SERVINGS

1 cup packed brown sugar
1¼ cups all-purpose flour, divided
½ tsp. salt, divided
1 cup water
1 tsp. lemon juice
2 tsp. baking powder
5 Tbsp. butter, divided
¾ cup 2% milk
5 cups sliced peeled apples
½ tsp. plus ⅛ tsp. ground cinnamon, divided
½ tsp. ground nutmeg
1 tsp. vanilla extract
1 Tbsp. coarse sugar
Whipped cream, optional

1. In a saucepan, combine brown sugar, ¼ cup flour and ¼ tsp. salt. Add water and lemon juice; cook and stir over medium heat until thick. Cover and set aside.

2. In a bowl, combine baking powder and remaining flour and salt. Cut in 3 Tbsp. butter. Add the milk and mix just until moistened (a few lumps will remain); set aside.

3. Arrange apples in a 1½-qt. baking dish; sprinkle with ½ tsp. cinnamon. Add nutmeg, vanilla and remaining butter to sauce; pour over apples. Drop dough by spoonfuls over sauce. Combine the remaining cinnamon and coarse sugar; sprinkle over dough. Bake at 350° for 55 minutes or until top is brown and apples are tender. Serve warm, with whipped cream if desired.

1 SERVING: 260 cal., 7g fat (4g sat. fat), 20mg chol., 304mg sod., 47g carb. (33g sugars, 2g fiber), 3g pro.

GRANDMA'S RICE PUDDING

You can whip up this classic dessert on short notice if you keep cooked rice on hand.
Cooked rice can be frozen in an airtight container for up to three months.
Just thaw it in the refrigerator or microwave when you're ready to use it.
—*Margaret DeChant, Newberry, MI*

PREP: 10 MIN. • BAKE: 45 MIN. • MAKES: 6 SERVINGS

1½ cups cooked rice
¼ cup raisins
2 large eggs
1½ cups whole milk
½ cup sugar
½ tsp. ground nutmeg
Additional milk, optional

1. Place rice and raisins in a greased 1-qt. casserole. In a small bowl, whisk the eggs, milk, sugar and nutmeg; pour over rice.

2. Bake, uncovered, at 375° for 45-50 minutes or until a knife inserted in the center comes out clean. Cool. Pour milk over each serving if desired. Refrigerate leftovers.

1 CUP: 197 cal., 4g fat (2g sat. fat), 79mg chol., 52mg sod., 36g carb. (23g sugars, 0 fiber), 5g pro.

APPLE
PANDOWDY

BREAD PUDDING WITH NUTMEG

I make this bread pudding recipe for my dad on his birthday and holidays. He says it tastes exactly like the bread pudding he enjoyed as a child.
—*Donna Powell, Montgomery City, MO*

PREP: 15 MIN. • BAKE: 40 MIN. • MAKES: 6 SERVINGS

- 2 large eggs, room temperature
- 2 cups whole milk
- ¼ cup butter, cubed
- ¾ cup sugar
- ¼ tsp. salt
- 1 tsp. ground cinnamon
- ½ tsp. ground nutmeg
- 1 tsp. vanilla extract
- 4½ to 5 cups soft bread cubes (about 9 slices)
- ½ cup raisins, optional

VANILLA SAUCE
- ⅓ cup sugar
- 2 Tbsp. cornstarch
- ¼ tsp. salt
- 1⅔ cups cold water
- 3 Tbsp. butter
- 2 tsp. vanilla extract
- ¼ tsp. ground nutmeg

1. In a large bowl, lightly beat eggs. Combine milk and butter; add to eggs along with sugar, salt, spices and vanilla. Add bread cubes and, if desired, raisins; stir gently.

2. Pour into a well-greased 11x7-in. baking dish. Bake at 350° for 40-45 minutes or until a knife inserted 1 in. from the edge comes out clean.

3. Meanwhile, for sauce, combine sugar, cornstarch and salt in a saucepan. Stir in water until smooth. Bring to a boil over medium heat; cook and stir until thickened, about 2 minutes. Remove from the heat. Stir in the butter, vanilla and nutmeg. Serve with warm pudding.

1 PIECE: 419 cal., 19g fat (11g sat. fat), 118mg chol., 534mg sod., 56g carb. (40g sugars, 1g fiber), 7g pro.

MARBLED ORANGE FUDGE
The dreamy Creamsicle flavor of this soft fudge brings on the smiles.
Bright orange and marshmallow swirls make it perfect for events and get-togethers.
—Diane Wampler, Morristown, TN

PREP: 30 MIN. + CHILLING • MAKES: ABOUT 2½ LBS.

1½ tsp. plus ¾ cup butter, divided
3 cups sugar
¾ cup heavy whipping cream
1 pkg. white baking chips (10 to 12 oz.)
1 jar (7 oz.) marshmallow creme
3 tsp. orange extract
12 drops yellow food coloring
5 drops red food coloring

1. Grease a 13x9-in. pan with 1½ tsp. butter; set aside.

2. In a large heavy saucepan, combine the sugar, cream and remaining butter. Cook and stir over low heat until sugar is dissolved. Bring to a boil; cook and stir for 4 minutes. Remove from the heat; stir in chips and marshmallow creme until smooth.

3. Remove 1 cup and set aside. Add orange extract and food coloring to the remaining mixture; stir until blended. Pour into prepared pan. Drop the reserved marshmallow mixture by tablespoonfuls over the top; cut through with a knife to swirl. Cover and refrigerate until set. Cut into squares.

1 PIECE: 109 cal., 3g fat (2g sat. fat), 7mg chol., 12mg sod., 20g carb. (15g sugars, 0 fiber), 0 pro.

LEMON BERRY DUMP CAKE
This sweet-tart cake recipe is so much fun to make with my grandkids.
They love just dumping it all in and watching it magically become a pretty, delicious dessert.
—Nancy Heishman, Las Vegas, NV

PREP: 10 MIN. • BAKE: 45 MIN. + COOLING • MAKES: 15 SERVINGS (3 CUPS LEMON TOPPING)

6 cups fresh or frozen blueberries
1 tsp. ground cinnamon
¾ cup butter, melted
1 pkg. lemon cake mix (regular size)

TOPPING
2 containers (6 oz. each) lemon yogurt
1 container (8 oz.) frozen whipped topping, thawed
½ cup marshmallow creme
⅓ cup lemon curd
Additional blueberries, optional

1. Preheat oven to 350°. Toss blueberries with cinnamon; spread into a greased 13x9-in. baking dish. Drizzle with half the melted butter. Sprinkle with cake mix; drizzle with remaining butter.

2. Bake until golden brown and fruit is bubbly, 45-55 minutes. Cool on a wire rack.

3. Beat together yogurt, whipped topping, marshmallow creme and lemon curd. Serve dump cake with yogurt mixture and, if desired, additional blueberries.

1 SERVING: 340 cal., 15g fat (9g sat. fat), 31mg chol., 297mg sod., 48g carb. (33g sugars, 1g fiber), 3g pro.

PUMPKIN CREAM TIRAMISU

Pumpkin isn't only for pies. Now you can take the classic fall vegetable and enjoy it in a tiramisu-style dessert. I promise after one bite, you'll add this recipe to keeper files.
—*Pam Peters, Fernie, BC*

PREP: 1 HOUR + CHILLING • BAKE: 15 MIN./BATCH + COOLING • MAKES: 12 SERVINGS

½ **cup butter, softened**
1 **cup sugar**
1 **large egg, room temperature**
¼ **cup honey**
½ **cup solid-pack pumpkin**
1 **tsp. dark rum**
2⅓ **cups all-purpose flour**
2 **tsp. ground cinnamon**
1½ **tsp. baking soda**
1½ **tsp. ground ginger**
1 **tsp. ground cloves**
½ **tsp. salt**

TIRAMISU

2¼ **cups solid-pack pumpkin**
1½ **tsp. ground cinnamon**
¾ **tsp. ground ginger**
¼ **tsp. ground cloves**
3 **cups heavy whipping cream**
¾ **cup sugar**
12 **oz. cream cheese, softened**
¼ **cup dark rum**
½ **tsp. ground cinnamon or nutmeg**

1. Preheat oven to 350°. In a large bowl, cream butter and sugar until light and fluffy, 5-7 minutes. Gradually beat in the egg and honey. Add pumpkin and rum; mix well. In another bowl, whisk flour, cinnamon, baking soda, ginger, cloves and salt; gradually beat into creamed mixture.

2. Cut a ¾-in. hole in the tip of a pastry bag or in a corner of a food-safe plastic bag. Working in batches, pipe dough to form 2½-in. logs, 2 in. apart, onto parchment-lined baking sheets. Bake 12-14 minutes or until the cookies are golden and set. Cool on a wire rack.

3. In a large bowl, mix pumpkin and spices. In a small bowl, beat cream until it begins to thicken. Add sugar; beat until soft peaks form. Fold a third of the whipped cream mixture into the pumpkin mixture. In a small bowl, beat cream cheese until smooth. Beat in remaining whipped cream until combined. Arrange a third of the cookies in a single layer in a 13x9-in. baking dish; brush with rum. Top with a third of the pumpkin filling. Spread with a third of the cream cheese mixture. Repeat layers twice. Refrigerate, covered, 8 hours or overnight. Sprinkle with cinnamon.

1 PIECE: 635 cal., 40g fat (25g sat. fat), 132mg chol., 432mg sod., 63g carb. (40g sugars, 3g fiber), 7g pro.

GRANDMA'S SECRET
When whipping cream, keep the cream and your equipment cold. Cream whips better at a lower temperature, so it's best to chill the bowl you're creating it in, and the beaters (or whisk), too.

RECIPE INDEX